WITHDRAWN

the knight
in history

Also by Frances Gies:

JOAN OF ARC (1981)

In collaboration with Joseph Gies:

WOMEN IN THE MIDDLE AGES (1978)
THE INGENIOUS YANKEES (1976)
LIFE IN A MEDIEVAL CASTLE (1974)
MERCHANTS AND MONEYMEN (1972)
LEONARD OF PISA *(juvenile)* (1969)
LIFE IN A MEDIEVAL CITY (1969)

the knight in history

FRANCES GIES

1817

HARPER & ROW, PUBLISHERS, New York

CAMBRIDGE, PHILADELPHIA, SAN FRANCISCO, LONDON
MEXICO CITY, SÃO PAULO, SINGAPORE, SYDNEY

Copyright acknowledgments follow page 255.

Photographs not credited in the captions are from the author's collection.

FIRST EDITION

Designer: Barbara DuPree Knowles

Maps by Frank Ronan

LIBRARY OF CONGRESS CATALOGING IN PUBLICATION DATA

Gies, Frances.
The knight in history.

Bibliography: p.
Includes index.
1. Knights and knighthood—History. I. Title.
CR4509.G54   1984   929.7′1   84-47571
ISBN 0-06-015339-3

To Paul
"a verray, parfit gentil knight"

contents

List of Illustrations

maps

acknowledgments

This book was researched at the
Harlan Hatcher Graduate Library of the University of Michigan,
the Library of Congress, and the McKeldin Library
of the University of Maryland.

Special thanks are due to
David Herlihy of the history department of Harvard University,
who read the manuscript and made valuable suggestions,
and to my husband, Joseph Gies, who took photographs,
contributed his editorial skills, and wrote the chapter
on Bertrand du Guesclin. I am also grateful to Hallam Ashley
for his help with local Norfolk history.

what
is a
knight?

◄§ YOU CALL YOURSELF KNIGHT; WHAT IS THAT?
—Wolfram von Eschenbach, *Parsifal*

OF ALL THE many types of soldier that have appeared on the military stage in the course of time, from the Greek hoplite, the Roman legionary, and the Ottoman janissary to members of the specialized branches of modern armed forces, none has had a longer career than the knight of the European Middle Ages, and none has had an equal impact on history, social and cultural as well as political.[1] Knights fought on the battlefields of Europe for six hundred to eight hundred years, some scholars dating their emergence as early as the eighth century, some as late as the tenth. They were still prominent, though increasingly obsolescent, in the sixteenth century, long after the introduction of firearms and the advent of the national state.

Originally a personality of mediocre status raised above the peasant by his possession of expensive horse and armor, the knight slowly improved his position in society until he became part of the nobility. Although knights remained the lowest rank of the upper class, knighthood acquired a unique cachet that made knighting an honor prized by the great nobility and even by royalty. This cachet was primarily the product of the Church's policy of Christianizing knighthood by sanctifying the ceremony of knighting and by sponsoring a code of behavior known as chivalry, a code perhaps violated more often than honored, but exercising incontestable influence on the thought and conduct of posterity.

The institution of knighthood summons up in the mind of every literate person the image of an armor-plated warrior on horseback, with the title "Sir," whose house was a castle, and who divided his time between the pageantry of the tournament and the lonely adventures of knight-errantry. The image has the defect of being static, and it represents a concept that belongs more to legend and literature than to real life. Yet the real historical figure of the knight is not totally at odds with the popular image. He did indeed wear plate armor, but plate superseded mail only late in his long career. The "Sir"—"Messire" in French—also came late and in England still exists as a title of honor or of minor nobility. A knight sometimes lived in a castle, but the castle was rarely his own. He participated in tournaments, but the tournament's character as pageant developed only in its decadence. He was certainly prone to adventure in his often short life, but nearly always in company and in search of income rather than romance.

In England and America the popular image of the knight is preponderantly English, thanks to the overpowering appeal of the King Arthur story. Real knights, however, originated in France and were unknown in England until the Norman Conquest. The French-Welsh-English creators of the Arthur literature, who grafted onto a grain of historical fact a mass of legend about a sixth-century British chieftain, ended by creating a bizarre time warp in which knights in gleaming plate armor galloped anachronistically through the primitive political countryside of post-Roman Britain.

Though change was continuous, one may usefully divide the knight's long history into three stages: first, the emergence of the armored, mounted soldier in the turmoil-filled ninth and tenth centuries; second, the development of the mature institution of knighthood in the eleventh through the thirteenth centuries, the age of the architects of the King Arthur legend; and third, the decay of the institution as a consequence of the rise of new social forces in the late Middle Ages and early modern times.

The knight may be defined from three different standpoints, each of them important: the military, the economic, and the social.

He was first and foremost a soldier, as identified by the Latin term for him, *miles,* and the Anglo-Saxon *cniht,* cognate of "knight." He was invariably mounted; in most languages the medieval vernacular word that replaced *miles* denoted horseman: French, *chevalier;* German, *Ritter;* Italian, *cavaliere;* Spanish, *caballero.* Again invariably, he was clad in armor. Thus militarily he was an armored cavalryman.

Economically, the knight was a component of the system known to historians as feudalism. In this dominant economic (and political) order of the Middle Ages, a lord granted land to a vassal in return for military and other less important services. Lord and vassal swore an oath, of protection and support on the part of the lord, of loyalty on the part of the vassal. At the height of feudalism, the knight was the cornerstone of the institution. He may be said to have formed its basic currency. The lord's grant of land to his vassal was typically in return for the service of a specified number of knights, whose swords the vassal was able to secure in his turn by granting land to them through a similar exchange of oaths. Lord, vassal, and knight were free men, tied together by their mutual promises.

The economic prototype of the knight, then, was a free man, holding land, and owing feudal military service. Details of practice varied widely. In Germany up to the thirteenth century some knights were household retainers who shared characteristics with serfs. Throughout Europe and throughout the Middle Ages, many knights were landless and not strictly speaking part of the feudal system. Finally, in the late Middle Ages, knights ceased to perform feudal military service in return for grants of land and became plain professional soldiers, differing only in prestige, equipment, and pay scale from other men-at-arms.

Socially, even the protoknights of the early period were set apart by their expensive equipment and horses. Gradually professional pride matured into class consciousness, which was enhanced by the Church's sponsorship. The soldiers of the earlier period may or may not properly be called knights, but the full development of knighthood came only with the acquisition of class identity.

The Western European knight may be summarized as a mounted, heavily armed and armored soldier, in most times and places a free man and a landholder, and, most significantly, a member of a caste with a strong sense of solidarity.

This book will attempt to trace the development of the medieval knight from first appearance through rise to gradual eclipse, and to assess his impact on history, using real-life knights as examples.

It will first describe the genesis of the knight and his tenth-century manifestation, a crude and violent figure virtually uncurbed by a society that had lost control over its military class. The efforts of the Church first to tame and then to harness the brute bestowed on him a dawning consciousness of belonging to an "order," a chosen cadre with duties and disciplines prescribed by the Church, to which he came to owe a special allegiance.

The maturing eleventh-century knight, his self-image further enhanced by the designation "soldier of Christ," a radical concept of Pope Gregory VII, undertook the unparalleled adventure of the First Crusade. Social and economic motives as well as religious ones impelled him. One motive proved ephemeral: many landless knights went to the East with thoughts of acquiring estates, but few remained. Nevertheless, the Crusade gave further impetus to the rise of the knightly class, through the broadening effect of travel, which helped lift the knight from petty provincial to European gentleman-soldier, and through his role in "the army of the Lord," combating "God's enemies."

In the twelfth century, some of the same social and economic forces that lay behind Crusading led knights into an unexpected and even anomalous pursuit. Certain of them became "troubadours," lyric poets who flourished in the sophisticated climate of southern France and who produced a body of verse that, in addition to its influence on European literature, had a high intrinsic value, now unfortunately obscured by the lapse of Provençal from an international literary language to a local dialect. The troubadours' poetic successors, knights of northern France and of Germany, carried on the tradition as trouvères and minnesingers. Narrative poetry and prose, influenced by the troubadours, also swelled the twelfth-century literary Renaissance, reaching a climax in the Arthurian romances, a multiauthored accumulation that fixed the image of the medieval knight for himself, his contemporaries, and posterity.

The knight-errant heroes of the Arthur stories had historical counterparts whose adventures, if less fabulous, were genuine enough as they roamed Europe earning a living in tournament and battle. Those of William Marshal of England, who became the trusted counselor of kings, have been preserved in a valuable chronicle. By the thirteenth century, political developments had attached the knights firmly to the nobility and modified their role from the strictly military. The rise of a money economy and subsequent inflation increased the expenses of knighthood and created a new class of men eligible to become knights who no longer wished to be knighted but opted to remain squires. Simultaneously, commoners—rich peasants and merchants—began to invade the knightly class.

The Church's ideal of the "soldier of Christ" was best realized in the Military Orders that fought the infidel in Spain, eastern Europe, and above all the Holy Land. The Knights Templars, Hospitalers, Teutonic Knights, and Spanish Orders of Calatrava, Santiago, and Alcantara performed their military duties with a monastic discipline that contrasted with the unruly individualism of the traditional knights. The Templars, the most celebrated of the Orders, were drawn into the unknightly profession of banking, which led first to their enrichment and then to their downfall.

The Hundred Years War (1337–1453) worked the final transformation of the western European knight from landed vassal to professional soldier. The careers of two knights, the Breton hero Bertrand du Guesclin and John Fastolf, an English knight of middle-class origins who reaped a fortune from the war, illuminate aspects of fourteenth- and fifteenth-century knighthood.

In the end the knight was absorbed into the standing army of the new national state, where he quickly lost his distinctive identity. More enduring was the influence on manners and morals of "chivalry," an ambiguous word that sometimes refers to the corps of knights themselves, sometimes to the panoply of tournament and heraldry, sometimes to the knightly code of conduct. The title of knight survived as a lower rank of nobility and as a conferred civil or military honor. The panoply long enjoyed popularity, especially in the circles of royalty, and even made a memorable farewell appearance in the age of Victoria. The code of conduct, with its invocation of generous sentiments, has never lost its appeal, and is permanently enshrined in the literature of chivalry.

the
first
knights

◦§ IN THE BEGINNING . . . NO MAN WAS HIGHER IN BIRTH THAN ANY
OTHER, FOR ALL MEN WERE DESCENDED FROM A SINGLE FATHER AND
MOTHER. BUT WHEN ENVY AND COVETOUSNESS CAME INTO THE WORLD,
AND MIGHT TRIUMPHED OVER RIGHT . . . CERTAIN MEN WERE APPOINTED
AS GUARANTORS AND DEFENDERS OF THE WEAK AND THE HUMBLE.
—*The Book of Lancelot of the Lake*

MEDIEVAL MORALISTS

believed that at an early stage knights had been chosen as the sword arm of society, to enforce justice and protect the helpless. This event had occurred in antiquity, and Old Testament heroes such as Judas Maccabeus and King David were included in the roll of knights. The real entry of the knight into history was no such dramatic phenomenon, but a gradual coalescing of social and technological elements over a long period of time.

Long though its germination took, the rise of knighthood was a medieval event, not a Roman continuation. Rome possessed its own class of "knights" (*equites,* horsemen), originally the cavalry wing of the Roman army and source of the army's officers. This class had by the end of the Republican period abandoned its military role and become army contractors, tax farmers, and exploiters of public resources. They formed the lower segment of the upper class, just below the senators, a status memorialized in the theaters and arenas throughout the Empire, where the first rows were reserved for the senators, the next several for the knights.[1] Contrary to the assumption of some nineteenth-century historians, however, this Roman "Equestrian Order" had no historical connection with medieval knighthood.

Scholarly controversy still clouds the emergence of the medieval knight.[2] Records for the critical period are scarce, and semantic problems—the relationship between late-Roman terms for certain kinds of soldiers and Latin terms used in the early Middle Ages—compound the difficulty. Terms used for social classes in the time of Charlemagne and those of the eleventh century are equally ambiguous. The prejudices of early modern historians also inhibited understanding. In the nineteenth century, when feudal society was regarded as backward, barbaric, and chaotic, a school of German scholars headed by Heinrich Brunner attempted to prove that feudalism had originated not in ancient German tribal custom but in eighth-century France. Brunner traced its beginnings to the adoption by Charles Martel of the Muslims' cavalry arm and tactics. To support his new cavalry corps, Charles seized church lands and granted them as "benefices" to the mounted soldiers, thereby inventing the fief. These first knights became, according to Brunner, the ancestors of the medieval nobility.[3]

Brunner's theory was elaborated and refined by two twentieth-century historians, French medievalist Marc Bloch and American Lynn White, Jr. Bloch, writing in the 1930s, proposed that the nobility of the early Middle Ages, both the Roman senatorial class and the Germanic chiefs, had disappeared by the eighth century; what took its place was a new class distinguished not by birth but by power derived from the king's service. Pedigrees of the medieval nobility could be traced back only to the "crucial turning-point of the year 800," shortly before which the class had its origins in the professional warrior of the time, with his horse, armor, shield, lance, and sword. "As the logical consequence of the adoption, [in] about the tenth century, of the stirrup, the short spear of former days, brandished at arm's length like a javelin, was abandoned and replaced by the long and heavy lance. . . ." Added to stirrup and lance were helmet and chain mail. These improvements made the warrior's equipment far more expensive, affordable only by a rich man or a rich man's vassal. Therefore the Carolingian kings bestowed lands—benefices—to support and equip their fighting men, who formed a new aristocracy.[4]

In the 1960s Lynn White embellished the theories of Brunner and Bloch, making the stirrup the "keystone" of "Brunner's magnificent structure of hypotheses." White moved the arrival of the stirrup in western Europe back to the first part of the eighth century and attributed its adoption to "Charles Martel's genius." "Feudal institutions, the knightly class, and chivalric culture" were born from "the new military technology of the eighth century."[5]

Recent scholarship has favored a more complex picture of the origins of knights, medieval nobility, and feudalism. Most historians now do not believe that knights originated in the eighth century, or that they were the founders of either the medieval nobility or feudalism. The consensus is rather that there was a genuine nobility of blood and birth in the time of Charlemagne and his successors, that it was indeed enriched by the king's grants of land and office, but that its origins lay not in a class of mounted warriors recently raised from obscurity but in the old Frankish aristocracy. This Carolingian nobility, with continuing transfusions of new blood including that of

CAROLINGIAN WARRIORS,
FROM A NINTH-CENTURY
IVORY PLAQUE, WEAR
CONICAL HELMETS AND
CARRY ROUND SHIELDS.
(LOUVRE)

knights, was the source of the nobility of the High Middle Ages.[6] Pedigrees are difficult to trace (and not only before the "crucial turning-point of the year 800" but in most cases before the year 1000) not because the families were parvenu, but because the concept of family in the ninth and tenth centuries differed from that of the eleventh and twelfth centuries.[7] "The noble kins of the Carolingian and post-Carolingian world," writes a modern authority on early medieval sociology, ". . . present to the historian an oddly horizontal rather than vertical aspect, very different from the later dynasties of counts, castellans, and, by the twelfth century, even knights. . . ."[8]

Patronymics—family names—had not yet appeared. Families were not the monolithic arrangements of the later age when feudalism was at its height. Much of the land in Europe in the tenth century was still held not by the conditional terms of feudal tenure but unconditionally as "allods," land that could be sold or bestowed freely as the owner chose. On his death, the land was commonly divided equally among his heirs. Primogeniture, with principal family property passing from father to eldest son, or any variant form of undivided inheritance, was not yet the rule.

In this new picture, feudalism did not emerge suddenly out of the military needs of Charles Martel, but grew slowly out of the confluence of Germanic and Roman social institutions, with strong influence from a third source, the Christian Church.[9] The personal association of lord and vassal has been found to have roots in both Germanic and Roman society. An ancient German custom was the *comitatus,* the association of a young warrior with an older one, in which the young man pledged loyalty and service in return for maintenance by the older. A similar Roman custom provided patronage, protection, and support of a client in return for his allegiance. Still another form of mutual association was the Franks' practice of commendation, in which a freeman voluntarily bound himself to a lord, giving up his freedom and pledging his fealty while placing himself under the lord's protection.

The other great basic of feudalism, the conditional grant of land, had its origin in the Church. Forbidden to sell its lands, the Church invented the benefice (favor) or *precarium* (response to prayers), allowing a layman use of Church land without giving him title to it.

Feudalism was in essence the association between lord and armed followers supported by the conditional gift of land. Although its origins can be traced to the early Middle Ages, not until the thirteenth century did it reach maturity, and in some regions, notably Italy, it never became the dominant system. By the thirteenth century the most feudalized areas of Europe—northern France, the Low Countries, England, and Germany—no longer recognized the existence of allodial land, land owned outright. All lands were regarded as fiefs. In southern France and Spain, on the other hand, allodial property never completely disappeared, while in Italy the allod remained the principal form of land tenure throughout the Middle Ages.

The military revolution, too, seems to have been gradual, though

BRONZE EQUESTRIAN
STATUE OF CHARLEMAGNE,
NINTH CENTURY. NOTE
THE ABSENCE OF STIRRUPS.
(*LOUVRE*)

in light of the long Greek-Roman standstill in weapons technology its changes were dramatic.[10] The Roman soldier fought on foot, with short sword, protected by a shield and a few pieces of light armor. The knight of the High Middle Ages fought on horseback, completely sheathed in heavy armor, carrying a long sword and heavy lance. With the lance gripped under his arm, his body secured to his horse by saddle and stirrups, he could deliver his blow with the mass and strength of the horse united to his own, creating the sometimes overrated but nonetheless effective technique of shock combat.

The technical innovations embodied by the knight, including the nailed horseshoe and the stirrup, can be traced all the way back to the central Asian nomads who invaded the Near East and Balkans at the beginning of the Middle Ages. The first documented evidence of the stirrup is from North Korea in the fifth century A.D. The Avars, originally from Mongolia, seem to have brought the stirrup when they established themselves in the 550s in what became Hungary. From the Avars the device passed to the Byzantines, then to the Arabs.[11] The first pictorial evidence of the stirrup in western Europe dates only from the ninth century, but archeological evidence shows that it was known at least a century earlier. Whether Charles Martel's "genius" was responsible for adopting it cannot be proved or disproved, but what emerges from the mass of literary, archeological, and pictorial evidence is first, that the stirrup was probably not widely used till long after its initial arrival in Europe, and second, that mounted shock combat was not a decisive element in the campaigns of Charles Martel and his immediate successors, or indeed for some time afterward. Even as late as the Battle of Hastings (1066), it was apparently not the rule. David C. Douglas, the authority on William the Conqueror, describes the battle as offering no evidence of "the 'classic' use of cavalry—that is to say a massed charge of heavily armed horsemen, riding knee-to-knee, using their mounts to overwhelm their opponents, and then attacking with lances and swords."[12] The famous Bayeux Tapestry, executed in England a few years after the battle, shows the Normans equipped with stirrups but carrying light lances which, like the spears or javelins of the infantry, are thrown at the enemy rather than driven by the force of the horse. That decisive changes took place in military technology between the eighth and the twelfth centuries is beyond question, but perhaps it is more appropriate to describe them as evolutionary than as revolutionary.

The medieval knight can thus be seen emerging from the cavalry of Carolingian times, his status changing with innovations in military technique and the feudalization of Europe. A final element came in

THE NORMAN ATTACK AT HASTINGS. SPEARS ARE THROWN RATHER THAN USED AS LANCES IN SHOCK COMBAT. (*BAYEUX TAPESTRY, PHAIDON PRESS*)

the Christian Church's attempts first to restrain and then to harness his violent behavior.

The knightly title *miles* began to appear in France during the disorders of the tenth century;[13] whether these knights had their origins as free peasants or as descendants of lesser nobility seems to vary with the region. In status they occupied the lowest echelon of the upper class, and the scholarly consensus is that they were not yet considered noble. Their land holdings were small; as late as the period of the Domesday Book (1086), after the Normans had brought feudalism and knighthood to England, a knight's normal fief placed him "only just above most well-to-do peasants."[14] The very name that the Anglo-Saxons gave the Norman *miles* after the Conquest signaled his minor status: *cniht,* a man of modest standing who rendered military service to a lord, heretofore as a foot soldier.

In Germany, where royal authority remained strong and feudalism was slow to develop, the early history of knighthood followed a different course. The place occupied by free men in France, as territorial administrators, household officials, and knights, was filled in Germany by a hereditary group of servile retainers called ministerials. They could not marry without the lord's consent, were subject to the same taxes as serfs, could not plead their cases in public courts, could not acquire or sell property without the lord's consent, and could even be bought and sold. This "servile aristocracy," which German kings and princes employed to counterbalance the power of the nobles, gradually acquired fiefs and vassals of their own and finally freedom, merging into the lower nobility to form the *Ritterstand* (knight class). Some of the descendants of ministerials eventually became members of the high nobility, while others distinguished themselves in politics, literature, and intellectual life.[15]

Little is known about the life-style, training, and rituals of the early knights, in either France or Germany. Probably they underwent a term of apprenticeship and on coming of age were presented with sword and spurs. If there was a formal ceremony, the Church took no part in it.

The transitional state of the knight in the tenth century has been illuminated by the researches of French scholar Georges Duby in the region of Mâcon, in central France. There much of the knight's land was still allodial, that is, free of feudal obligation. He lived on his demesne, in a walled "curia" that consisted of dwelling house, servants' quarters, barns, storage buildings, dairy, dovecote, bakehouse, pigsty, byre, and sometimes a chapel, often arranged in a square around a central yard where straw and hay were stacked. Nearby were the houses of the peasants, who paid him a small rent and owed him labor services, mainly at planting and harvest times. The activities involved in the agricultural production that provided most of his livelihood were carried on by serfs, who doubled as domestic servants, and who enabled him to be absent for extended periods without loss of income. At intervals the knight served a tour of duty in the local castle, built in the ninth and tenth centuries as part of the public defense system against Viking and Saracen raiders, under the orders of a castellan whose office had become hereditary.[16] A few castles were of masonry, usually small rectangular stone towers. Most were timber-and-earthwork constructions of the motte-and-bailey pattern, with moats and palisade walls girdling a mound topped with a wooden tower. A neighboring courtyard usually contained the lord's —castellan's—residence and barracks for the garrison knights.[17]

The knight's armor in this early period, and for a long time after, consisted exclusively of a helmet and hauberk or body armor. The helmet was solid iron, conical or round. The hauberk was of chain mail, fabricated principally by a time-consuming hand process in which wire was wound around a rod in a helical coil and then cut entirely down one side of the rod, producing a number of open rings. The two ends of each ring were annealed and hammered flat, and the hauberk, in form a shirt or coat, was fashioned by linking the rings and closing them by overlapping and riveting the flattened ends. The length and style of the hauberk varied. In the Bayeux Tapestry hauberks are long, reaching to the knees, divided front and back for riding, and with wide sleeves. An opening at the throat was laced tight, and close-fitting mail coifs, or hoods, worn under the helmet, helped to protect neck and chin, but the nose and eyes were at first left exposed. The "nasal," a bar protecting the face, was added to some helmets in the eleventh century and became common in the twelfth. Simultaneously, mail leggings made their appearance: in the Bayeux Tapestry the Norman leaders wear them.

On his left side the tenth-century knight carried a long shield made of wood covered with leather, vertically concave toward his body, rounded at the top and pointed at the bottom. The shield hung from a strap around his neck and was gripped in his left hand by a shorter strap. On his right side, a broad-bladed sword in a scabbard of wood covered with leather was belted to his waist. He might also carry an axe with a fan-shaped blade and a light lance with a leaf-shaped head. His spurs were of goad form, with a single sharp point.[18]

ELEVENTH-CENTURY KNIGHTS CARRYING SPEARS AND KITE-SHAPED SHIELDS WITH ROUNDED TOPS. (VIE DE ST. AUBIN, *BIBLIOTHÈQUE NATIONALE, MS. NOUV. ACQ. LAT. 1390, F. 7V*)

HAUBERKS, HELMETS, AND SWORDS ARE LOADED ON NORMAN SHIPS
FOR THE INVASION OF ENGLAND. CHAIN MAIL IS SCHEMATICALLY
DEPICTED IN HAUBERKS WITH DIVIDED SKIRTS.
(*BAYEUX TAPESTRY, PHAIDON PRESS*)

In his person, the real-life knight of the tenth century had little in
common with the courtly heroes of the Round Table. Ignorant and
unlettered, rough in speech and manners, he earned his living largely
by violence, uncontrolled by a public justice that had virtually disappeared. Civil disputes and criminal cases alike had ceased to be ad-
judicated by the enfeebled royal power and instead were settled by
the sword. The unarmed segment of the population, the Church and
the peasants, were victims or bystanders. In the words of Georges
Duby, "Moral obligations and the persuasion of their peers were all
that could impose a limit to [the knights'] violence and greed."[19]

The prevailing anarchy stimulated remedial action. This came
from the Church in a development that had profound effects on the
knights and on the medieval nobility. Two related movements were
launched in the tenth and eleventh centuries: the "Peace of God" and
the "Truce of God." These two great innovations presaged the powerful assertion of Church authority summarized by historians as
Gregorian reform, paving the way for the mighty movement known
as the First Crusade.[20]

The Church's motivation in initiating the Peace and Truce of God
had two aspects. First, there was self-interest, mainly the defense of

its own property and personnel and of the peasants and merchants whose tithes, rents, and services provided part of its income. Political self-interest also came into play, as when in 994 and 1025 the bishops of Mâcon, Chalon, and Autun convened peace councils at Anse, on the Saône, to prevent Count Otto-Guillaume of Mâcon from asserting authority in Church territory, particularly that of the great abbey of Cluny. The councils at Anse were instigated by the count's secular rivals, King Robert the Pious of France and the count of Chalon. The Church lent its support because it hoped to free itself from the count's power and indeed from lay control in general.[21]

Self-interest, then, was one aspect of the Church's peace offensive. A second was idealism. The Church believed in peace as an absolute good, one that favored order, justice, and the indivisibility of Christianity. "How fair is the name of the peace and how beautiful is the repute of the unity which Christ left to his disciples when he ascended into heaven," began the preamble to the canons set forth by one of the councils.[22]

In the Peace of God, the Church's peacemaking efforts were directed toward protecting certain classes at all times, in the later Truce of God, toward protecting all classes at certain times. Both movements sought only to limit and contain the knights' violent proclivities.

The Peace of God was first pronounced in 989 at a council of bishops at the abbey of Charroux, in Aquitaine. Spiritual sanctions were threatened against anyone who plundered or violated a church, struck an unarmed member of the clergy, or robbed "a peasant or other poor man." The prohibition was later extended to attacking other unarmed laymen—specifically merchants—and to destroying mills or vineyards and attacking a man on his way to or from church.[23]

To implement the Peace of God, local councils assembled nobility, knights, and peasants in the open fields. There, in an atmosphere of evangelical enthusiasm, oaths to keep the peace were sworn on saints' relics. To underline the sacred character of the occasion, miracles of healing were performed.[24] Chronicler Ralph Glaber describes such a council at which those present "were inflamed with such ardor that . . . with outspread palms and with one voice [they] cried to God, 'Peace, peace, peace!' that this might be a sign of perpetual covenant for that which they had promised between themselves and God."[25] Another chronicler, Adhémar of Chabannes, described a Peace Council held at Limoges in 994 at the behest of the abbot of the monastery of St. Martial. After a three-day fast, the assembly met in the open air on a hill outside the city. "The bodies and relics of the saints were solemnly conveyed there from all parts, while the body of St. Martial, the patron of Gaul, was borne from its sepulchre, so that everyone was filled with immeasurable joy. All sickness everywhere ceased, and the duke [of Aquitaine] and the nobles [*principes*] concluded a mutual pact of peace and justice."[26] Violators of the peace oath were threatened with excommunication.

Early in the eleventh century the second movement emerged. The Truce of God was less broadly evangelical, more focused on the knights and nobility. With respect to their favorite occupation, fighting, an ascetic discipline was imposed. Like penitents required to fast on certain days, knights were made to forgo the pleasure of war on Sundays and holy days and to refrain from acts of violence at any time in churches and in certain areas around churches. When the list of truce days had gained at least a degree of acceptance, it was slowly lengthened till it included Thursday, Friday, and Saturday, all the saints' days, and all of Advent and Lent.[27]

In 1041 a Peace Council at Toulouges, in southern France, spelled out rules combining the chief elements of both the Peace and the Truce movements:

> No man may commit an act of violence in a church, or in the space which surrounds it and which is covered by its privileges, or in the burying-ground, or in the dwelling-houses which are, or may be, within thirty paces of it. . . . Furthermore, it is forbidden that anyone attack the clergy, who do not bear arms . . . or do them any wrong; likewise it is forbidden to despoil or pillage the communities of canons, monks, and religious persons. . . . Let no one burn or destroy the dwellings of the peasants and the clergy, the dovecotes and the granaries. Let no man dare to kill, to beat, or to wound a peasant or serf, or the wife of either, or to seize them and carry them off. . . . The bishops . . . have solemnly confirmed the Truce of God, which has been enjoined upon all Christians, from the setting of the sun of the fourth day of the week, that is to say, Wednesday, until the rising of the sun on Monday, the second day. . . .[28]

How much the Church's sanctions actually affected the warriors' behavior is conjectural, but their impact on knightly psychology and hence on the institution of knighthood was significant. The collective oaths helped to create a class consciousness that included acknowledgment of a personal responsibility to the Church and to the unarmed population. From prohibiting attacks on the clergy and the poor, the Church next advanced to prescribing a knightly mission as active protector of both. A council in Narbonne in 1054 expanded the terms of the Truce of God in these words: "Let no Christian kill another Christian, for there is no doubt that he who kills a Christian spills the blood of Christ."[29] This startling assertion, which few knights could accept literally, carried an implication with enormous potential consequence: the knight was justified in exercising his profession of war only if he did it against the enemies of Christ.

The Church had already moved toward sanctifying the knight with formulas for blessing his sword that had begun to appear in the tenth century and became common in the eleventh. Shortly after 1070 the ceremony of knightly investiture known as "dubbing," usually in a church, is first mentioned in French sources.[30] With this ritual of initiation the Church adopted knighthood, just as it had many other lay institutions, such as pagan holidays and sanctuaries.

The Church had first confronted the knights and imposed limits to their depredations. It had then prescribed an ascetic discipline for them as a group, while persuading them that they were at heart good and honorable and deserving of its blessing. Logically, it remained only to enlist their services for the Church's own purposes. From the Council of Narbonne to that of Clermont and the concept of the knight as the "soldier of Christ," the holy Crusader, was the final step.

knights
of the
first crusade

⊷ DO YOU KNOW WHAT GOD HAS PROMISED THOSE
WHO TAKE THE CROSS?
BY GOD! HE HAS PROMISED TO REWARD THEM WELL!
PARADISE FOR EVERMORE.   —Early twelfth-century Crusading song

⊷ LET NONE OF YOUR POSSESSIONS DETAIN YOU, NO SOLICITUDE FOR
YOUR FAMILY AFFAIRS, SINCE THIS LAND WHICH YOU INHABIT, SHUT IN
ON ALL SIDES BY THE SEAS AND SURROUNDED BY MOUNTAIN PEAKS, IS
TOO NARROW FOR YOUR LARGE POPULATION; NOR DOES IT ABOUND IN
WEALTH; AND IT FURNISHES SCARCELY FOOD ENOUGH FOR ITS CULTIVA-
TORS. HENCE IT IS THAT YOU MURDER ONE ANOTHER, THAT YOU WAGE
WAR, AND THAT FREQUENTLY YOU PERISH BY MUTUAL WOUNDS. LET
THEREFORE HATRED DEPART FROM AMONG YOU, LET YOUR QUARRELS
END, LET WARS CEASE, AND LET ALL DISSENSIONS AND CONTROVERSIES
SLUMBER. ENTER UPON THE ROAD TO THE HOLY SEPULCHRE; WREST
THAT LAND FROM THE WICKED RACE, AND SUBJECT IT TO YOURSELVES.
THAT LAND WHICH AS THE SCRIPTURE SAYS "FLOWETH WITH MILK AND
HONEY" WAS GIVEN BY GOD INTO THE POSSESSION OF THE CHILDREN OF
ISRAEL.

JERUSALEM IS THE NAVEL OF THE WORLD; THE LAND IS FRUITFUL
ABOVE OTHERS, LIKE ANOTHER PARADISE OF DELIGHTS.
   —Urban II at Clermont, according to the
Historia Hierosolymitana (History of Jerusalem), by Robert the Monk

ON NOVEMBER 27, 1095,
Pope Urban II preached the First Crusade at Clermont, in central
France, in an open field outside town, in a scene reminiscent of the
Peace of God councils. Chroniclers report that the vast crowd wept
and applauded by stamping on the ground,[1] their enthusiasm culminating in a great cry of "God wills it!"[2] Adhémar, bishop of Le
Puy, who later became the pope's legate, a churchman of noble
origin who had been trained as a knight, came forward, knelt, and
took the vow to go to Jerusalem. The pope gave him his blessing
and named him leader of the Crusade.[3] Urban then "instituted a
sign well suited to so honorable a profession by making the figure
of the Cross . . . the emblem of the soldiery . . . of God. This
. . . he ordered to be sewed upon the shirts, cloaks, and tunics of
those who were about to go."[4] Nobles and knights then followed
Adhémar's example, kneeling to take the vow.

During the eight subsequent months that Urban toured France
preaching the Crusade, thousands of knights enlisted under the banners of great regional princes such as Count Raymond of Toulouse,
Count Hugh of Vermandois (brother of the king), Count Godfrey
of Bouillon, Count Robert of Flanders, Duke Robert of Normandy,
and Bohemund d'Hauteville, the Norman lord of Taranto in southern Italy. Five knightly armies took the field, setting out in 1096 by
land and sea for Constantinople, their base of operations for the
offensive against the Saracens.[5]

The knights came from France and neighboring lands: Lorrainers,
Normans, Flemings, Burgundians, northern French, southern
French, Germans, Italians. Their condition varied from region to
region as to social standing, life-style, and the degree to which they
were involved in a feudal hierarchy, but all had been affected by
changes that had taken place since the year 1000 in knights' status,
in the laws of inheritance, and in the philosophical concept of knighthood. These changes, in fact, combined to supply much of the motivation for the Crusade.

Contemporary chronicles focus on the princely leaders, leaving

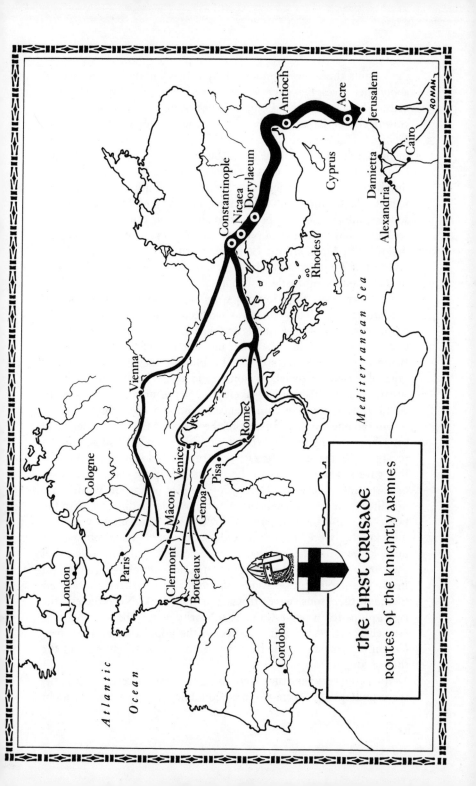

the first crusade
routes of the knightly armies

the knights almost anonymous. Many names and bits of information about their lives, however, are preserved in local documentary records. Those of central France, which supplied the single largest contingent of Crusaders, have been the subject of the study by Georges Duby mentioned in the first chapter. Duby's research, mainly in the records of the great abbey of Cluny, provides information about some of the men who fought in the First Crusade: their numbers, place in the social scale, marriage and inheritance customs, feudal relationships and obligations, and way of life. From other sources, information can be gleaned about their training, armor and weapons, and how they supported themselves. Among the knights described by Duby are the Le Hongre brothers, whose family lands lay west of Tournus, and who were vassals of the Gros family, lords of the neighboring castle of Uxelles.

In many ways the Hongres were typical of the contemporary knightly family. Of five sons, two had become monks, two responded to the preaching of the Crusade and went off to the Holy Land, never to return, the fifth, Humbert, became sole heir of the family estate.[6] Behind the varying fates of the Le Hongre men lay the series of gradual but drastic social, economic, and legal transformations in the situation of knights that had taken place in the course of the eleventh century, by more than coincidence in time for the Crusade.

On the one hand, as a result of the Peace of God movement and the Christianizing of knighthood, the title of knight had acquired a prestige that made even great lords proud to assume it, a prestige that gave a new cohesion to the two-tiered upper class. The lords, or castellans, a very small group of families of ancient wealth and nobility, exercised independent control over large districts, with the power to command and punish, tax, try, and exact military service. The knights were small landholders, subject to vassal obligations but exempt from the castellans' other powers, and with powers of their own within their restricted territories. Simple knights might marry the daughters or sisters of castellans; castellans chose their own and their sons' wives from their own rank. Nevertheless, the two groups felt a powerful class solidarity as members of the military elite, segregated from the rest of the population by their profession of arms and united by the ceremony of knighting and the title of knight.

But at the very time they were rising in the social scale, the knights were undergoing a catastrophic economic squeeze which brought about changes in family structure and inheritance customs that in turn profoundly affected the institution of knighthood. The ancient custom of dividing the inheritance equally among sons and daughters had diminished land holdings to the point where many heirs were reduced to poverty and peasant status.[7] A general European agricultural crisis around the year 1000 may have aggravated the problem.[8] The mechanism by which the historic change was brought about is not known, but by the end of the eleventh century the system of partition of estates had been supplanted nearly everywhere by that of undivided inheritance.[9]

In many areas this took the form of primogeniture, inheritance by the eldest son. In the region where the Hongres lived, the commonest form was the *frérèche* or *fraternitas* (brotherhood), in which the estate was owned intact by all the male relatives but administered by a single heir (not necessarily the eldest).[10] In either form of undivided inheritance, marriage and the founding of a household was limited to one or at most two sons. Where primogeniture was the rule, younger sons had to leave home to find a livelihood either in the Church or by the sword. In the area where the Hongres lived, they might remain at home but were subject to the supervision of the head of the family, who alone became truly an adult *(senior)*. The younger sons were perpetual "bachelors," "youths" *(juvenes)*, and they had to leave home, if not to seek a livelihood, at least to seek fortune and freedom.

In the early eleventh century, knighthood still constituted an open class. Anyone could belong who could afford a warhorse, armor, equipment, and peasants to work his lands in his absence. But the caste was scarcely threatened from below. The great medieval commercial revival, though already under way, had as yet enriched few merchants or peasants. On the contrary, in at least some areas, the knightly class was subject to losses, as impoverished members could no longer afford to equip themselves. In the first decades of the eleventh century, Duby found, the number of knights in the Mâcon region declined. One district, Merzé, had seven knights in the year 1000; one died without heirs, and two did not leave sufficient inheritance for their sons to maintain the rank; by the time of the First Crusade, descendants of these two knights were peasants, serving as stewards for a castellan who held land in their village. Only four knightly families were left, and no new ones rose from the peasantry or the bourgeoisie to replace those that had been lost.[11]

This demographic erosion of the knightly class, which in some regions actually threatened it with extinction, was counteracted in the course of the century by certain other changes. The knights' financial basis was strengthened by the general economic upturn and the new family customs with respect to succession. The title *miles* became more widely applied and was now attached to a surname, usually the name of the principal family estate. As family solidarity strengthened and individualistic ownership declined, knightly status began to be regarded as hereditary. After 1050 knighthood was commonly handed down from father to son; what had been a rank became a hereditary caste, closed to new members and locking in the old ones. In short, it became an "order," whose qualifications for membership were those of birth; neither peasant nor merchant could gain entrance, no matter how rich they might be.[12]

As knighthood became hereditary, the upper class grew more and more feudalized. In England following the Norman Conquest a symmetrical pyramid of vassalage was established, with the king at the top, the great barons under him, then the lesser lords, and finally the knights. In central France the feudal system was less neatly organized and showed a weaker sense of hierarchy. Where in Norman England

HOMAGE: THE VASSAL PLACES HIS HANDS BETWEEN HIS LORD'S AND KISSES HIM AT THE CLOSE OF THE CEREMONY. (*BIBLIOTHÈQUE ROYALE ALBERT IER, BRUSSELS, MS. 5, F. 285V*)

feudal tenure was the dominant form of landholding, in central France it was not. The allod still prevailed, and land in feudal tenure made up only a small part of each knight's or castellan's holding.

A crisscrossing network of homages had grown up among the castellans, but as a rule these merely guaranteed friendly relations and mutual security rather than establishing domination and subordination. Sometimes a castellan held a piece of land far from his own castle and therefore hard to defend or exploit. By conceding it as a fief to a lord who lived nearer, he created a bond of friendship while freeing himself from an administrative problem. Vassalage also connected the knights with the castellans, with the great ecclesiastical establishments, and with one another. In the region of Mâcon, by the time of the First Crusade, all the knights in the neighborhood of a castle were vassals of the castellan; those in the neighborhood of a great sanctuary such as the abbey of Cluny were vassals of the abbot. Knights were also often vassals of other knights.[13]

Humbert Le Hongre owned allodial lands near Chapaize and held a fief of Landry Gros, lord of the castle of Uxelles.[14] Landry's father had given the Hongres this fief, taken from land that the abbots of Cluny claimed he had illegally seized from them, and which therefore had dubious title.[15] Humbert, like his father before him, swore fidelity to the castellan; he promised gratitude and friendship and pledged not to do him any injury. In addition Humbert acknowledged the obligations of "aid and counsel" toward the lord of Uxelles. "Aid" included *ost*, or regular military services limited to forty days in a year, and *chevauchée*, mounted service on a shorter expedition or as an escort. Humbert also mounted castle guard in the garrison of Uxelles for specified periods every year. All these forms of service dated back two or three centuries, but where they had once been "public" duties, in the service of the king, they had long since become "private," in the service of a local lord.

The obligation of "counsel" required Humbert to attend the lord's court, advise on policy, take part in proceedings of justice, witness legal documents, and on occasion serve as hostage for the lord. In return, the lord undertook to respect Humbert's rights, to defend them when they were threatened by others, and to lend his influence on Humbert's behalf when necessary.[16]

Between two castellans, though a technical relation of lord and vassal might exist, it was never one of domination and dependence. Between a castellan and a knight, it was: the knight was legally and socially inferior. Yet his subordination at that time and place was typically moderate. Usually he still owned some land outright and did not depend on land granted by the lord. In frontier zones, lords often competed for knights' vassalage, offering greater advantages for lighter obligations.[17] Finally, most knights held fiefs from more than one lord. Besides his principal lord, the castellan of Uxelles, Humbert Le Hongre held a fief of the abbot of Cluny and one of the castellan of Bourbon-Lancy, 100 kilometers distant.[18] A vassal so situated was not severely subject to a lord; he could not be constrained to obey a command he considered unreasonable.

At the time of the First Crusade, knights' fiefs were typically a few acres of field or vineyard, or a single *mansus* (land sufficient to support a household). Often a fief was not land, but a church, a mill, rents, or a portion of tithes or taxes. These two could be subinfeudated, or regranted to other knights, often at several removes. In 1080 the count of Chalon was the eminent possessor of a church granted in fief to the castellan Lébaud de Digoine, who in turn had granted it to his vassal Hugues Lébaud, who had granted it to Seguin Rongefer, who had granted it to Josseran de Fautrières. Humbert Le Hongre held jointly with a neighboring knight three small parcels of land in fief from the lords of Bourbon-Lancy. Humbert and his neighbor in turn conceded them to two other knights, so that three small pieces of land were responsible for tying together six men in feudal arrangements.[19]

The knight of the eleventh century remained a country gentleman, sharing many of the interests and concerns of the peasants and closely associated with them, but from time to time escaping his agricultural pursuits to hunt, to mount castle guard, to attend the lord's assemblages, to go on pilgrimage, to accompany the lord on a journey, and above all to exercise the military profession that defined his position in society. He did not work his own lands. He might direct their exploitation if he did not employ a steward, and perhaps on rare occasions he might take part in harvest or haymaking, but he did not work with his hands. He was not a laborer; the drudgery of life he left to household servants, plowmen, herdsmen. His house at the center of the village was no castle, but a larger, better-constructed, and better-furnished version of those of the peasants, surrounded by outbuildings for the animals and storage of grain and wine. His prosperity depended not on his lord but on the weather and the harvest.

The knights of a single castle district formed a sort of extended family, linked to one another by professional solidarity and to the castellan by vassal relationships. Many had lived together for periods in the castle as boys while they underwent preparation for knighthood. During their periodic service of castle guard and when war threatened, they again lived together in the castle. At intervals they assembled for the lord's council and justice. Furthermore, they were nearly all kin, close or distant. Constrained after the year 1000 to marry within their own class, they usually married in their local neighborhood outside certain degrees of relationship. They also shared an ancestral bond as descendants of the ancient nobility.[20]

Though the decline in the knightly population had been arrested, their numbers remained small. Duby was able to identify at the time of the First Crusade only 98 knightly families in the Mâconnais region, unevenly distributed in 150 parishes. Some villages counted several knights; others had none. They were sparse in areas under Church domain, and more numerous in forest regions where land had been reclaimed for cultivation.[21] The contemporary chronicles of the great eleventh-century expeditions vastly exaggerate the numbers of knights, claiming 100,000 for the First Crusade and 50,000 in William the Conqueror's army. In fact, these two armies, including both knights and foot soldiers, probably numbered about 30,000 and 7,000 respectively.[22] On the eleventh- or twelfth-century battlefield, a few hundred knights represented a very considerable force.

The apprentice knight typically underwent training in the company of other boys in the household of his father's lord. Evidence of the existence of a dubbing ceremony is manifested in France in the last quarter of the century. In the German Empire dubbing did not appear until a century later, and then it was limited to the sons of royalty. In France it seems to have been practiced at all social levels, from the sons of kings and counts to the sons of castellans and of ordinary knights. Basically it consisted of the arming of the new knight, particularly of girding on the sword, which was done by his lord or by a powerful relative, though not necessarily by a person of superior rank. (A count might dub a future king.) The sword was usually a gift to the new knight from his sponsor. Several references indicate that the ceremony had taken on a religious character even at this early date; it was usually held on a religious holiday and in the presence of a priest.[23]

With respect to his armor and weapons, the knight made only very gradual progress. Helmet, shield, and mail armor remained his defensive equipment, lance and sword his weapons. Missile weapons were left to the foot soldiers. The knight scorned the bow as beneath his dignity, probably more because of its low cost than for the sometimes stated reason that fighting at a distance was cowardly (foot soldiers also fought hand to hand). In any case, the bow would have been awkward if not impossible for the mounted armored knight to use.[24]

The cost of warhorse and armor continued to rise. The warhorse —"*destrier*" or "charger"—bred for size and strength, might cost as much as fifty sous (shillings), five times the price of a good cow. The knight typically required several for himself and his squires. Armor was still more expensive; in 1080 the Le Hongre brothers' lord, Landry Gros, gave the abbey of Cluny a *mansus* in return for mail armor worth 100 sous. Armor and weapons were an important part of a family's patrimony.[25]

The revenues of a knight's lands were supplemented by booty. In the incessant petty wars of western Europe, prizes were horses and cattle, forage and food. In a great expedition such as the First Crusade, to this booty were added, in the words of the chroniclers, "gold and silver, and many ornaments,"[26] "houses filled with goods of all kinds,"[27] and "great riches."[28] The chronicler Raymond d'Aguilers wrote of the capture of Antioch, "How great were the spoils . . . it is impossible for us to say, except that you may believe as much as you wish and then add to it."[29] The valuables went to the knights; the foot soldiers shared the provisions.[30]

A more uniquely medieval source of knightly income was ransom. A prisoner taken in battle or siege was held until his relatives raised the required sum, whose size depended on his rank and soon became a source of pride. A captor had no need to haggle over the ransom of a noble captive whose vanity was gratified by the high price exacted from his dependents.

Traditionally, the fief was regarded as payment for the knight's services, or conversely the service as rent paid for the land.[31] But already in the eleventh century knights received money payments for service, usually in times of crisis or special need. As early as 991 Fulk Nerra of Anjou, at war with the count of Brittany, had knightly mercenaries among his troops.[32] Although eleventh-century Normandy was far more feudalized than central France, William the Conqueror in his English expedition had not only a large number of Flemish and other mercenary knights but compensated his own Norman knights, his vassals, with "generous provision." After the Conquest he settled his knights on lands held in feudal tenure, but on later occasions he again hired large numbers of knights for cash.[33] William's son William Rufus "energetically emptied his father's treasuries," partly in paying mercenaries. "Knights fixed their own rate of pay," complained chronicler William of Malmesbury.[34] William Rufus was described as "a wonderful merchant and paymaster of knights."[35] In the twelfth century knight hire became increasingly common.*

Irrespective of the form of his compensation, the medieval knight relished war for its own sake. In company with his peers, with the promise of booty to be won, he rode to battle exactly as to a tournament, which in the eleventh century, at least for the knights, it much resembled.

War was both profession and sport. The small private wars seldom involved anything that amounted to political significance. They were

---

*Another source of income, the *fief-rente*, which appeared early in the twelfth century, was a feudal arrangement that substituted a money payment for a grant of land but, unlike mercenary hire, involved homage and fealty and was passed from father to son.[37]

fought over a right that had been violated or a piece of land that had been usurped, or in order to violate a right or to usurp a piece of land. The national state did not exist. Patriotism had not yet been invented. In its absence the only large, transcendent cause for which Europeans could fight was the Christian religion. The idea of fighting in the name of God was introduced by a number of eleventh-century wars against the Muslims, especially the wars of the Reconquest in Spain. A powerful and radical pope, Gregory VII, gave the idea of holy war the impetus that made possible the Crusades.[36]

Gregory, famous for his "Gregorian Reform" of the Church, and his investiture struggle with German Emperor Henry IV, promoted a revolutionary theory of the relationship of the laity to the Church that proved to be of foremost importance to the knightly class. Building on the Peace of God and Truce of God movements, Gregory boldly carried the Church's intervention in worldly affairs a long step further. The interests of the Church took precedence over all others, according to Gregory. The role of the laity, and of the knights in particular, was to serve those interests, both in secular politics and elsewhere. In case of conflict, a knight's loyalty to the Church superseded his loyalty to his lord and even canceled his oath. Cleverly adopting feudal vocabulary, Gregory declared that knights were "the vassals of St. Peter."

Conservatives among the feudal nobility and clergy reacted strongly. In their eyes the pope's concerns should be limited to matters of faith. Gregory's pretensions threatened to reduce kings to the status of "village bailiffs," wrote one conservative churchman.[38] Another protested, "Hitherto, knights were bound by the covenant of the oath. They were shocked by injuries to their lord and avenged his wrongs; they protected his power, defended his dignity and remained vigilant for the sake of their own salvation; and it seemed equal to sacrilege if they rebelled against their vassal-duty. Now . . . knights are armed against their lords . . . right and wrong are confounded, sanctity of the oath is violated."[39]

Gregory demanded obedience from temporal rulers in worldly as well as spiritual matters, and to exact it he was prepared to resort to armed force. The laymen who would fight the pope's battles were *milites Christi*, knights of Christ. For centuries the Church had stood strictly for peace, in the tradition of St. Martin of Tours: "I am the soldier of Christ; I am not permitted to fight." Gregory discarded this pacifist ideology in favor of the "theory of the two swords": the pope, a representative of St. Peter, held two weapons, a spiritual blade to be drawn by his own hand, and a secular one to be drawn at his command by nobles and knights.

Gregory did not rely merely on theological reasoning to persuade. He added a powerful inducement: service as a "soldier of Christ" would be paid by total remission of sins. A knight, he said, could hardly hold secular lords dearer than the pope, "for they confer what is but wretched and transitory," that is, land and booty, while the pope promised "eternal blessings, absolving [the knights] from all sins." Those who fought for Gregory against Henry IV would win "[St. Peter's] blessing in this life and in the life to come."[40]

Gregory's vision of the Christian soldier, who wins salvation by his sword, provided the psychological and ideological motivation for the Crusade. Gregory's successor and protégé, Urban II, wielded the instrument forged by his predecessor with history-making effect. In the "great stirring of the heart in all the Frankish lands"[41] that he set in motion, the knights enthusiastically accepted the role of "the army of the Lord" fighting against "God's enemies and ours."[42]

In fact, the success of Urban's appeal far outran his own expectations. He may have intended no more than the enlistment of a modest army to aid Byzantine emperor Alexius Comnenus, who had appealed for help against the Turks. From the varying reports of his sermon, all written at second hand, it is not certain that Urban even mentioned Jerusalem, but the holy city was seized on by popular imagination as at once a more definite and a more inspiring goal than the mere succor of persecuted Christians and churches in Asia Minor. The Jerusalem the Crusaders pictured was the celestial city of the Book of Revelations, with gates of pearl, walls studded with precious stones, and streets paved with gold, with "no need of the sun, neither of the moon, to shine in it, for the glory of God did lighten it,"[43] where the water of life flowed and the tree of life bore leaves "for the healing of the nations."[44]

The magical attraction of the idea of Jerusalem was reinforced by economic and social motivations. The prospect of acquisition of land was inviting for younger sons excluded from inheritance by primogeniture. To land, booty, and adventure was added for many like the Hongres the chance to escape from the tutelage of the head of the family. Yet the main appeal was undoubtedly religious. "Let those who have hitherto been robbers now become soldiers," Urban proposed, according to one version of his address. "Let those who formerly contended against their brothers now fight as they ought, against the barbarians. . . . On one side will be . . . the enemies of God, on the other his friends,"[45] whose reward would be the remission of sins, in the novel form of the Crusading indulgence. The value of the indulgence was heightened by the ambiguity of the existing penitential system, which left Christians unsure that the penances they did were equal to their sins. Although the intricate theology of the indulgence was not yet worked out, it was understood that the sinner received absolution by an act of grace.

The Crusade was closely connected with an older form of penance popular with the knightly class: the pilgrimage. The Hongres's lord, Bernard Gros, went on pilgrimage to Rome in 1050 to atone for his land disputes with the abbey of Cluny.[46] The armed pilgrimage of the Crusade might be seen as a superior form in which a knight could win total remission of his sins through skill and valor. Significantly, "pilgrimage" was the term by which contemporaries referred to the Crusades, or alternatively "journey to the Holy Land," or "journey to Jerusalem." The Latin term for "Crusade" did not appear until the thirteenth century, the vernacular not until the eighteenth (along with "feudalism," "Gothic," and "Middle Ages"). The custom of pilgrimage itself contributed to the Crusade, as pilgrims were easily convinced that it was intolerable for the Holy Places to be in the hands of the infidels.

The chronicler Fulcher of Chartres described the departure of the Crusading knight: "Oh, how much grief there was! How many sighs! How much sorrow! How much weeping among loved ones when the husband left his wife so dear to him, as well as his children, father and mother, brothers and grandparents, and possessions! . . . The wife reckoned the time of her husband's return. . . . He commended her to the Lord, kissed her, and promised as she wept that he would return. She, fearing that she would never see him again, not able to hold up, fell senseless to the ground; mourning her living husband as though he were dead. He, having compassion, it seemed, neither for the weeping of his wife, nor . . . for the grief of . . . friends, and yet having it, for he secretly suffered severely . . . went away with a determined mind. What, then, can we say? 'This is the Lord's doing; it is marvelous in our eyes.' "[47]

The knightly armies of the Crusade were preceded eastward by the ragtag throng of the "People's Crusade," a bizarre product of Urban's appeal quite unforeseen by him. Inspired by two charismatic leaders, Peter the Hermit and Walter the Penniless (actually an impoverished German knight), this horde made up of bands numbering some tens of thousands (100,000, the chroniclers exaggerated), entirely out of the control of the Church or the princes, made a calamitous march through central Europe and the Balkans to perish at the hands of the Turks on the road to Nicaea in the fall of 1096.

In sharp contrast to the disorganized march of the rabble, the campaign of the knights was a model of efficiency. Its five armies, led by the great regional princes of France, Flanders, and Norman Italy (no kings took part), arrived in Asia Minor intact and in fighting trim, well-supplied through the able support of the Italian merchants and mariners, who had their own interests in the venture. Three years of march, battle, and siege were climaxed by the storming of Jerusalem on July 15, 1099.

The success of this most remarkable of medieval military operations reflects well not only on the Crusade's leadership but on the training, equipment, and morale of the individual knight who bore the hardships and fought the battles. Despite his near anonymity, the knight is the central actor in the story. Without repeating the well-known history of the Crusade, we may profitably examine his conduct in this largest single event in the annals of knighthood.

The factor that made a knight a Crusader was the Crusading vow, introduced by Urban at Clermont. By it the knight swore to march to Jerusalem and pray at the Holy Sepulchre. The cross sewn on his clothing was the public sign of the commitment. Vow and cross gave the clergy a measure of control over enlistment, allowing them to screen out those who were "unfit for bearing arms" and who would be "more of a hindrance than an aid"[48] The same two elements conferred a temporary ecclesiastical status on the Crusader. With vow and cross, the Crusader acquired privileges similar to those enjoyed by pilgrims. By becoming a kind of temporary cleric, he made himself subject to Church courts and therefore exempt from lay jurisdiction. The Church promised to protect his lands and family during his absence and granted him freedom from tolls and taxes, a moratorium on debts and exemption from interest payments, and delay in the performance of vassal services or in judicial proceedings.[49]

Of the approximately 30,000 fighting men in the Crusade, perhaps 4,000 were knights, the rest foot soldiers. An undetermined number of unarmed pilgrims, including women and children, accompanied the troops. Modest compared with modern armies, the Crusading army was nevertheless very large by medieval standards. To the local populations it looked huge. The Armenian chronicler Matthew of Edessa likened the "formidable and immense throng" to "locusts who cannot be counted or the sands of the sea which are beyond the mind's calculation."[50]

Organization and financing were improvised. Urban had named Bishop Adhémar leader (dux) of the Crusade, and Adhémar, fighting in person at their side, lent unity to the five armies, but he was in no sense a commanding general. There was no central command structure, even after arrival in Syria. Each prince continued to lead his own troops. Under the princes, lesser nobles, some with their own vassals, formed their corps, and parties of knights from the same region banded together to elect their own leaders. In combat, the knight fought essentially as an individual. He might seize the initiative, sometimes to the dismay of his leaders, to lead a scaling party, signal for an advance, or impulsively begin a skirmish. The knights were also capable of acting in concert; at Antioch they successfully pressed the leaders to continue the march to Jerusalem.[51]

Not surprisingly, strife was chronic among the leaders, who quarreled from Constantinople to Jerusalem (should the city be a possession of the Church or be ruled by one of them as a king?). But at critical moments they were able to resolve or overlook their differences and come effectively to each other's aid. Also noteworthy was the degree of discipline that the normally unruly knights accepted.

Both nobles and knights pledged or sold their lands to outfit and provision themselves. Achard de Montmerle, scion of a castellan family of the Mâcon region, mortgaged his patrimony to the abbey of Cluny to finance his participation.[52] Others sold their allodial lands outright, often to the Church. In a foreshadowing of future policies, Robert Curthose pledged his duchy of Normandy for 10,000 silver marks borrowed from his brother William Rufus, king of England, raised by William through a heavy tax on his English subjects.[53] There is no record of the fiscal arrangements of the Hongres in the First Crusade, but in the following century their knightly descendants pledged and sold lands to finance Crusading.[54]

Most knights provided their own horses and equipment, as for normal military expeditions. Two leaders, Bohemund d'Hauteville and his nephew Tancred, supplied some of their knights' equipment and horses,[55] and Raymond of Toulouse set up a fund of 500 marks

na a la arte de melerene. Ga
bruel li fires de la vile le reaut
a grant ioie a toutes ces ges
et fift bele chiere et li rendi la

gaaing. Li vaillant hoins q
grant souffraite auoit eue pst
auet lui gent acheual. t a pie
tant comme il en pot auoir

CRUSADERS FORAGING: LEFT, THEY CROSS THE JORDAN WITH A STOLEN
FLOCK OF SHEEP; RIGHT, GODFREY OF BOUILLON SLAUGHTERS A CAMEL.
(ROMAN DE GODEFROI DE BOUILLON, *BIBLIOTHÈQUE NATIONALE,*
MS. FR. 22495, F. 78)

to replace losses, after which "our knights boldly attacked the enemy
because those who had worthless and worn-out horses knew they
could replace their lost steeds with better ones" (Raymond d'Aguilers).[56] On the final march to Jerusalem, "our knights and more afflu-
ent people" bought Arabian horses.[57]

The knights' armor was also normally their own. Crossing a
"damnable mountain" in the Anti-Taurus range in 1097 in the heat
of summer and impeded by their armor, the knights "stood about
gloomily . . . trying to sell their shields, fine armor, and helmets for
three to five deniers, or whatever they could get. . . ."[58] Later they
"undertook to buy arms and fit and repair them."[59]

Transport and supplies were furnished at least in part by the
leaders. Throughout the long journey to Constantinople, the Crusad-

ers sought market rights, the opportunity to buy food. In the Balkans the count of Toulouse "bestowed many gifts upon the king of the Slavs [probably Bodin, a local prince] so that the Crusaders could buy in peace and look for the necessities of life."[60] When these were denied, they resorted to foraging; in other words, looting. The anonymous knight who recorded the deeds of the followers of Bohemund d'Hauteville and Tancred reported crossing the Balkans in "very rich country": "We . . . stayed for some days trying to buy provisions, but the inhabitants would sell us none. . . . So we seized oxen, horses, and asses, and anything else we could find. . . ."[61]

Once they arrived in the Holy Land, the Crusaders were supplied in part by sea—at Antioch first by a Genoese fleet that put in at nearby Port Simeon, later by English pilgrim ships, and at Jerusalem by another Genoese fleet. Raymond d'Aguilers praised the men "who dared to sail through the strange and vast surface of the Mediterranean and the [Atlantic] Ocean out of love of Crusading. The English . . . set sail on the Anglican Sea, and thus rounding the coast of Spain, bearing across the Ocean and ploughing through the waves of the Mediterranean, after great trials arrived at Antioch and Latakia in advance of our army. The English as well as the Genoese assured us commerce from Cyprus and other islands. . . . Daily these ships sailed to and fro over the sea."[62]

Away from the coast, the armies had to fend for themselves, which they did with fair success. The ripened harvests, Fulcher of Chartres wrote, were "prepared for their subsistence by God," though the native population doubtless took a different view.[63]

In military technology and technique, the First Crusade produced few innovations.[64] As in all medieval warfare, pitched battles played a minor role. Two were fought against the Turkish chief Kilij Arslan, near Nicaea and at Dorylaeum. The Crusaders also fought off sallies by the garrison of Antioch, repelled the relieving forces of Ridvan and Kerbogha, and routed an Egyptian army at Ascalon to bring the Crusade to a triumphant close. But sieges played the central role, with the Crusaders usually the besiegers, always at a disadvantage against defenders behind high walls. Yet Nicaea, Antioch, and Jerusalem were successively taken, the siege of Antioch occupying the entire winter and spring of 1097–1098. Lesser sieges were conducted at Ma'arrat al-Nu'man southeast of Antioch and at 'Arqah near Tripoli.

In the field, the Crusaders organized their troops in "battles,"

CRUSADING KNIGHTS MEET SARACENS, SOME OF WHOM
ASK FOR BAPTISM, WHILE OTHERS CONTINUE TO FIGHT.
(LES CHRONIQUES DE FRANCE, *BRITISH LIBRARY, MS. ROYAL 16G VI, F. 442*)

successive arrays of knights and foot soldiers that attacked in turn.
In the fight against Kerbogha near Antioch there were six "battles,"
each a double line, with foot soldiers in the first, knights in the
second.[65] The Turks, operating in large bands of light cavalry and
relying on mounted archers, preferred the fast strike and the surprise,
ambushing and attacking convoys and detached parties. At Dorylaeum they fell upon part of the Crusading army "with clashing of
weapons and shrieking" and "fiercely let loose a shower of arrows,"
driving the Crusaders in flight. The timely arrival of the rest of the
army saved the day. "It is their custom to use such arms," wrote
Fulcher. "They were all cavalry. We, on the other hand, were both
infantry and cavalry."[66] Kerbogha's army at Antioch, without the
advantage of surprise, was overpowered by the feudal array and after
a brief struggle, "when they realized the ensuing fight would be
waged hand-to-hand with swords rather than at a distance with
arrows," fled into the mountains.[67]

Yet the Crusaders came to admire the enemy, whom Urban had
called "that wicked race." The anonymous author of the *Gesta Francorum,* himself a knight, wrote after Dorylaeum, "What man, however experienced and learned, would dare to write of the skill and

prowess and courage of the Turks...? They have a saying that they are of common stock with the Franks, and that no men except the Franks and themselves are naturally born to be knights. This is true, and nobody can deny it, that if only they had stood firm in the faith of Christ and holy Christendom, and had been willing to accept One God in Three Persons, and had believed rightly and faithfully that the Son of God was born of a virgin mother, that he suffered, and rose from the dead and ascended in the sight of his disciples into Heaven, and sent them in full measure the comfort of the Holy Ghost, and that he reigns in Heaven and earth, you could not find stronger or braver or more skillful soldiers, and yet by God's grace they were beaten by our men."[68]

THE SIEGE OF ANTIOCH: CRUSADERS SCALE THE CITY WALLS.
FROM THE THIRTEENTH-CENTURY *HISTOIRE DE JÉRUSALEM.*
(BIBLIOTHÈQUE NATIONALE, MS. FR. 9081, F. 44)

SICKNESS AMONG THE CRUSADING KNIGHTS AT ANTIOCH; SOME FLEE THE EPIDEMIC (BELOW, RIGHT). *(BIBLIOTHÈQUE NATIONALE, MS. FR. 9081, F. 65V)*

In the siege, the Crusading knights used all the techniques established by European experience: blockade, starving the enemy into surrender; siege machines; mining; escalade (assaulting the walls with scaling ladders); and ruse or bribery.

A prolonged blockade sometimes caused more suffering among the besiegers than the besieged. At Antioch "both the rich and the poor were desolate from hunger," and the knights "ate the shoots of beanseeds growing in the fields and many kinds of herbs unseasoned with salt; also thistles . . . also horses, asses, and camels, and dogs and rats."[69] At Ma'arrat al-Nu'man, according to Fulcher, the Crusaders resorted to cannibalism, cutting "pieces from the buttocks of the [dead] Saracens . . . which they cooked."[70] At Jerusalem food supplies were adequate but the Crusaders suffered terribly from thirst, the Turks having filled up the wells and springs.[71]

Siege machines included the battering ram, the catapult and ballista for hurling missiles, and the wooden tower to attack walls. Usually they were constructed on the spot. At Nicaea the Crusaders "had machines made, battering rams, sows [for undermining walls], wooden towers, and petrariae [stone throwers]. . . . Our enemy and we retaliated alternately with all our might in the struggle. Often, armed with our machines, we dashed on the city, but with the strong wall obstructing us, the assault was brought to nought. Often the Turks, often the Franks, struck by arrows or by stones, died."[72]

At Nicaea the Crusaders undermined a tower. "Men were assigned to do the digging, with *arbalistae* [crossbowmen] and archers to defend them on all sides. So they dug to the foundations of the wall and fixed timbers and wood under it and set fire to it." The tower collapsed during the night, but the Turks hastily improvised a new wall and "when day came no one could harm them on that side."[73] The city finally fell after the Crusaders fought off a relieving army, and a surrender was negotiated by the Byzantine emperor.

At Antioch the Crusaders built a number of "castles" (assault towers) to try to storm the walls, but finally they resorted to trickery. A Turkish leader opened the gate—according to Fulcher because Christ appeared and commanded him to "return the city to the Christians,"[74] according to other accounts because he was suitably bribed.[75]

At Ma'arrat al-Nu'man, the defenders "hurled stones from catapults, darts, fire, [also] hives of bees and lime upon our men," but under cover of a barrage of rocks and missiles the knights scaled the walls and by nighttime had captured most of the towers. Awaiting morning for the final assault, the knights were chagrined to find not only the enemy gone, but the pilgrims who had accompanied the army busy seizing "the lion's share of booty and houses . . . while the knights . . . found poor pickings."[76]

The conquest of Jerusalem, like that of Ma'arrat al-Nu'man, was a victory of siege technology, but it was also one of psychological motivation. The knights fought with renewed ardor, and at first with improvised siege weapons. When these failed, they sent a detachment to Jaffa where the Genoese admiral William Embriaco supplied "ropes, hammers, axes, mattocks, and hatchets" and the know-how to assemble the machines. Everyone fell to. "We pressed the work, we labored, built, and cooperated. . . . Only the artisans, who were paid from public collections, and the men of [Count] Raymond, who got wages from his treasury, worked for money." When the leaders of the army saw that the Saracens had strengthened the city's walls facing the new machines, they set to work during the night shifting the machines to a new position. "Believe me," wrote Raymond d'Aguilers, "the disjointing, transporting over a mile, and erecting of those machines was no small job." On the morning of July 14 the assault began. As the siege machines were pushed toward the walls, "defenders rained down upon the Christians stones, arrows, flaming wood and straw, and threw mallets of wood wrapped with ignited pitch, wax, sulphur, tow, and rags."[77]

That night both camps worked furiously to repair walls and weapons, and in the morning the assault was renewed. By noon the Crusaders, baffled and discouraged, were contemplating defeat when, Raymond reported, a solitary knight "whose name is unknown to me, signaled with his shield from the Mount of Olives to the count [of Toulouse] and others to move forward."[78] Spurred by his example, the knights renewed their attempts to scale the walls. The *Gesta* chronicler says that Litold, a Flemish knight from Tournai, was the first Crusader to set foot on the wall.[79] The gates were opened and the Crusaders poured into the city.

The slaughter that followed was reported in every contemporary chronicle, western European, Greek, Jewish, and Muslim. Raymond d'Aguilers wrote that dismembered bodies lay in the houses and streets, trampled by knights and men-at-arms, and exaggerated that "in the Temple of Solomon . . . Crusaders rode in blood to the knees and bridles of their horses."[80] According to Fulcher, "They did not spare the women and children."[81] Writing a century later, Archbishop William of Tyre declared that "the victors themselves were struck with horror and disgust,"[82] but contemporary writers record no such reaction. Rather, they excused the slaughter as "poetic justice [for] pagans who blasphemed God" (Raymond d'Aguilers).[83]

Many other instances of shocking brutality on the part of the Crusaders are recorded: the mutilation of Slav prisoners,[84] the slaughter of captives at Antioch and Albara, the torture of "hapless Muslims" at Ma'arrat al-Nu'man,[85] the mounting of heads on posts[86] or even use of them as missiles,[87] and the dismemberment of bodies in search for swallowed gold pieces.[88] The chroniclers notwithstanding, the barbarous behavior of the Crusading knights was not inspired wholly by the fact that the enemy were pagans. Massacre and torture were common enough in warfare in Europe and continued to be in the centuries to come. Brutality was an inescapable aspect of medieval soldiering, for knights as for others.

Whatever the relationship of religious fanaticism to the savagery, it did not repress the knightly proclivity for turning war into sport. At Antioch, Raymond extolled "the bravado of the army whose

furent en grant uolente treltuit deleltei
nef deleur guerref bien emploier. zmout
delirroient liheurement enprendre leur
prumier fet quetoutes lef Autref genz
lef en doutallent.

CRUSADERS BOMBARD NICAEA WITH HEADS OF DEAD ENEMIES.
(LES HISTOIRES D'OUTREMER, *BIBLIOTHÈQUE NATIONALE,*
MS. FR. 2630, F. 22V)

Delautre denlque lachies quele fu
lour leneldhie deni comede Alel lem
pereres coltentinf lafilt olter delpoir Acel

knights actually sang warlike songs so joyously that they seemed to look upon the approaching battle as if it were a sport."[89] Before the battle with Kerbogha, the Crusading leaders proposed to the Turks that the issue be settled by a combat between picked companies from each side, but the Turks refused.[90]

Though the prospect of acquiring land had been held out to the knights and though during the expedition many were apparently planning on settlement (they "got out of bed at midnight," says a chronicler, to seize villas in the plains of the Jordan),[91] only a handful actually stayed in the Holy Land. Even these remained for the most part not as settlers or landlords but as garrison soldiers. While a few of the Crusade's leaders—Godfrey of Bouillon, Bohemund and Tancred d'Hauteville, Baldwin of Boulogne—assumed titles of royalty and for a time lorded it over subject populations, nearly all the knights who had survived the fighting and the rigors of the expedition returned home. This was in marked contrast to the members of the other two major military expeditions of the time, the Norman conquests of England and Sicily. Syria and Palestine apparently had little appeal as permanent homes for the men of Europe.

The history of the later Crusades is essentially that of efforts to sustain and reinforce the garrisons left behind, a history in which a major role was played by the Military Orders: the Templars, the Hospitalers, and the Teutonic Knights, whose story will be told in another chapter.

Modern historians have pronounced a generally negative verdict on the Crusades. The cultural osmosis between Islam and the West, once credited to the Crusades, is now perceived as taking place mainly through other points of contact, chiefly in Italy, Sicily, and Spain. Viewed strictly from the perspective of the knightly class, however, the great adventure had profound and beneficial effects (whatever the fates of individual Crusaders). It provided a needed safety valve for surplus sons, such as the two Hongres who went on the First Crusade and the grandson of Humbert Le Hongre who perished on the Second. Crusading broadened the horizons of the rustic knight whose world had consisted of the village, the neighboring castle, and an occasional *chevauchée* or pilgrimage. Not only was he exposed to new scenes and ideas, but he mixed with knights and lords of other regions of France and of Europe. In the later Crusades he even met kings and emperors. This mingling of the European elite helped to counteract the feudal political fragmentation and was a factor in the development of national feeling. At the same time, the knights acquired a taste for travel and for luxury that enriched their life-style.

Most important, the Crusades, and above all the First Crusade, gave an immense impetus to the Christianization of knighthood, the idea of chivalry that had been fostered by the Peace of God and the Truce of God. One who had fought in the Holy Land wore the imaginary badge of the *militia Christi*, Christ's soldiery, in the eyes of the twelfth century surely the insignia of true knighthood.

the
tROUBaDOURS
and the
LiteRatuRe
of knighthood

IF THE event of the eleventh century that had the greatest impact on the knight was the First Crusade, the most important influence of the twelfth century on the knightly class lay in a totally different direction: the outpouring of chivalric literature, above all, that of troubadour poetry. The troubadours were knights, as were their successors, the trouvères of northern France and the minnesingers of Germany. Their verses demonstrate an inventiveness and sophistication that is startling after the simplicity and rough piety of the chroniclers of the First Crusade. Living amid the civilized court and castle life of southern France, these knight-poets reached the height of their fame three generations after the Crusade, toward the end of the "Renaissance of the twelfth century," with its great achievements in scholarship, law, science, philosophy, and historical writing.

Unlike the individually obscure Crusading warriors, the knightly troubadours left lasting records of their personalities in their verses, and in many cases considerably more is known of them. Arnaut Daniel, celebrated by Dante and Petrarch and translated by (among others) Ezra Pound, is one of those troubadours to have a *vida*, or biographical sketch, appended to the thirteenth-century manuscript of his poems.

"Arnaut Daniel was from the same region as Arnaut de Mareuil [another troubadour], from the bishopric of Périgord, from a castle called Ribérac, and he was a gentleman. He was accomplished in letters and loved to write songs. He abandoned his learning and became a jongleur, and adopted a fashion of composing in precious rhymes *(caras rimas)*, so that his songs were not easy to understand or learn. And he loved a noble lady of Gascony, wife of Lord Guillem de Buovilla, but the lady did not grant him the pleasure of love; so that he said:

'I am Arnaut who gathers the wind
And hunts the hare with the ox
And swims against the incoming tide.' "[1]

INITIAL FROM A MANUSCRIPT OF ARNAUT DANIEL'S POEMS SHOWS HIM IN A SCHOLAR'S CAP AND GOWN. *(BIBLIOTHÈQUE NATIONALE, MS. FR. 854, F. 65)*

The castle of Ribérac (now demolished) stood on the banks of the river Dronne, fifty miles northwest of Bordeaux. Built by the counts of Périgord (the Talleyrands) in the tenth century, it was the seat of a viscount. We do not know Arnaut Daniel's status in the castle, but the designation *gentils hom* shows that he was a son of a knight, possibly a lord. His accomplishment in "letters" suggests that he was a younger son intended for the clergy. Another troubadour described him as "Arnaut the scholar who is ruined by dice and backgammon, and goes about like a penitent, poor in clothes and money."[2] He seems to have been a friend of troubadour-knight Bertran de Born (fl. 1175–1196), to whom he addressed a poem.[3] From his verses, we may conjecture that he attended the coronation of the French king Philip II in May 1180,[4] the beginning of his period of productivity, which lasted until 1210. A story, probably apocryphal, that accompanies his *vida* says that he participated in a poetic competition at the court of Richard Lionheart.[5]

Such is the surviving information about the poet who "surpassed them all."[6] The estimate of many modern critics agrees with that of Dante and Petrarch, that he was the most gifted of the host of knightly poets who enriched Western literature with their outpouring of "Provençal" poetry in the twelfth and thirteenth centuries, stimulating similar literary movements in northern France, Spain, Germany, and Italy and permanently influencing the literary tradition of Europe.

Two elements distinguished the new poetry: it was written not in Latin but in the vernacular, the "mother tongue," and its customary subject matter was romantic love. Love was hardly a new theme for poets, but the Romans treated it realistically (Catullus), heroically (Vergil), or satirically (Horatius and Propertius). The Latin poetry of the early Middle Ages usually dealt with more serious philosophical or religious subjects; when a lady was praised, it was as a patroness. Romantic love introduced a new theme, one that idealized both the love object and the emotion experienced by the lover.[7]

The troubadours are usually referred to as "Provençal poets," but the term is slightly misleading, since only a fraction were natives of the ancient Roman province east of the Rhone. All wrote in "Provençal," the language of southern France, properly the *langue d'oc,* as opposed to the *langue d'oil* of northern France (*oc* and *oïl:* "yes"). A Romance language surviving only as a dialect, the *langue d'oc* is closer to modern Portuguese or Spanish than to French. Four hundred and sixty names of troubadours have been preserved. The origins of a little more than half are known; of these one quarter came from Provence and one quarter from neighboring Languedoc. The rest came mostly from Périgord, Gascony, Limousin, La Marche, Auvergne, Quercy, Poitou, Rouerge, Dauphiné, Vienne, Velay—in a word, from all over southern France, while a handful had their origins in northern Italy or in Spain.[8]

"Troubadour" *(trobaire)* derives from the word for the poet's activity, *trobar,* whose modern French cognate is *trouver,* to find; the troubadour was a "finder," a discoverer, inventor, creator. He was a composer of songs; troubadour poetry was meant to be sung. As a member of the knightly class, he was distinguished from the lower-class jongleurs, who were basically entertainers, not poets. (A modern scholar speculates that the jongleur, at first a juggler, acrobat, or magician, at some point added music to his act.) The troubadour might sing his own works or employ a jongleur to perform them. Some troubadours mention their jongleurs in their verse, or even address songs to them.

The *vidas* follow a fixed formula: the poet's country of origin, his social condition, an outline of his career with emphasis on his amorous adventures, and a brief criticism of his talents as poet and musician. Thus we are told where Arnaut Daniel came from, what social class he belonged to, the story of his life in brief including a frustrated love affair that supposedly inspired his poetry, and an evaluation of his work: that his versification was elaborate and his poems were consequently hard to understand. Neither the *vidas* nor the *razos* (stories or themes) that often accompanied them in the manuscripts, and that were evidently recited by jongleurs to introduce the poet's songs, are wholly reliable sources. Both are often demonstrably assembled and elaborated from scraps of information in the poems or in the verses of other poets, or even adapted from folklore or fiction. Arnaut's *razo* about the poetic competition at the court of Richard Lionheart is an anecdote that is also told about another troubadour. Nevertheless, some facts can be inferred from the *vidas* and *razos* about the class origins of the troubadours.

The troubadour was a knightly poet. He wrote for and about knights; he had the status of a knight even though his father was not always a knight. Many of the *vidas* state that the subject was a knight or son of a knight—often with the adjective "poor" preceding the "knight." Some troubadours were from castellan families, and occasionally there is evidence that the families had fallen on hard times. A few were great lords, usually patrons of troubadours, who had taken up poetry themselves: Richard Lionheart; Alfonso I of Aragon; Raimbaut d'Aurenga (of Orange); Ebles of Ventadorn; Savaric de Mauléon, seneschal of Poitou; Enric I, count of Rodez; Guillem, lord of Les Baux; Albert, son of the Marquis de Malespina. Some troubadours were middle class: the son of a cloth merchant, of a tailor, of a furrier, of a goldsmith, or simply "of a bourgeois." Some were clerics—monks, priests, or canons who had abandoned their profession, having, in the words of one *vida*, "fallen in love with the vain things of this world." A few were "of low estate," including, if we are to believe their *vidas,* two of the greatest, Marcabru (fl. 1129–1150), left on the doorstep of a rich man and by implication illegitimate,[9] and Bernart de Ventadorn (fl. 1150–1180), whose father was "a serving man who was a stoker and heated the oven to bake the bread in the castle [of Ventadorn]."[10] One troubadour, son of a poor fisherman, learned to play the viol and compose songs, and became a jongleur, whereupon "the dauphin [count] of Auvergne took him for his knight and clothed and armed him and gave him lands."[11] Eight of the *vidas* describe women troubadours *(trobaritz),* all depicted as noble, well-educated, and most as "very beautiful."*

In almost every *vida* the troubadour's knightly virtues are stressed: he was "a courtly man and eloquent," "a good knight and a good warrior," "a poor knight but clever and well-bred and skilled at arms," "a man of *pretz* and *valors*" (excellence and worth), or "a gentleman and handsome and charming and with natural sense." The great lords who were troubadours and patrons of troubadours had an additional knightly virtue: they were *"larcs,"* generous, open-handed.

Whether the troubadours originally wrote down their poems, or whether the songs were transmitted orally until their thirteenth- and

RUINS OF THE CASTLE OF VENTADORN (VENTADOUR),
IN SOUTH-CENTRAL FRANCE, WHERE TROUBADOUR
BERNART DE VENTADORN WAS BORN,
SON OF A CASTLE SERVANT.

*Scholar Meg Bogin presents the poems of seventeen in her *The Women Troubadours* (1976).[12]

fourteenth-century transcription is not known, but the versification is at times so complex that oral composition seems impossible. Yet some troubadours, like many of their fellow knights, may not have been literate. The *vidas* describe many as *ben enseignatz*, which could mean "well educated" or simply "well bred." Clerics who became troubadours were usually described as "lettered," implying Latin scholarship, as in the case of Arnaut Daniel.

The great majority of troubadours made their living from their poetry. Most seem to have belonged to the category of younger sons of knights or castellans who had to make their way in the world or were members of knightly families who had lost their lands. A few were sons of the bourgeoisie, perhaps looking for a way to better their social position. They were men of talent; as their *vidas* described them, they could "sing and compose well" and "play the viol," they had "good natural sense," they were "clever," "charming," "wise," and "eloquent." Turning troubadour was a means of upward mobility open to a man of intelligence, artistic ability, and social skill. All one had to do was find a patron.

In a few cases, the *vidas* tell us that a poor knight was taken in hand by a richer knight or great lord, and "clothed and armed" and given lands. More often the knight had to find his own sponsors, traveling from court to court, spending a few weeks or months, sometimes years, and then moving on. The *vidas* are full of their subjects' movements "from castle to castle" on their "travels through the world"—the world of the troubadours, comprising southern France, Lombardy, and northern Spain. That troubadouring was a viable profession supporting a large number of practitioners is testimony to the material wealth and taste of twelfth-century civilization in southern France. Has any modern time and place, even with the aid of printing, produced more poets, including perhaps a dozen of the first order? Certainly none has permitted a larger number of poets to make their living by writing poetry.

A scholar has compared troubadour poetry to a flower that seems suddenly to appear without root or stalk but that "buds, opens out and blooms in perceptible stages in the south of France in the twelfth century."[13] Root and stalk have been sought in classical literature, Christian thought, and the poetry of Moorish Spain. Ovid (43 B.C.– A.D. 18), a powerful influence on all medieval literature, was well known to the troubadours, as probably were early medieval poets who wrote in Latin, such as Boethius (c. 480–524), Venantius Fortunatus (c. 530–c. 603), Alcuin (c. 735–804), and Hrabanus Maurus

(776–856). Some of the troubadour music came directly from the Church, as did certain verse forms; even the terms in which earthly women were flattered in troubadour poems were often borrowed—daringly—from those used to praise the Virgin Mary: the troubadour "worshiped" his lady, there was "no woman like her."

Some scholars, on the other hand, consider the eleventh-century *zajal* and *muwashshah* of Muslim Andalusia as the source of troubadour poetry. Written to be sung, accompanied by lute or rebec (an early violin), these poems were distinguished by their lively measure, elaborate rhyme scheme, and sophisticated tone. Their themes were unrequited love, self-sacrifice, eternal fidelity, and love supreme over all else in the world. (There was even a Muslim forerunner of the women troubadours, blue-eyed, red-haired Wallada, daughter of Caliph Al-Mustaki and a Christian slave, herself a patron of scholars and poets.)

The cultural interchange between Muslims and Christians in Spain reached France by way of the French knights who fought in the Reconquest. Some took Muslim slaves back to France, or even married Muslim ladies. When the French captured Barbastro in northeast Spain in 1064, each knight was awarded a house with all it contained—furniture, servants, women, and children. A dispossessed Arab sent a Jewish merchant to ransom his daughters. The Jew found the conqueror in Moorish dress, seated on a divan, surrounded by Muslim girls. He refused all offers of ransom, saying that he had married one of the daughters and hoped she would give him sons. "Her Muslim ancestors did this with our women when they took this country. Now we do likewise." He then turned to the girl and in broken Arabic told her to take her lute and sing some songs for the gentleman. The Jew added, "I was surprised and pleased to see the knight show great enthusiasm as if he understood the words—though he continued drinking."[14]

The expedition against Barbastro was led by the duke of Aquitaine, whose son Guillem (William) IX (1071–1127) has been called the "first troubadour," on the strength of his being the first whose verses have survived. The chronicler Ordericus Vitalis pictures Guillem, whom he describes as "gay and lighthearted," entertaining "kings and magnates and throngs of Christians" with stories of his misadventures in the Crusade of 1101 in the Holy Land "using rhythmic verses with skillful modulations," as if such entertainment was already an accepted tradition.[15]

In the words of Guillem's *vida,* he was "one of the greatest courtiers in the world and one of the greatest tricksters of ladies, and a good knight at arms, and openhanded in giving, and he traveled a long time through the world to deceive women."[16] Chronicler-cleric William of Malmesbury characterized him more severely as "a buffoon and a man so inclined to evil that he indulged in all manner of vices before his return from Jerusalem. . . . He took nothing seriously, he turned everything into a joke and made his listeners laugh uncontrollably."[17]

Five of Guillem's eleven surviving poems[18]—the best known—are burlesques, including the riddle poem *"Farai un vers de dreyt nien"* (I'll write a verse about nothing at all) and the Rabelaisian *"Farai un vers, pos mi sonelh"* (I'll write a verse, then fall asleep), with its tale of a knight who pretends to be a deaf-mute in order to spend a week in "dalliance gay" with two married ladies who wish to ensure discretion. In another equally lusty song, *"Companho, tant ai agutz d'avols conres"* (Comrades, I have had such sorry company), he rails in earthy terms against the husband who too closely guards his wife's virtue; he hates a *cons gardatz* (a guarded cunt) as much as a fishing hole without fish; the man who first guarded cunt should have perished,

> For never was there a servant or guard
> Who was worse to his lord
> But I shall tell you about the cunt, what its nature is
> As a man who has done bad things with it and taken worse from it:
> Although any other thing decreases if someone steals from it, the cunt
> increases.

Thus in a private thicket when the wood is cut, two or three trees grow up where one stood before,

> And when the wood is cut down, it grows back even thicker,
> And the lord does not lose his revenue or his income from it;
> The devastation is lamented wrongly if there is no damage at all.

It is wrong to lament the devastation if there is no harm at all.[19]

One of William's poems is a *congé,* a farewell poem written at a time when he believed that he was dying. The remaining five are on themes that became characteristic for troubadours: *"d'amor e de joy e de joven"* (of love and joy and youth). One of his verses provides the first example in the vernacular of one of poetry's great favorite devices, the opening salute to spring, *"Ab la dolchor del temps novel"* (In the sweetness of the new season). After the singing birds and flowering hawthorn, the poem ends characteristically with a jolly reference to physical love:

> *Que tal se van d'amor gaban,*
> *Nos n'avem la pessa e·l coutel.*

> (Let others brag vainly about love,
> We have the food and the knife.)[20]

The early troubadours called all their poems simply *vers,* but Guillem IX's five love poems belong to the most popular troubadour genre, the *canso.* By mid-century other forms had emerged: the *sirventes* (satire), *tenso* (debate), *alba* (dawn song), *pastorela* (pastoral, usually a dialogue between a virtuous shepherdess and a seducing knight), the *cobla* (epigram), and the *planh* (lament on the death of a great personage).

Whereas so much of the terminology of medieval history and criticism is the invention of the eighteenth century, the terminology of troubadour poetry is wholly contemporary. The worldly, witty, and self-conscious verse was discussed and evaluated by its practitioners and their circles. Poets wrote verses criticizing and satirizing each other and theorizing about their own poetry. Literary controversy developed, with songs exchanged like challenges. Should poetry be clear and accessible, easy to understand, and social in nature *(trobar leu),* as in the verses of Bernart de Ventadorn and Raimon de Miraval, or should it be personal, allusive, and difficult, making use of colored words with overtones and nuances, like the poetry of Arnaut Daniel *(trobar clus)?* Marcabru boasted that he had written poems he himself could not understand. Should it be rough *(trobar braus),* with discordant, harsh words, or smooth *(trobar plan),* or delicate *(trobar prim)?*

Typically the songs were in stanza form, with usually seven or eight metrically identical strophes and a *tornada,* an envoi of two to four lines. Each poem had a different rhyme scheme and meter; some rhyme schemes were very complicated.

TROUBADOUR BOUND WITH A GOLDEN THREAD OF LOVE, FROM THE
FOURTEENTH-CENTURY MANESSE CODEX, A COLLECTION OF MINNESINGER VERSE.
(*UNIVERSITÄTSBIBLIOTHEK HEIDELBERG, COD. PAL. GERM. 848, F. 251*)

COURTLY LOVE: DAVID AND BATHSHEBA,
FROM THE ILLUMINATED BOOK OF THE OLD TESTAMENT.
(*PIERPONT MORGAN LIBRARY, MS. 638, F. 41V*)

The product of poets who were original and individual, troubadour poetry derives its distinctive unity from its very nearly unanimous subject matter: love as a means of a man's self-realization. What kind of love best achieved this end? The troubadours examined love in all its permutations, analyzed it, weighed it: physical love, in the setting of the court, with its manners and customs; the dreamlike love for a distant and unapproachable lady realized only in the imagination; love on a transcendental plane, for God or the Virgin Mary. They defined, in varying terms, good and bad love: *Fin' Amors* and *Fals' Amors*. *Fals' Amors* was always unbridled lust, but *Fin' Amors* could be otherworldly, or it could be earthly love controlled by reason and moderation or merely practiced according to the ideas of proper court behavior.

Earthly love had one invariable characteristic: it was adulterous. The object was always a married woman. With equal invariability her status was always higher than that of the poet, who approached her humbly and worshipfully, eager to "serve." Sometimes she was cruel and deceitful, sometimes kind, sometimes she remained unattainable. In the background of this two-character drama, played over and over in troubadour verse, hovered a pair of minor but essential elements, the jealous husband and the *lauzengier,* the throng of gossiping, cynical, malicious scandalmongers.

This "courtly love," to use the label invented by a nineteenth-century critic, has provoked more comment than almost any other aspect of medieval civilization. Gaston Paris, who coined the term in 1883[21] and whose views were accepted for many decades, deduced from the poetry an aristocracy that legitimized adultery and practiced it as an art. The game had a system of rules codified at the court of the counts of Champagne by Andreas Capellanus (André the Chaplain) in a work called *De arte honeste amandi (On the Art of Noble Love),* written in the 1190s. Paris accepted as realistic Andreas's picture of twelfth-century ladies and poet-knights entertaining themselves with mock trials at which varieties of amatory conduct were argued and judged and love was found to exist only "outside the bonds of wedlock," and at which decisions were pronounced on all the minutiae of adulterous love.[22]

Today, however, these "courts of love" are generally regarded as fiction, and Andreas's intention is perceived as satirical.[23] The "courtly love" of the troubadours is regarded by most scholars as having been either artificial convention or tongue-in-cheek wit. Sexual freedom, particularly before marriage, was an explicit medieval male prerogative. A twelfth-century nobleman of northern France was described by a chronicler intent on flattery as surpassing in his sexual exploits "David, Solomon, and even Jupiter"; his funeral was attended by ten legitimate and twenty-three illegitimate children.[24] No such freedom was accorded women. Adultery on the part of a wife cost a husband his honor and was therefore punished by disgrace or repudiation, with the lover often killed or castrated. Adultery with the lord's wife was the worst crime a vassal could commit. Yet this was precisely the aim expressed over and over by the troubadours, whose verses, far from being passed surreptitiously from lover to lady, were sung aloud in public.

The theme is so persistent and freighted with such emotional conviction that it seems as if some real motivation must lie behind it. It has been suggested that the married woman of higher rank was "a conduit of status" for the knightly poet.[25] A countess or chatelaine offered the "poor knight" an opportunity, in his own reiterated words, to enhance his *valors* (worth) and *pretz* (excellence). The troubadours flattered ladies to reach their lords; courtly love was ambitious flirtation.

Georges Duby, in his *Medieval Marriage* and in an essay "Youth in Aristocratic Society," goes further, asserting that troubadour poetry was an expression not only of the desire for upward mobility but of the frustrations, particularly strong in the twelfth century, that resulted from the knight's position in society. A knight was considered a "youth" until he had married, become the head of a house, and started a family. Younger sons, or even eldest sons unable to make a good match, might remain "youths" for a long time, even permanently. Although the troubadours glorified youth, the longed-for and often unreachable goal was to join the company of the adults. The poetry of courtly love may have been a gesture of defiance to the system, a "sublimated form of abduction."[26]

The traditional view of critics is that the poetry of the troubadours idealized women. Perhaps the reverse is true: the women in the poems already possessed a status from which the poets, through their verses, sought to borrow. Sometimes pictured as kind and beneficent, sometimes as cruel, capricious, and treacherous, the heroines of the poems always remained objects through which the poet tried to attain his goal of self-realization or, more concretely, position at court.

The ladies associated with the troubadours by the *vidas* and *razos* possessed all the attributes of the subjects of the verses: they were almost always great ladies, and invariably married. Arnaut Daniel was supposed to have fallen in love with "the wife of Lord Guillem de Buovilla." Gaucelm Faidit "fell in love with Maria de Ventadorn," lady of the castle of Ventadorn.[27] Guillem de Balaun's inspiration was "a gentle lady from Gabaudan, Guilhelma de Jaujac," whom "he greatly loved and served in deeds and songs."[28] Peire Rogier loved Ermengarde, viscountess of Narbonne, "and made his verses and cansos for her."[29] Raimbaut de Vaqueiras loved "the [married] sister of Marquis Boniface [of Montferrat],"[30] Richart de Berbezill "a lady, wife of Jaufre de Tonnay, a valiant baron of that area, and the lady was gentle and beautiful and gay and pleasant."[31] One troubadour, Uc Brunenc, from Rodez, loved "a [presumably wealthy] bourgeoise of Aurillac named Galiana, but she did not love him," whereupon he became a monk.[32] Raimon de Miraval's *razos* credit him with seven exploits of gallantry with seven high-born ladies.[33] Some love affairs attributed to the troubadours are demonstrably fictional, as in cases involving historical figures about whom we have external information. Sometimes the biographer patently borrows a story, as in the *razo* of troubadour Guillem de Cabestang, recognizable as "The Eaten Heart," a favorite folktale whose most famous version is "The Castellan of Coucy": a knightly lover is slain by his mistress's husband, who has his heart roasted and served to his unaware wife.[34]

The poets themselves were less indiscreet than their biographers. Usually the songs are addressed merely to a nameless "lady." Sometimes the subject is given a code name: Lady Better-than-Good, More Than a Friend, Best of Ladies, Good Neighbor. When "real" names are given, they are often unidentifiable.

Significantly, the ladies in troubadour songs are a faceless assemblage, with little to distinguish one from another. Eyes are neither blue nor dark but merely "beautiful," nor is hair color often mentioned. All the ladies display red mouths, white breasts, and slender white bodies, and all are endowed with the prescribed virtues: *pretz, sabers, cortezia, umiltatz* (excellence, wisdom, courtesy, humility).[35]

A song by Bertran de Born does explicitly what much troubadour poetry does in effect. Since his lady cares nothing for him, and since he can find no substitute, he will "cull from each a fair trait / To make me a borrowed lady / Till I again find you ready." From "Bels Cembelins," her color and eyes. From Aelis of Montfort, "Her straight speech free-running, / That my phantom lack not in cunning." From the viscountess of Chalais, "Her two hands and her throat." From Lady Anhes of Rochechouart, her "grace of looks." From Audiart at Malemort, "her form that's laced / So cunningly." From Miel-de-ben (Better Than Good) "Her straight fresh body, / She is so supple and young, / Her robes can but do her wrong." From Lady Faidita, "Her white teeth." From Bels Mirals, "Tall stature and gaiety." Finally,

> Ah, Bels Senher, Maent, at last
> I ask naught from you,
> Save that I have such hunger for
> This phantom
> As I've for you, such flame-lap,
> And yet I'd rather
> Ask of you than hold another,
> Mayhap, right close and kissed.
> Ah, lady, why have you cast
> Me out, knowing you hold me so fast!

> *(Translation by Ezra Pound)*[36]

Eighteen of Arnaut Daniel's songs have survived, seventeen of them *cansos*.[37] The other is a *sirventes* satirizing, in terms surpassing Guillem IX in their coarseness, the conventions of courtly love which the other songs demonstrate: the Lady Ena seeks to impose a condition on her suitor, Bernart de Cornil, to which, transgressing the code of lovers, he refuses to accede; the whole world of knights and troubadours is torn by the controversy, with some condemning Bernart, others defending him. The lady's condition, an "unnatural" form of intercourse that shocked Arnaut's early-twentieth-century editor, is debated—and rejected—in a tour de force of versification: five verses of nine lines each and a four-line *tornada*, each verse with a single rhyme, and the *tornada* continuing the rhyme of the final stanza. At the same time, the song is full of plays on words, including a series of puns on "Cornil," Bernart's place of origin.*[38]

Arnaut's *cansos* are written in a different spirit, though with sensuality and irony, but display the same virtuosity of craftsmanship. In one, admired by Dante and translated by Ezra Pound, Arnaut uses

*Some scholars question Arnaut's authorship.

a rhyme scheme in which, besides interior rhymes, each line rhymes with a corresponding line in the other stanzas—almost a third of the syllables are governed by rhyme. Alliteration and assonance also tie the poem together. The lines are segments of the more customary eight-syllable line, and the sounds, rough and smooth, produce the onomatopoeic effect of the wind in the trees and the chattering birds. (Ezra Pound's translation accomplished the difficult feat of reproducing meter and rhyme scheme, although he did not attempt the onomatopoeia; but the unfortunate result was to emphasize the poem's mechanics and obscure the meaning, at the same time employing jarring archaisms. The two verses given below are accompanied by James Wilhelm's literal translation.)

L'aura amara	The bitter breeze
Fa·ls* bruoills brancutz	Makes the leafy copses
Clarzir	Whiten
Que·l doutz espeissa	That the soft one thickens
ab fuoills,	with leaves,
E·ls letz	And the happy
Becs	Beaks
Dels auzels ramencs	Of birds on branches
Ten balps e mutz,	It holds stammering and mute,
Pars	Both paired
E non-pars;	And unpaired.
Per qu'eu m'esfortz	And so I strive
De far e dir	To do and say
Plazers	Pleasant things
A mains, per liei	To many, because of her
Que m'a virat bas	Who has turned me from high
d'aut,	to low,
Don tem morir	So that I fear to die
Si·ls afans no m'asoma.	If she doesn't heal my torments.
Tant fo clara	It was so clear,
Ma prima lutz	My first bright glimpse,
D'eslir	When I selected

*In Provençal poetry, words are often combined, with letters omitted, the omission indicated by a dot: *fa·ls* is a contraction for *fa los.*

Lieis don cre·l cors	Her for whom the heart
los buoills,	believes the eyes,
Non pretz	I don't value
Necs	Base
Mans doz aigonencs;	Messages worth two angevins;
D'autra s'es dutz	By another very rarely
Rars	Is my prayer
Mos preiars,	Drawn forth;
Pero deportz	And so it's a delight
M'es ad auzir	For me to hear
Volers,	Good will,
Bos motz ses grei	Good words with nothing harsh
De liei don tant m'azaut	From her for whom I exult so
Qu'al sieu servir	That at her service
Sui del pe tro c'al	I stand from the feet up to my
coma. . . .	hair. . . .[39]

The theme is not difficult to understand. The poet is cast out by his lady; still he loves her, he hopes for her love, he sends his song to the king of Aragon, and he expresses his devotion. The biographer who blames Arnaut's "precious rhymes" for his songs' obscurity was to the point; it is the poem's extreme compression that makes it difficult. But the compression supplies the essential poetic ingredient, the poet's feeling of violent constriction and repression.

In Petrarch's words, Arnaut was the "great master of Love,"[40] and love is invariably his subject (here again the rhymes are between corresponding lines in the stanzas).*

En cest sonet coind'e leri	In this gay, charming air
Fauc motz e capuig	I will put words so honed
e doli,	and pared
E serant verai	that when they've passed
e cert	beneath
Quan n'aurai passat	my file, they'll be true
la lima;	and sure;
Qu'Amors marves plan'e	for love at once smooths
daura	and gilds

---

*In this translation by Anthony Bonner no attempt has been made to reproduce the rhyme scheme.

Mon chantar, que de liei mou	my song, which proceeds from her
Qui pretz manten e governa.	whom Merit guides and sustains.
Tot jorn meillur et esmeri	I continually improve and purify myself, for I serve the gentlest lady
Car la gensor serv e coli	
Del mon, so·us dic en apert	in the world (and say so openly
Sieus sui del pe tro qu'en cima,	I am hers from head to toe,
E si tot venta·ill freid'aura	and even amid cold winds,
L'amors qu'inz el cor mi plou	the love raining within my heart
Mi ten chaut on plus iverna. . . .	keeps me warm in harshest winter. . . .
No vuoill de Roma l'emperi	I do not want the Empire of Rome,
Ni c'om me'en fassa apostoli,	nor to be elected Pope, if I
Qu'en lieis non aia revert	cannot return to her for whom
Per cui m'art lo cors e·m rima;	my heart burns and cracks;
E si·l maltraich no·m restaura	and if she does not cure my ills
Ab un baisar anz d'annou	with a kiss before the new year,
Mi auci e si enferna.	she'll kill me and condemn herself.
Ges pel maltraich qu'ieu soferi	Yet in spite of the ills I suffer,
De ben amar no·m destoli	I shall not desist from loving,
Si tot me ten en desert,	even though I remain in solitude,
C'aissi'n fatz los motz en rima.	for I can still set words to rhyme.
Pieitz trac aman c'om que laura,	Love makes my lot worse than that
C'anc plus non amet un ou	of a peasant—yet the lord of Montcli
Cel de Moncli n'Audierna.	did not love Audierna one whit more.

Ieu sui Arnautz qu'amas
  l'aura,
E chatz la lebre ab lo bou
E nadi contra suberna.

I am Arnaut who gathers the
  wind
and hunts the hare with the ox
and swims against the incoming
  tide.[41]

Dante's favorite among Arnaut's *cansos* was not a technical display of virtuosity such as "*L'aura amara,*" but "*Sols sui qui sai,*" a poem with a simple metrical arrangement and a rhyme scheme in which each line in the seven-line stanza rhymes with a corresponding line in the others; what Dante admired was the harmony between the means of expression and the ideas expressed, the "lucid and graceful and elevated order of construction."[42]

. . . D'autras vezer sui secs e
  d'auzir sortz,
Qu'en sola lieis vei et
  esgar;
E jes d'aisso no · ill sui fals
  plazentiers
Que mais la vol non ditz la boca · l
  cors;
Qu'eu no vau tant chams, vauz
  ni plans in puois
Qu'en un sol cors trob aissi bos
  aips totz:
Qu'en lieis los volc Dieus triar et
  assire.

. . . I am blind to others, and
  their retort
I hear not. In her alone, I see,
  move,
Wonder. . . . And jest not. And
  the words dilate
Not truth; but mouth speaks
  not the heart outright:
I could not walk roads, flats,
  dales, hills, by chance,
To find charm's sum within
  one single frame
As God hath set in her t'assay
  and test it.

Ben ai estat a maintas bonas
  cortz
Mas sai ab lieis trob pro mais que
  lauzar:
Mesura e sen et autres bos
  mestiers,
Beutat, joven, bos faitz e bels
  demors.
Gen l'enseignet Cortesia e la
  duois;
Tant a de si totz faitz desplazens
  rotz

And I have passed in many a
  goodly court
To find in hers more charm
  than rumor thereof . . .
In solely hers. Measure and
  sense to mate,
Youth and beauty learned in all
  delight,
Gentrice did nurse her up, and
  so advance
Her fair beyond all reach of
  evil name,

PAGE FROM A MANUSCRIPT OF ARNAUT DANIEL'S "LO FERM VOLER." (*BIBLIOTECA AMBROSIANA, MILAN, MS. G R71 SUPERIORE, F. 78*)

*De lieis no cre rens de ben sia a
    dire. . . .*

*Ma chansos prec que no·us sia
    enois,*
*Car si voletz grazir lo son e·ls
    motz*
*Pauc preza Arnautz cui que
    plassa o que tire.*

To clear her worth, no shadow
    hath oppresst it. . . .

The song begs you: Count not
    this speech ill chance,
But if you count the song
    worth your acclaim,
Arnaut cares lyt who praise it
    or who contest it.

(*Translation by Ezra Pound*)[43]

Arnaut's most famous poem, *"Lo ferm voler,"* was a sestina, a form invented by Arnaut and imitated by a number of poets, including Dante and Petrarch. This poem has been called "a high point of *trobar clus*" (difficult troubadour poetry).[44] Six rhyming words are used, repeated in each subsequent stanza in a fixed pattern in relation to the preceding one, the rhyming words of the *tornada* repeating the last three of the last stanza. Arnaut's poem plays throughout on the words *l'oncle* (uncle or kinsman) and *l'ongle* (claw or nail) and on *verga*, which can mean "rod" or "Virgin" and *vergier* (orchard). At least two levels of meaning are present: the literal one, the thoughts of the lover whose love is firm against the attacks of slanderers, who longs for his lady and loves her more than his family, and whose love will bring him joy in paradise; and the allegorical one, the debate between mind and spirit, with Arnaut's affirmation of *Fin'Amors,* the perfect form of profane love, which he hopes will take him to paradise.

Lo ferm voler q'el cor m'intra	The firm desire which enters
No·m pot jes becs escoissendre ni ongla	my heart cannot be taken from me by the beak or nail
De lausengier, qui pert per mal dir s'arma;	of that talebearer whose evil words cost him his soul,
E car non l'aus batr'ab ram ni ab verga,	and since I dare not beat him with a branch or rod,
Sivals a frau, lai on non aurai oncle,	I shall at least, in secret, free from any spying uncle,
Jauzirai joi, en vergier o dinz cambra.	rejoice in love's joy, in an orchard or in a chamber.
Quan mi soven de la cambra	But when I think of that chamber
On a mon dan sai que nuills hom non intra	which, to my misfortune, no man enters
Anz me son tuich plus que fraire ni oncle,	and is guarded as if by brother or uncle,
Non ai membre no·m fremisca, neis l'ongla,	my entire body, even to my fingernail,
Aissi cum fai l'enfas denant la verga,	trembles like a child before a rod,
Tal paor ai que·ill sia trop de m'arma.	such fear I have of not being hers with all my soul.
Del cors li fos, non de l'arma.	Would that I were hers, if not in soul
E cossentis m'a celat dins sa cambra!	at least in body, hidden within her chamber;
Que plus mi nafra·l cor que colps de verga	for it wounds my heart more than blows of rod

Car lo sieus sers lai on ill es non intra;	that I, her serf, can never therein enter.
Totz temps serai ab lieis cum carns et ongla,	No, I shall be with her as flesh and nail
E non creirai chastic d'amic ni d'oncle. . . .	and heed no warnings of friend or uncle. . . .
C'aissi s'enpren e s'enongla	As if with tooth and nail
Mos cors en lei cum l'escorssa en la verga;	my heart grips her, or as the bark the rod;
Qu'il m'es de joi tors e palaitz e cambra,	for to me she is tower, palace and chamber
E non am tant fraire, paren ni oncle:	of joy, and neither brother, parent nor uncle
Qu'en paradis n'aura doble joi m'arma,	I love so much; and in paradise my soul
Si ja nuills hom per ben amar lai intra.	will find redoubled joy, if lovers therein enter.
Arnautz tramet sa chansson d'ongla e d'oncle,	Arnaut sends his song of nail and uncle
A grat de lieis que de sa verg'a l'arma,	(by leave of her who has, of his rod, the soul)
Son Desirat, cui pretz en cambra intra.	to his Desirat, whose fame all chambers enters.
	(Translation by Anthony Bonner)[45]

Arnaut Daniel has been described as the culmination of the troubadour poets; to Dante he was "the better craftsman of the mother tongue *(il miglior fabbro del parlar materno)*."[46]

In the first decade of the thirteenth century, a historic calamity devastated the world of the troubadours. Pope Innocent III, alarmed by the Albigensian heresy that had spread through southern France, turned to the weapon his predecessors had forged for war with the Muslims. An army of knightly Crusaders mobilized in northern France invaded the land that had proved equally hospitable to poets and heretics. Poetry fell victim along with heresy. The aristocracy of the South was ruined, and many of the troubadours fled to Spain and Italy to find new patrons. Raimon de Miraval appealed in verse to Pedro II of Aragon, begging him to recover "Montégut and Carcassonne":

Puois poiran dompnas e drut
Tornar el joi q'ant perdut.

(Then ladies and lovers can
Return to the joy they have lost.)[47]

But the environment that had created and fostered the troubadours was lost, never to be recovered. The surviving singers prudently abandoned the theme of earthly love for praise of the Virgin and other religious themes. Suddenly the troubadour was gone. Not, however, without sending a powerful wave of poetic impulse through Europe that reached far into the future.

Beginning in the late twelfth century, northern France had its own knightly poets, the trouvères (again, "finders"), who like the troubadours composed and sang their own verses. Like them, the trouvères' status was knightly; like them, they ranged in class origin from great lords, like Count Thibaut IV of Champagne, to knights like Gace Brulé and a few commoners like Rutebeuf of Troyes. The types of their poetry were essentially the same as those of the troubadours, with northern French names; the pervasive theme remained "courtly love."

In the thirteenth-century kingdom of Sicily, during the enlightened reign of Holy Roman Emperor Frederick II (1205–1250), lyric poetry in vernacular Italian appeared, modeled after the Provençal. The erudite emperor himself contributed verses to the movement. Tuscan poets also began to write in the "mother tongue," and in the last half of the thirteenth century a school of lyric poets appeared, characterized by the "sweet new style" *(dolce stil nuovo)* described by Dante, who practiced it himself: a serious, refined, and delicate treatment of love. Besides Dante, its major exponents were Guido Cavalcanti, Guido Guinizelli, and Cino da Pistoia. In the thirteenth century vernacular lyric poetry also made its appearance in Spain and Portugal, where poets wrote verses in the troubadour tradition. Simultaneously Germany and Austria adopted the love lyric, and the minnesingers (*Minne:* love), knights whose origins were mostly in the class of ministerials, the unfree household retainers of the German empire, circulated among the courts performing their songs. Of the more than 300 known minnesingers, the most famous was Walther von der Vogelweide (c. 1170–c. 1230). A poor knight who, like the troubadours, wandered from castle to castle, Walther wrote in the tradition of courtly love, like the best of the troubadours distilling his own poetic flavor.[48]

The chief contribution of northern France and Germany to the literature of knighthood, however, lay in a different direction, though this too was influenced by the tradition of the troubadours. The narrative literature of the North, both poetry and prose, exerted influence in turn on the self-image of the knight and on his manners and mores, and through the knightly class it came to influence not only the literature but the manners and thought of Europe. It also provided the modern world with most of its notions about knights.

In the eleventh century, before the troubadours appeared on the scene, a mass of epic poetry came into being. The *chansons de geste* were orally transmitted, and had a single common subject: the exploits of Charlemagne and his followers. No one knows who composed, transmitted, or finally recorded them in writing. The *chansons de geste* sang war rather than love, and vaunted the knightly virtues of honor, courage, and loyalty. The most famous was the *Chanson de Roland*, written down by an unknown pen just before the First Crusade. The *Chanson de Roland* tells the story of the ambush of Charlemagne's rearguard in the pass of Roncesvaux in the Pyrenees following his expedition against the Muslims in Spain in 778. The hero Roland (an obscure historical figure) confronts overwhelming odds and with knightly pride, and knightly obstinacy, refuses to summon help by blowing his ivory horn (olifant) until it is too late; finally, alone amid his fallen companions, he sinks to the grass,

> His olifant and sword beneath him placed,
> Turning his head to face the pagan host,
> He wished that Charles and all the Franks might say,
> "The noble count has died a conqueror!"[49]

In the late eighth century of the real Roland and Charlemagne feudalism was barely germinating and "knight" was neither a title nor a concept, but the authors of the *Chanson de Roland* and its companion eleventh-century epics unhesitatingly dressed their tales in the forms of their own day, a literary custom that continued long after.

A different spirit informed the narrative poetry that originated in northern France at the end of the twelfth century. The *romans*, so called because they were written in the "Romance" language, the vernacular, were frankly fiction, stories of chivalry, love, and adventure that owed much of their spirit and ideas to troubadour poetry. One group, known as the "romances of adventure," or the "matter of France," dealt with knights, their exploits, and their ladies. In such tales as *Galeran, Joufroi, Flor et Blancheflor,* and *Amis et Amiles,* love was idealized, but in a very different sense from that of troubadour poetry. The lovers were young couples who, after adventures that were romantic but reasonably realistic, ended by getting happily married. A second group, the "romances of antiquity" or "matter of Rome," developed new versions of classical themes: the *Roman de Thèbes, Roman de Troie,* and *Roman d'Eneas.* Most influential, however, and by far the best known today, was a third group of romances dealing with the "matter of Britain."

Whether a King Arthur ever existed is uncertain.[50] The only contemporary British chronicler, Gildas (died c. 570), recounts the sixth-century invasion by the "abominable Saxons" and the opposition organized under Ambrosius Aurelianus who "alone of the Roman race had escaped the disasters of the epoch." The British resistance was climaxed by a great victory at Mount Badon. No mention is made of Arthur. Nor is Arthur mentioned in the account of the Saxon invasion in Bede's *Ecclesiastical History,* written in 731.

A compilation begun not long after and completed at the end of the eighth century by a chronicler known as Nennius, the *Historia Britonum (History of the Britons),* is the only documentary basis for the Arthur story, and the first source to mention Arthur, identified only as a *dux bellorum* (leader of wars, or general) who "fought against [the Saxons] in those days together with the kings of the Britons." The *Historia* lists Arthur's "twelve battles," the last on Mount Badon, where "he alone in one day killed nine hundred and sixty men; and in all the battles he was victor." Some elements that were developed in later versions of the King Arthur story also appear, principally the figure of a miracle-working youth who became Merlin. The source of the *Historia*'s information about Arthur is unknown.

Over the next four centuries nothing was added to historical information, but piece by piece a rich Arthurian myth was constructed. Chronicler William of Malmesbury (born c. 1095), reframing the *Historia Britonum* to make a more interesting and consistent story, commented about the "warlike Arthur": "This is the Arthur concerning whom the idle tales of the Britons rave wildly even today—a man certainly worthy to be celebrated, not in the foolish dreams of deceitful fables, but in truthful histories; since for a long time he sustained the declining fortunes of his native land and incited the uncrushed courage of the people to war."[51]

Not long after, the Arthur story was given its greatest impetus and almost its final historical form by a Welsh cleric named Geoffrey of Monmouth. In his *Historia Regum Britanniae (History of the Kings of Britain)*,[52] written in about 1136 in a Latin prose of style and originality, Geoffrey in effect created the medieval romance of Arthur, with many of the elements familiar to us today. According to Geoffrey, he found most of his information in "a certain very ancient book in the British tongue" given him by the archdeacon of Oxford. Whether such a book existed or was a literary device of Geoffrey's, or possibly a figurative reference to a body of oral tradition, Geoffrey combined, rearranged, and elaborated his material into a strong, integrated narrative. He made Arthur for the first time a king and introduced in addition to Merlin the personae of Uther Pendragon, Gawain, Guinevere, Mordred, Kay, and Bedevere. He added the seduction of Arthur's mother, the lady Igerna, by Uther, Mordred's usurpation and his treacherous abduction of Guinevere, and Arthur's final departure, mortally wounded, to the Isle of Avalon.

What gave Geoffrey's narrative dramatic power in its own time and appeal for subsequent ages was his medievalizing of the story. King Arthur's court is the court not of a sixth-century British chieftain but of a twelfth-century king, modeled after contemporary Anglo-Norman prototypes. He has vassals, whom he rewards with gifts of land. After conquering France, he divides it among his nobles, exactly as William the Conqueror had in fact done with England a few decades before Geoffrey wrote. The nobles live in castles, first built in Europe in the ninth century and in England in the eleventh, and Arthur's court is crowded with knights. Knights and nobles comport themselves in accordance with twelfth-century chivalric ideas. Arthur "developed such a code of courtliness in his household that he inspired peoples living far away to imitate him."[53] The knights wear their own livery and armorial devices, and "women of fashion" adopt the colors of their knights; "they scorned to give their love to any man who had not proved himself three times in battle."[54] At the great plenary court at Caerleon after Arthur conquered France, "the knights planned an imitation battle and competed to-

gether on horseback, while their womenfolk watched from the top
of the city walls and aroused them to passionate excitement by their
flirtatious behavior,"[55] exactly as really happened in twelfth-century
tournaments.

Geoffrey's immensely popular work was widely adapted and trans-
lated into several vernacular tongues. The outstanding adaptation
was that of a scholar named Wace, born at about the same time as
Geoffrey, in the Isle of Jersey, and educated in the Norman city of
Caen.[56] Wace dedicated his *Brut (Brutus)*,* a poetic paraphrase of
Geoffrey's prose history completed in 1155, to the famous queen of
France and England, Eleanor of Aquitaine. Written in French in
the form used by the poetic romance, Wace's work told the story

BATTLE OF YVAIN AND GAWAIN, ILLUSTRATING
CHRÉTIEN DE TROYES'S *YVAIN. (PRINCETON UNIVERSITY LIBRARY,
GARRETT MS. 125, F. 52)*

*Brutus the Trojan, legendary great-grandson of Aeneas, was supposed to have jour-
neyed to England, where he founded New Troy (London) and gave his name to the
British race.

vividly and dramatically, with detailed descriptions of battles and feasts, much dialogue, and an emotional content not present in Geoffrey's original. He added several details to the story, from Celtic myth, the most significant of which was the Round Table.[57] Carrying Geoffrey's medievalizing further, Wace made Britain a model feudal kingdom and described battles as clashes of mounted knights in shock combat. Wace's Arthur had matured into the paragon of knighthood, in the tradition of the romances: "a very virtuous knight," "a stout knight and a bold . . . and large of his giving. He was one of Love's lovers; a lover also of glory. . . . He ordained the courtesies of courts, and observed high state in a very splendid fashion."[58]

Shortly before the end of the century a Saxon poet and cleric called Layamon wrote an adaptation of Wace, the first account of Arthur in English vernacular. Layamon expanded and embellished the story, notably with an account of the construction of the Round

MARRIAGE OF YVAIN AND LAUDINE. CONTRARY TO THE TRADITION OF COURTLY LOVE, LOVERS IN THE ROMANCES USUALLY MARRIED. (*PRINCETON UNIVERSITY LIBRARY, GARRETT MS. 125, F. 38*)

Table, and a detailed description of Arthur's final transportation to Avalon. The wounded Arthur is made to say:

" 'And I will fare to Avalon, to the fairest of all maidens, to Argante the queen, an elf most fair, and she shall make my wounds all sound; make me all whole with healing draughts. And afterwards I will come again to my kingdom, and dwell with the Britons with [much] joy.' Even with the words there approached from the sea a boat, floating on the waves; and two women therein, wondrously fair: and they took Arthur and put him quickly in the boat and departed. . . ."[59]

Such was the contribution of the chroniclers to the King Arthur story, a fragment of shadowy history upon which they embroidered an imperishable substance of myth and romance. From the chroniclers the work now passed into the hands of the poets.[60]

The imagination and wit of Chrétien de Troyes (fl. 1165–1190) lent a new mystical-magical aura to the story.[61] Besides using Wace, Chrétien took from Celtic sources the major figures of Lancelot and Perceval, Camelot as Arthur's capital, and the theme of the Holy Grail. Tristan was already a figure familiar to poets, one of whom, known only as Thomas of England, seems to have introduced him into the Arthurian story in about 1170.

All these additions wrought a change in the role of Arthur. The central character of Geoffrey of Monmouth was reduced to the role of a bystander in Chrétien's five romances (*Erec et Enide, Cligès, Lancelot, Yvain,* and *Perceval),* in each of which the central character was a knight-errant. His adventures included not only tournaments and combats but supernatural experiences with dragons, giants, enchanted castles, spells, and magic rings. Chrétien showed the influence of troubadour poetry in his idealization of secular love as well as in his poetic technique. Lancelot's adulterous affair with Guinevere and Tristan's with Iseult were the essence of "courtly love."

Other poets took up the Arthurian theme. Notably, the minnesinger Wolfram von Eschenbach painted a vivid picture of King Arthur's court and the Round Table and further developed the theme of the Grail, building his story on the knight's search, beyond adventure, human love, and even the brotherly spirit of the Round Table, for the meaning of life.[62]

The last significant medieval addition to the Arthurian literature was an anonymous collection of adaptations in French prose produced in the thirteenth century, known as the Vulgate Cycle, which added the final, and in many ways crowning, Arthurian figure, Gala-

had.[63] Translated into many languages, the Vulgate Cycle provided the chief source of Sir Thomas Malory's English-language *Morte d'Arthur*, which was published in 1485, virtually marking the end of the Middle Ages.

Aside from its intrinsic literary value, and its influence on European thought and culture, chivalric literature played an important part in the history of knighthood. It contributed to fixing the self-image of the knight and to strengthening his esprit de corps. It helped define standards for knightly behavior, some of which were implicit in knightly life-style itself, some, the religious and moral, set down in the codes of chivalry that began to appear late in the twelfth century.

The rules of conduct that the poetry of the troubadours prescribed were mainly social: a knight should be courteous, generous, well-spoken, discreet, faithful in the service of love; he should have

THE KNIGHTLY VIRTUES: THE KNIGHT RESCUES THE MAIDEN IN DISTRESS.
(BRITISH LIBRARY, HARLEIAN MS. 4431, F. 98v)

"*pretz e valors,*" excellence and worth, as well as good sense.

From the *chansons de geste* came a different model, also secular: a knight should be brave, loyal, and honorable, and he should perform deeds that would earn him glory.

The guidelines added by the Arthurian romances supplied a religious note reminiscent of the Peace of God and the "soldier of Christ" of the First Crusade.

When Chrétien de Troyes's Perceval leaves home to seek King Arthur, his mother tells him, "You will soon be a knight, my son. . . . If you encounter, near or far, a lady in need of help, or any damsel in distress, be ready to aid her if she asks you to, for all honor lies in such deeds. When a man fails to honor ladies, his own honor must be dead. . . . Above all, I beg you to go to church, to pray to Our Lord to give you honor in this world and grant that you so lead your life that you may come to a good end."[64] He finds a sponsor who knights him, fastens on his spurs, girds on his sword, and kisses him, saying that he has given him

> La plus haute ordene avec l'espee
> Que Diex ait faite et commandee

C'est l'Ordre de chevalerie
Qui doit estre sanz vilonnie. [65]

(With the sword, the highest Order
That God has created and ordained,
The Order of chivalry
Which must be without wickedness.)

The sponsor echoes Perceval's mother in his advice: "If you find a man or a woman, or an orphan or a lady, in any kind of distress, you'll do well to lend them your aid if you know how and are able. And one more lesson I have for you . . . go willingly to church to pray to Him who made all things."[66]

The Vulgate *Lancelot* carried the advice further. When Lancelot expresses his desire to become a knight, the Lady of the Lake explains the significance of knighthood to her foster son: Once men were equal, but when envy and covetousness came into the world and might began to triumph over right, it became necessary to appoint defenders for the weak against the strong, and they were called knights. "They were the tall and the strong, and the fair and the nimble, and the loyal and the valiant and the bold." A man thus chosen had to be "merciful without wickedness, affable without treachery, compassionate toward the suffering, and openhanded. He must be ready to succor the needy and to confound robbers and murderers, a just judge without favor or hate. He must prefer death to dishonor. He must protect the Holy Church, for she cannot defend herself."

Each of the arms that the knight bore carried symbolic meaning. The shield protected him as he must protect the Holy Church from all malefactors, whether robber or infidel. As the hauberk guarded his body, he must defend the Church. As the helmet shielded his head, he must shield the Church from all who wished to injure her. The two edges of his sword signified that the knight was the servant of both Our Lord and of his people. The point signified the obedience the people owed the knight. The horse also symbolized the people, who must support him; the knight guarded them night and day, and therefore the people must provide him with the necessities of life. As the knight guided his horse, he must guide the people.

He must defend and maintain the church, and widows and orphans. "Knights must have two hearts, one as hard as a diamond, the other as soft and pliant as warm wax." The hard heart must be inexorable toward traitors and felons, the soft heart merciful toward those who claimed pity.

Such were the requirements of knighthood, and those who could not fulfill them did well not to seek that estate, since they ran the danger of being disgraced here in this world and afterward with the Lord God.

Did any man exist who possessed all these virtues? Lancelot asked. Yes indeed, said the Lady of the Lake, even before Christ, and she listed the "very good knights" John the Hircanian, Judas Maccabeus and his brother Simon, King David, and after Christ's passion "Joseph of Arimathea and his son King Galahad and their descendants."[67]

Chrétien's *Perceval* was again unmistakably echoed in a late twelfth-century didactic poem, *L'Ordene de chevalerie (The Order of Chivalry)*, in which a Frankish knight explains to Saladin the rules and ceremonies of knighthood.[68] A hundred years later, the most famous and influential statement of the chivalric code, the *Libre del orde de cauayleria (Book of the Order of Chivalry)* by Spanish poet and theologian Raymond Lull, borrowed freely from the *Ordene* and from the Lady of the Lake's advice in the Vulgate *Lancelot*. Widely circulated in Latin and French, it was translated into English and printed by William Caxton in 1484.[69]

Through all these forms, adaptations, reiterations, and interpretations, the Arthurian romances made a deep impression on the knightly class that was their unvarying protagonist. Elements of the romances were acted out in courts and castles. Beginning in the thirteenth century, and growing more elaborate as time progressed, in England, France, Flanders, and the Holy Land "Round Tables" were organized—feasts and tournaments in imitation of those at Camelot. Sometimes participants took the names of Arthur, Lancelot, Galahad, Gawain, Yvain, or Perceval. In 1344 Edward III founded in imitation of King Arthur the order of knights that became the Order of the Garter.[70]

To whatever degree the knight of the High Middle Ages consciously tried to be faithful to the courtly image of the troubadours and the heroic examples of the *chansons de geste*, while modeling himself after Lancelot and Perceval and heeding the injunctions of the Lady of the Lake, these powerful images and standards could not fail to influence his self-perception. The knight of the twelfth and thirteenth century was, above all in his own eyes, measurably above the crude, uncivilized warrior of the tenth century.

William Marshal:
knighthood
at its zenith

◦§ MANY NOBLE MEN BY THEIR INDOLENCE
LOSE GREAT GLORY, WHICH THEY COULD HAVE
IF THEY ROVED THROUGH THE WORLD.
NOT CONSONANT WITH EACH OTHER
ARE IDLENESS AND GLORY, I THINK,
FOR NO GLORY IS WON
BY THE RICH MAN, WHO IDLES EVERY DAY.

—Chrétien de Troyes, *Cligès*

◦§ THEY SOJOURNED IN ENGLAND
ALMOST A YEAR, IN WHICH HE DID NOTHING
BUT ENGAGE IN JOUSTS
OR IN THE HUNT OR THE TOURNEY.
BUT TO THE YOUNG KING IT WAS NOT PLEASING,
HIS COMPANIONS ALSO
WERE TERRIBLY BORED,
FOR THEY PREFERRED TO ROAM RATHER
THAN TO SOJOURN, IF THEY COULD WANDER.
FOR KNOW WELL, IT IS THE GIST,
THAT A LONG SOJOURN DISHONORS A YOUNG MAN.

—*L'Histoire de Guillaume Maréchal*

THE ROMANCES of adventure and the Arthurian romances centered around the exploits of fictional knights-errant. Through the accident of history we possess the biography of a real knight-errant, William Marshal, a unique document that owes its existence to the fact that its knight hero rose to become a great baron and played a powerful political role. Shortly after his death his eldest son employed William's squire, John d'Erley, to write, with the aid of a trouvère whose name is unknown, *The History of William Marshal (L'Histoire de Guillaume Maréchal).*[1] Composed in the form of a verse romance, the biography is in French, the language of the twelfth-century English court and literature. Though the work was designed to glorify its subject, and therefore embroiders his role, the authors were contemporaries and sometimes eyewitnesses of the events they record* and the biography was aimed at a knowledgeable contemporary audience. Many of the facts are externally verifiable. Its picture of society may be romanticized, but it nevertheless reveals much about the manners, customs, and values of the knightly class of the twelfth century.

William Marshal was the son and grandson of court officials of King Henry I of England. His grandfather Gilbert, a small Wiltshire landholder, the first member of the family about whom anything is known, became royal marshal, in charge of the king's horses. Gilbert and his son John, William's father, successfully defended by judicial duel (trial by combat) their right to the office of marshal and its hereditary status. Taking the term "Marshal" first as a title and later as a surname, John married a member of his own middling social class, the heiress of another small Wiltshire landholder, and by her had his first two sons, Gilbert and Walter.[2]

Until the death of Henry I in 1135, and for the first years of the reign of King Stephen, John Marshal remained a minor official and petty landholder, neither wealthy nor powerful. But when Henry I's

---

*John d'Erley is first mentioned in connection with William Marshal in 1186, and the anonymous trouvère seems to have joined him in 1180; the poem was completed in 1226.

EFFIGY ON WILLIAM
MARSHAL'S TOMB IN THE
TEMPLE CHURCH, LONDON.
*(DEPARTMENT OF THE
ENVIRONMENT)*

daughter Matilda (once empress of Germany, now countess of
Anjou) invaded England in 1139 to challenge Stephen's rule, John
seized the opportunity the civil war offered. Shrewd, ruthless, and
able, he first sided with Stephen, seizing castles in the king's name
and holding them for his own benefit. When Matilda began to gain

the upper hand, he switched loyalties, managing at the same time to get rid of his first wife by annulment and to make a more advantageous marriage with Sibile, sister of the future earl of Salisbury. This marriage produced four sons and two daughters. The second son, born about 1144, was William.*[3]

Of William's early childhood the *History* narrates a single picturesque incident. Besieging Newbury Castle in 1152, King Stephen granted its commandant a truce to confer with John. John asked for a further truce while he petitioned Countess Matilda for aid. The king agreed, but required the surrender of one of John's sons as hostage. William, the youngest, was chosen. When John used the respite to provision and garrison the castle, Stephen threatened to hang the young hostage unless John surrendered. John defied him, sending word that he "had the anvils and hammers with which to forge still finer sons." The boy was led out to be hanged, but his innocent confidence so touched the king's heart that he picked him up and carried him back to camp.[4] Later someone proposed that they catapult William over the castle wall, but good-hearted Stephen forbade it, saying, "William, you will never be harmed by me."[5]

William spent two months as prisoner of the king at Newbury. His mother sent a servant to spy. Peering into the king's tent, the man saw William and the king playing "knights" with plantain weeds. As the servant watched, the boy struck off the clump of leaves that represented the head of his opponent's knight. Catching sight of his mother's servant, he greeted him with a shout: "Welcome, Wilikin! How is my lady mother? How are my sisters and brothers?" The terrified servant fled and narrowly escaped.[6]

The civil war ended in 1153 with a treaty by which Stephen was to rule for the rest of his life and be succeeded by Matilda's son, Henry Plantagenet, count of Anjou. Stephen died the following year, and Henry became king as Henry II. Young William was returned to his parents and John Marshal was rewarded for his services to Matilda with life revenues from valuable manors in Wiltshire. With these, plus estates he had inherited from his father and other scattered lands, he had substantially improved his economic situation over that of his

*The chronology of the *History*, particularly in early episodes, is confused. In 1216, according to the *History* (verse 15510), William said that he was "over 80," i.e., born before 1136. However, the marriage of John Marshal and Sibile took place no earlier than 1141, and William, the second son, seems to have been six to eight years old in the episode that follows.

father, but he was still not in a position to provide for his sons. By primogeniture, the eldest, Gilbert, would inherit the office of marshal and John's lands; the others would have to fend for themselves.[7]

In 1156 William was sent to Normandy to be educated as a knight in the castle of a powerful cousin, William of Tancarville, chamberlain to the duke of Normandy.[8] The *History* records that twelve-year-old William wept on saying goodbye to his mother and sisters and brothers, like any adolescent off to school for the first time, then rode away, accompanied by two servants.[9]

William's apprenticeship as a squire involved training with lance and sword, caring for his master's weapons and armor, looking after his horses, helping him dress, waiting on him at table, and carving his meat. From the songs and romances sung in the castle hall he absorbed the ideology of knighthood.

At the age of twenty, in about 1164, William was knighted. The ceremony took place during an episode in the war between Henry II of England and Louis VII of France, when Henry called on William of Tancarville to assist his ally, Count John of Eu.* Meeting Count John and William de Mandeville, earl of Essex, at Drincourt (now Neufchatel-en-Bray), northeast of Rouen, the lord of Tancarville decided to knight William in anticipation of the battle.[10]

The dubbing ritual had by this time undergone complete Christianization, with the ancient blessing of the sword expanded to a religious investment of every element of the ceremony. As described in *L'Ordene de chevalerie*, nearly contemporary with William Marshal, the candidate first was bathed, the bath symbolizing the washing away of his sins. Then he was clothed in a white robe symbolizing his determination to defend God's law, with a narrow belt to remind him to shun the sins of the flesh. In the church, he was invested with his accoutrements: the gilded spur, to give him courage to serve God; the sword, to fight the enemy and "protect the poor people from the rich." Finally, he received the *colée*, a blow of the hand on the shoulder or head, "in remembrance of Him who ordained you and dubbed you knight."[11]

---

*Paul Meyer, the editor of the *History*, believed that the authors had misplaced the order of events and that William was knighted either in 1164 or in 1167, but that the battle which the *History* names as its occasion actually occurred in 1173. Other considerations make this unlikely, however; the *History* makes no mention of Henry II's eldest son in the battle, although Meyer thought it must be part of his struggle against his father.[12]

KNIGHTING;
THE SPONSOR GIRDS ON BELT AND SWORD, WHILE
OTHER PARTICIPANTS PRESENT THE SPURS. *(BRITISH LIBRARY, MS. 11843, F.1)*

As often happened when knighting took place on the eve of battle, time cut short the ceremony in William's case. Before the knights and barons of the army, he donned a new mantle, the gift of his sponsor, the lord of Tancarville, who girded on his sword and gave him the *colée.*[13]

There followed his first battle, in which English and Norman knights successfully defended Drincourt. William, lance broken in the first charge, his horse wounded, flung himself into the hand-to-hand fighting through the streets while the townspeople cheered from their windows.[14] At the feast that night celebrating the victory, a knight commented on William's performance: William, he said, had fought to deliver the town rather than to take prisoners for ransom or to seize horses and equipment. He had behaved, in other words, like the ideal rather than the real knight. Such behavior was admired, but only to a point. The earl of Essex reminded William that a knight could not afford to disdain booty. "Marshal," he said, "give me a gift, for love and for recompense." "Surely," agreed William, "what?" "A crupper, or a horse collar." "But God bless me, I have never owned one in my whole life." "Marshal, what are you saying? Today you had forty or sixty, before my own eyes! Will you refuse me?" The assembled company burst out laughing.[15]

A truce concluded, William returned to Tancarville poorer than he had left, for his horse had died of its injuries. He could only afford to replace him with a cheap packhorse, and even that only by selling his new robe.[16] But the lord of Tancarville, deciding that William had learned his lesson, soon presented him with a warhorse on the occasion of the announcement of a tournament near Le Mans.[17] In it, his first, William enjoyed a brilliant success.

The *History of William Marshal* is the major historical source for general information about the tournament before the thirteenth century, although presumably these occasions for sport and training date

THE TOURNAMENT IN THE TWELFTH AND THIRTEENTH CENTURIES CONSISTED OF A WAR-IMITATIVE MELEE RATHER THAN INDIVIDUAL JOUSTS. *(BRITISH LIBRARY, ADDIT. MS. 12, 228, F. 150B-151)*

TWELFTH-CENTURY
KNIGHTS CONTINUE TO
WEAR LONG COATS OF
MAIL AND CONICAL
HELMETS AND TO CARRY
KITE-SHAPED SHIELDS
ROUNDED AT THE TOP IN A
REPRESENTATION OF A
BRONZE CASKET KNOWN AS
THE "TEMPLE PYX."
(BURRELL COLLECTION,
GLASGOW MUSEUM)

back to the eleventh century and even the tenth.[18] In William's time and much later, the tournament did not involve individual jousting. Instead it consisted of a "melee" in which two sides fought a mock battle. Ground rules varied. Sometimes the knights vied for ransoms, arranged beforehand; sometimes the victors also captured horses, arms, and armor of the vanquished. In either case there was usually a prize for the knight who performed best. The two parties donned their armor in refuges at either end of the field, mounted, and galloped toward each other, lances couched. An unhorsed knight fought on foot with his sword. Armor was still light enough to permit this maneuver and to allow an unhorsed knight, provided he was not wounded, to rise from the ground. A hauberk weighed only twenty to thirty pounds, and even when pieces of plate armor were added, a knight carried no more than about forty pounds of iron, whose weight furthermore was well distributed.[19] The contest was not confined to the field; combatants ranged the countryside, which was supplied with refuges where they could rest and rearm. On occasion, foot soldiers joined in the melee. The fighting continued until dusk, when the knights assembled to award the prize and raise ransom money for their captive friends.

In his first tournament, William heeded the advice of his elders on looking out for himself. Overthrowing his first adversary, he seized his horse and exacted a pledge for ransom, then captured two more prisoners and confiscated their horses and equipment. By the tournament's end, he had handsomely equipped himself and his retinue.[20] In William's second tournament, which, with his lord's permission, he attended alone, he unhorsed an opponent, successfully defended his prisoner against five other knights, and for his performance won a splendid warhorse from Lombardy.[21]

In the war-imitative spirit of the tournament, it was not regarded as unsporting for several knights to attack a single knight or to take prisoner a wounded man. William's biographers record how at din-

LATE TWELFTH-CENTURY ARMOR: A CRUSADER WEARS A SURCOAT OVER MAIL, A ROUND HELMET, A MAIL COVERING FOR HIS NECK (VENTAIL) AND MAIL GAUNTLETS AND STOCKINGS. (*BRITISH LIBRARY, MS. 2A XXII, F. 220*)

TWELFTH-CENTURY TOURNAMENT: KNIGHTS BATTLE AS LADIES WATCH.
QUEEN GUINEVERE POINTS TO HER FAVORITE, LANCELOT.
(MORGAN LIBRARY, MS. 806, F. 262)

ner during one tournament William caught sight of a knight of the opposing party who had fallen in the street and broken his leg. William "rushed outside, ran to the groaning knight, took him in his arms, armor and all, and carried him into the inn," not to succor him, but to present him for ransom to his dinner companions with the words: "Here, take him to pay your debts!" The *History* applauds William's knightly generosity on this occasion, as always, commenting that he "very willingly gave fine gifts and horses and *deniers*."[22]

The mock battles were realistic enough to be dangerous, with numerous casualties, and even fatalities (one of William's sons died in a tournament). Weapons were not blunted as in later practice. Violent behavior often overflowed into riot and even insurrection. Both the Church and lay authority strove to control such excesses.

Though the *History* pictures most of William's tournaments as before masculine audiences, other sources suggest that already ladies attended, decked in the colors of their favorites and cheering them on with the "flirtatious behavior" ascribed by Geoffrey of Monmouth to the ladies of Camelot.

A colorful element of chivalry that grew out of the tournament soon after the First Crusade was the science and art of heraldry.[23] Helmets had grown more massive, with three forms becoming popular, round-topped, flat-topped, and conical, all fitted with a face guard with slits for vision and openings for ventilation. The evolution ultimately resulted in the "great helm," a flat-topped cylinder completely enclosing the head and making the wearer unrecognizable with the visor closed.[24] Consequently identifying crests began to be added, becoming common in the thirteenth century along with insignia painted on shields and embroidered on surcoats or tunics (which were the original "coats of arms"). In time, as the insignia were elaborated into complex family histories, heraldry developed its own recondite vocabulary.

By the time William returned to England in 1167, his father and stepbrothers Gilbert and Walter had all died. The family estates and the office of marshal went to William's remaining elder brother, John. Shortly after his return, William's uncle, the earl of Salisbury, was summoned for an expedition to suppress a revolt in Poitou, part of the vast region of southwest France acquired by Henry II through his marriage to Eleanor of Aquitaine. William joined his uncle. In an ambush near Lusignan, southwest of Poitiers, his uncle was killed and William wounded and taken prisoner. He was ransomed by Queen Eleanor, and though the campaign was a failure, it thus brought William to the attention of the king.[25]

In 1170, Henry II decided to crown his fifteen-year-old son Henry in the interest of preparing a peaceful succession without, however, relinquishing his own royal authority. The younger Henry was known henceforth to his English subjects as the Young King. To head his household and take charge of his military training, Henry II chose William Marshal.[26]

The Young King was tall, fair-haired, and affable, and according to William's biographers courteous, generous, and "the handsomest of all the princes in the world, whether Saracen or Christian."[27] He was also a typical twelfth-century ruling-class youth, irresponsible, rebellious, pleasure-loving, spendthrift. His endless demands for money and power were accompanied by little taste or talent for administration.[28] In 1173 he quarreled violently with his father over the marriage settlement of his youngest brother, John, demanded Normandy, England, or Anjou as compensation, and sought the backing of his father-in-law, Louis VII of France, as well as that of the barons of England and Normandy. Fearing an attempt to depose him, Henry II started north from Limoges, where the quarrel had taken place, taking the Young King with him. At the castle of Chinon the younger Henry slipped away at night with his household. By this act of rebellion, he declared war against his father, and to fight it, arranged to be knighted. King Louis sent his brother and other barons to the ceremony, but the Young King chose William Marshal to gird on his sword and give him the ritual *colée*.[29]

Young Henry proceeded to Paris, where he was joined by his brothers Richard (Lionheart) and Geoffrey. A council of French barons pledged support to the Young King, some of the English magnates declared for him, and many of the lords of Aquitaine joined the uprising. Four of the Young King's household knights deserted to his father, but William and the majority followed their master.[30]

The *History* says nothing of William's part in the rebellion, which lasted a year and a half, ending in defeat. In the fall of 1174 Henry II signed separate treaties with his sons and with Louis reestablishing previous conditions; the Young King was given two Norman castles and 15,000 pounds. William took part in the peace council, was a witness to the treaty, and in the following spring accompanied the two Henrys to England.[31]

The next year the Young King and his household, who "preferred to wander rather than to sojourn," set out for the continent in search of adventure, beginning for William twelve years of knight-errantry.[32]

Henry's cousin, the count of Flanders, introduced him to the world of tournaments. In these William acted as bodyguard for the Young King and planned his tournament strategy. Observing Count Philip's trick of biding his time until the other combatants had tired themselves, William had Henry let it be understood that he would not enter the lists, and when combat raged at its height, he and his men charged onto the field and won the day for their chosen side.[33]

In 1177 William entered into a partnership with a Flemish knight named Roger de Gaugi, with whom he traveled for two years from tournament to tournament. In one ten-month period the pair took prisoner 103 knights.[34] William displayed other knightly talents besides fighting ability. At Joigny, south of Sens, while waiting for his opponents to arm, he entertained knights and ladies by singing while they danced. A young jongleur improvised on the spot a song with a refrain, "Marshal, give me a good horse." As the first of his opponents cantered onto the field, William mounted without a word, unhorsed him, and presented the captured horse to the jongleur.[35]

In 1179 William rejoined the Young King's household, continuing to fight in local tournaments and occasionally venturing to a larger, more distant contest. Henry sent William at the head of his knights to one near Anet, west of Paris, where they arrived late to find the party from Henry II's Angevin territories on the point of defeat. William's attack routed the knights of the king of France, some of whom fled on foot to the top of a mound surrounded by palisade and moat, tethering their horses to the pales. William dismounted, waded the moat, climbed the mound, and grasped the reins of "two fine horses," but as he was leading them out of the moat, two young French knights galloped up and seized them. This was against the rules, but William was at the moment powerless to protest. Remounting his own horse he presently came upon a scene in which fifteen French knights were besieged in some farm buildings by a superior Angevin force. The defenders offered to surrender to William, who accepted, led them away, and released them, a piece of generosity that cannot have been popular with his own party, who lost the ransoms. The tournament over, William sought out the uncle of the young knight who had taken one of the two captured horses. The uncle ordered the horse restored. Someone suggested that William give the knight half the horse and that the two men throw dice for the other man's half; William won. The second young knight was a member of a baron's household; the baron instructed him to return the horse; again it was suggested that William give him half the horse, and William complied. William told the knight to estimate its value, and the young man, thinking that William carried no money and that he could get the horse cheaply, priced it at fourteen pounds, though it was worth more than forty. William produced seven pounds and made off with the horse.[36]

The last splendid tournament attended by William as a member of the Young King's household was held at Lagny, east of Paris, in the fall of 1179, possibly to celebrate the coronation of Philip II of France. Henry's household was expanded for the event to two hundred knights, including a number of "bannerets," knights with half a dozen followers of their own.[37] Among these William appears for the first time. Now in his thirties, still unmarried, still landless, still a "youth," he had nevertheless achieved high status.

The following year William found himself an unwilling protagonist in a situation worthy of a troubadour *canso* or an Arthurian romance. Jealous members of the younger Henry's household circulated a rumor that William was the lover of the Young King's wife, Margaret of France. At Henry II's Christmas court at Caen in 1182,

HOUSE IN MARTEL, ON THE DORDOGNE RIVER,
WHERE THE YOUNG KING DIED AND WILLIAM MARSHAL
PROMISED TO FULFIL HIS MASTER'S CRUSADING VOW
BY VISITING THE HOLY LAND.

William challenged his accusers to judicial combat. When the Young King, who was torn between suspicion and his need for William's aid, forbade it, William sought and received a safe conduct out of Normandy.[38]

The *History* asserts that William had lucrative offers for his services from three great lords. He refused all but a minor grant of land from the count of Flanders, put aside his armor and weapons, and went on pilgrimage to Cologne.[39]

In February 1183, the Young King and his brother Geoffrey launched a fresh rebellion against their father.[40] This time Henry II gained the support of his redoubtable son Richard, and the younger Henry found himself besieged in the castle of Limoges. He sent for William.[41]

The *History* narrates a curious and revealing incident: en route to a rendezvous with two former companions-at-arms, William was resting by the roadside, when a man and a woman rode by, the woman complaining of weariness. William mounted his horse, overtook and questioned them. The man proved to be a monk, eloping with the lady. They had forty-eight pounds in cash, and the monk explained that he intended to lend the money and live on the interest. Usury shocked William more than elopement: "By the sword of God! I don't care—that will not do!" He ordered his squire to seize the money, which he shared with his two friends.[42]

William joined the Young King near Périgueux and they proceeded to Martel, on the Dordogne, where Henry fell seriously ill. It soon became evident that he was dying. After receiving the last rites, he made a request to William: he had taken a Crusader's vow but had never made the journey to the Holy Land. Giving William his Crusader's cloak with the red cross on the shoulder, he begged him to take it to Jerusalem, to the Holy Sepulchre.[43]

Though the Young King's short lifetime had been squandered in extravagant living and sterile rebellion, his contemporaries mourned. Count Philip of Flanders lamented, who would now patronize the "poor knight"? Who would give him "horses and arms and *deniers?*"[44] The troubadour Bertran de Born, protégé of Eleanor of Aquitaine, composed a *planh* (lament) for "the death of the young English king," a blow to the world of chivalry, the world of *pretz* and *jovens,* of excellence and youth, leaving the "courtly nobles and the jongleurs and the troubadours" weeping, since death, "that fell warrior," had taken away the king "who made the most liberal hand seem stingy." Bertran concluded with a plea that Christ pardon the Young King's sins and, like a medieval lord welcoming a knightly guest to his castle hall,

> Bid him go in with his honored companions
> Where there is no grief or sadness.[45]

William faithfully carried out his promise to journey to the Holy Land. The *History* says that Henry II gave him "two fine horses" and a hundred Angevin pounds for his pilgrimage. After visiting England to bid goodbye to his friends and family, he went off to fight the infidels. The *History* records rather cryptically, "He remained two years in Syria. There he did as many deeds as any man could do, even in seven years. His exploits are still recounted in many places before honest men. I have not described them here because I was not a witness and I have not been able to find anyone who could tell me half. Departing the Holy Land, he took leave of King Guy and his men, and of the Templars and the Hospitalers."*[46]

On returning to France in 1187, William began a new chapter in his life by entering the service of Henry II, whom he met in Normandy.[47] His days of knight-errantry were over. The king gave him a fief in Lancashire in return for vassal service in the form of counsel in Henry's struggle with the French king Philip II and his own son Richard. So helpful was William's counsel that it won him a reward that was the dream of every wandering knight: the promise of marriage to an heiress. The lady, Isabel de Clare, eighteen-year-old daughter of the earl of Pembroke, had inherited lands in Wales and Ireland that would make her husband one of the most powerful barons in England.[48]

In July 1189, before he could fulfill the promise, Henry died at the castle of Chinon, after concluding a humiliating treaty with Philip and Richard. Although William had fought against him, Richard recognized his loyalty and courage and welcomed his continuance in the royal service, confirming his father's gift of Lady Isabel and her inheritance. The marriage took place in London in 1189.[49]

*This passage indicates that William left the Holy Land after the coronation of Guy of Lusignan, king of Jerusalem, in mid-September 1186; other evidence suggests that he departed before the fall of Jerusalem to Saladin, probably at the end of 1186 or the beginning of 1187.

William was now in his early forties, and suddenly the lord of princely estates in three lands. These included the honor (large feudal estate of a tenant-in-chief of the king) of Striguil, with three demesne manors and some sixty knights' fees (fiefs sufficient to support a knight, about 600 acres apiece), and the marcher (border) lordship of Striguil, a hundred square miles on the Wye estuary dominated by the castle of Chepstow; the county of Pembroke in southwestern Wales, with its castle; the lordship of Leinster in Ireland, comprising the modern counties of Kildare, Carlow, Kilkenny, Wexford, Queens, and a part of Kings; and half the barony of Longueville in Normandy, with the service of forty or fifty knights.[50] In 1194 his elder brother John Marshal died, leaving William the family lands and the office of king's marshal, which by this time, like the office of his superior, the royal constable, involved important military duties.[51] In 1199 he became earl of Pembroke.[52]

William now passes from the orbit of this book, a knight who through his own prowess and royal favor gained the ranks of the upper nobility. He became King John's most trusted counselor and captain, smoothing his succession to the throne and remaining loyal during the disorders of the English barons that led in 1215 to Magna Carta. It was William who was sent to London to tell the barons that "for the sake of peace and the welfare and honor of his realm" the king would grant the concessions they demanded, and who was a chief negotiator at Runnymede.[53] Civil war broke out after Runnymede and the barons invited Prince Louis of France to be their king. Louis invaded England, and in 1216, in the midst of the fighting, John died, leaving William to serve as regent for the young Henry III. Under William's command, loyalists defeated barons and invaders, and in 1217 William concluded a treaty with Louis granting amnesty to the barons.[54] Shortly before he died (May 14, 1219), he joined the Templars. He was buried in the Temple church in London.[55]

William Marshal is a conspicuous example of the upwardly mobile knight of the twelfth century, a period that witnessed a general upward movement by the entire class. Exactly when knights came to be considered noble is controversial and regional history varied, but the general consensus is that in the course of the thirteenth century they came to be accepted everywhere as belonging in the ranks of the aristocracy.

In addition to the Christianization of knighthood and its enhanced social status, political changes took place that had dramatic impact. These took varying forms in the German Empire, France, and England but were roughly parallel.

In the Empire, the unfree ministerials, household knights of servile status, rose to become members of the lesser nobility. Serving the emperor or the Church, they had already absorbed some of the prestige of their masters. They were further elevated by deliberate policy, as the Hohenstaufen emperors, particularly Frederick Barbarossa and Henry VI, employed their servile knights against the rebellious nobility. German ministerial knights fought for the Hohenstaufens in Italy, garrisoned their castles, accompanied Frederick Barbarossa on his Crusade, tutored the Hohenstaufen sons, governed their cities, and administered their domains. A ministerial, Markward of Anweiler, who had been Henry VI's tutor, served as regent during the minority of Frederick II. Ministerials were largely responsible for the German literature of chivalry, explaining and justifying the consciousness of the class that they had joined. By the thirteenth century, most of the ministerials had eliminated their disabilities and established themselves as free, able to give and receive fiefs, to testify in court, and to marry as they pleased. In some regions they were called "noble" as early as the twelfth century.[56]

In France, the twelfth century witnessed the strengthening of the royal power alongside the growth of the great regional principalities, such as Flanders, Burgundy, Champagne, Provence, and Savoy, whose counts and dukes, like the German emperors, looked for knightly support against the local lords, the castellans. Counts, dukes, and king exerted themselves to break up the close relationship between the local lord and his knights and to enlist the knights in their own service, making them direct vassals and encouraging the transfer of judicial and other local power from castellan to knight. Knights acquired the title "sire," previously reserved for castellans, and assumed armorial bearings in imitation of the upper aristocracy. As the thirteenth century progressed, their life-style grew more expansive. They moved out of the villages where they had long lived in familiar intimacy with the peasants and built fortified manors, miniature castles with a tower or two, often surrounded by moats. These petty fortresses served more of a social than a military purpose. They were visual symbols of the change in the knight's relationship with the peasants, from neighbor-protector to governor, with powers of police, justice, and taxes.[57]

Georges Duby's study of the Mâcon region shows that knights had been forced to borrow money in the twelfth century, mainly from each other; early in the thirteenth century they had recourse to pledging part of their lands to the Church or to merchants. After about 1230 they began to sell their lands or to turn over their allodial lands to the Church or to a lay lord and take them back in fief, in return for cash. Thus the Hongre family, which had sent knights on the First Crusade, pledged and sold lands in the twelfth century to raise money to go on the Third Crusade, and in the thirteenth century borrowed against pledges, sold lands to the abbey of Cluny, and sold their homage for other allods to the abbey of St. Philibert in Tournus and to the duke of Burgundy.[58]

The result was that at least in central France, where feudalization had previously been only partial and feudal obligations had weighed lightly, the knights now had to submit to powerful lords, kings and counts and dukes, while the castellans sank in status to become scarcely distinguishable from the knights.[59]

In England, a partnership of royal power with feudal hierarchy had been founded by the Norman Conquest. Henry II's expansion of the central government apparatus—justice, administration, and finance—brought about the enlistment of knights in a role unique to England. The knights who had originally come over with William the Conqueror had been granted land to support their service and had thereby become administrators of estates. Gradually they had acquired public responsibilities outside their feudal obligations, especially in the area of justice. Where in France many knights entered royal service and so became part of the bureaucracy that grew with the growth of royal power, in England the knights' participation in government came by way of their local administrative function, leading to their important part in the foundation of Parliament.[60]

The institution that introduced the English knights to their new responsibilities was the "Grand Assize" set up by Henry II in 1179 to settle property disputes. The sheriff, administrator of the shire (county), appointed four knights who in turn elected twelve knights, "free and lawful men of the vicinity," to form a "jury," in the medieval sense, a court of inquiry of men acquainted with the case, who viewed the property in question, discussed the issue with appropriate parties (neighbors), paced the boundaries, and pronounced as to the "greater right." When verdicts were questioned, four "knights of the shire" were commissioned to bring the court record to the king's court and defend it.[61] Out of this practice grew that of summoning a representation of knights to the king's Great Council. In 1213, in a moment of crisis, King John called four knights from each shire "to speak with us about the affairs of the kingdom"; later the king from time to time asked the shire courts to send two, three, or four knights, sometimes elected by local knights, sometimes appointed by the sheriff, as representatives to discuss taxes, report on local affairs, or bring the political support of the shires to his aid.[62] In this role the English knights were used against the English barons as the Hohenstaufen emperors had used their ministerials against their nobles or the French king and magnates had used knights against the castellans.

English knights served in other functions in the shire, aiding and advising the sheriff and serving in local office, as sheriffs themselves, as coroners, and as forest officials.[63] These duties heightened the knights' pretensions; early in Henry II's reign, his justiciar, Richard de Lucy, himself from a family of knights, was moved to remark, "It was not the custom in the old days for every petty knight to have a seal."[64]

Another change introduced by Henry II that worked a major transformation in the situation of English knights was the increasing substitution of paid service for service based on feudal tenure. Mercenary soldiers had been employed long before the twelfth century (see Chapter 3), but an important innovation, the beginning of a new way of organizing a war economy, was "scutage" (shield tax, from *scutum*, shield), the imposition of a tax as a substitute for unreliable and short-term feudal service, with the revenue used to hire mercenaries. This device was particularly necessary in Henry II's wars to defend his extensive continental empire. In 1166 he required his tenants-in-chief, his major vassals, to inform him of the names of all their vassals who held land by military service. The king's purpose was to use the list as the basis for a tax to be levied in lieu of such service. At first collected from the barons, this tax was eventually collected directly from the knights.[65] A treatise on the English Exchequer (treasury office), written about 1179, explained scutage in benevolent terms:

> Occasionally, when enemies threaten or attack the kingdom, the king orders that a certain sum be paid from each knight's fee such as one mark or one pound to provide wages or bonuses for soldiers. For the king prefers to expose mercenaries rather than his own people to

the chances of war. This payment, because it is reckoned according to the number of shields, is called shield-money.[66]

Scutage enabled vassals to avoid burdensome military duties while providing the king with an army of experienced soldiers prepared to undertake a long campaign. Along with later tax measures for war finance, it made possible the development of the professional army.

Scutage was an aspect of two fundamental historic trends in twelfth-century Europe that profoundly affected the knights. The first was the increasing concentration of power in the hands of a few kings and great princes that gradually professionalized warfare. The second was the economic upturn from the depressed state of the ninth and tenth centuries to the Commercial Revolution of the eleventh and twelfth centuries that raised living standards and inflated prices. A knightly life-style now demanded luxuries. William Marshal's biographers, writing in the second quarter of the thirteenth century, apologized for the modest size of William's retinue when he set out for France in the 1150s. "The time was not then so proud as in our days; a king's son would ride with his cape trussed up, without any other baggage; now there is hardly a squire who does not want to have a pack horse."[67] The dubbing ceremony itself had come to include elaborate gifts and costly celebrations. The knights' new duties in service to kings and great lords involved travel, suitable clothing, and often contributions in the form of "aids" to the lord on special occasions. The price of knightly equipment, too, had mounted to the point where the initial outlay might cost a knight a year's income.*[68] The old round or conical helmet of the Bayeux Tapestry was replaced in the late twelfth and early thirteenth century by the larger helm, a flat-topped cylinder that gradually evolved into more rounded forms to better ward off blows. Mail gauntlets (mufflers) were added to extend the sleeves of the hauberk, under which a padded waistcoat called an acton or gambeson was worn to protect against bruises. The first pieces of plate armor appeared on elbows and knees.[69] The heavier armor increased the premium on strong horses, whose price accordingly rose.

In England, as the cost of knighthood increased, some knights with small landholdings clubbed together to pay the expenses of the

---

*In Genoa, in the first half of the thirteenth century, a helmet cost from 16 to 32 shillings, a hauberk from 120 to 152; with accessories, a total of about 200 shillings, or 800 grams of gold.[70]

THIRTEENTH-CENTURY
IVORY CHESS PIECE
SHOWING FLAT-TOPPED
HELM, SURCOAT, HAUBERK,
AND STRAIGHT-TOPPED
SHIELD. (*ASHMOLEAN
MUSEUM*)

service of one of their number. Others actually abandoned knighthood, as evidenced by a clause in the 1217 reissue of Magna Carta forbidding the gift or sale of land equivalent to a knight's fee and consequently owing the service of a knight. Those who remained knights, like their French counterparts, often had to pledge their lands and sometimes their armor to raise money.[72]

William the Conqueror's *servicium debitum,* the knight service of his tenants-in-chief, provided a theoretical total of about 5,000 knights. In the thirteenth century, King John and King Henry III could raise knightly armies of only 300 or 400 for service on the continent. In 1258 Henry's barons complained that there were so few knights in some counties that it was impossible to assemble a Grand Assize of twelve; in 1295, Essex, one of the most highly feudalized of English counties, numbered only twenty-four active resident knights, plus eleven who were too old or ill for service.[73]

In both England and France the economic pressures of the thirteenth century gave birth to a new social category, the sons of knights who were entitled by birth to knighthood, but who now remained squires (in France *écuyers* or *damoiseaux*). From the middle of the century, squires multiplied until they were more numerous than knights. In one district of the Mâconnais, all eligible men were knights in 1230, but by 1270 there were four *damoiseaux* to one knight. Some men died as *damoiseaux* but transmitted their nobility to their sons, who might become knights or remain *damoiseaux*.[74]

Thus the thirteenth century, apogee of knighthood, actually saw the number of knights decreasing all over Europe. The phenomenon provoked a strange new legal action in England, "distraint of knighthood," by which the royal authority enforced knighting on those deemed able to afford it—a radical extension of the principle of the 1217 Magna Carta. In 1224 Henry III, preparing for an expedition to Gascony, ordered every adult freeman who held land equivalent to a knight's fee to take up arms and be knighted. In 1242 a knight's fee was defined as land yielding a yearly income of twenty pounds, a level gradually raised by inflation to one hundred pounds. The measures raised revenues, but there is no evidence that they produced many knights.[75]

While the old knightly class was contracting and displaying a reluctance to assume the expenses and responsibilities of its rank, for the first time it experienced an infusion from below. The new affluence of the thirteenth century created rich peasants and merchants who aspired to rise in the social scale. Kings and princes encouraged their ambitions, but the knights, having climbed to the rank of nobility, now tried to shut the door to newcomers. Rules governing the inheritance of noble status were more strictly defined by the knightly class; nobility, stated the French legal text known as the *Etablissements de Saint Louis* (c. 1270), had its origins in the father's knighthood. Whereas a man whose mother was noble and whose father was a commoner could previously claim nobility on the maternal side, now if he were knighted, the fraud must be exposed and his spurs cast in the mire. Furthermore, commoners must not assume the powers and privileges of nobles, even without the title. Georges Duby records instances in the thirteenth century in which Burgundian merchants purchased fiefs but were denied homage or feudal service. The fief of a commoner was pronounced inferior to that of a noble, and gentlemen could not be vassals of a bourgeois, "for noble fief does not belong to a bourgeois or a non-noble," in the words of a late thirteenth-century legal document. Not only did commoners continue to hold noble fiefs, as Philippe de Beaumanoir recorded in his *Coutumes de Beauvaisis* (c. 1283), but they had the effrontery to compete for administrative office. The nobles denounced these "villeins" and the "bad princes" who surrounded themselves with them. In spite of their protests, the newcomers continued to infiltrate the nobility, through marriage, purchase of land, and royal service.[76]

Royal authority encouraged the infiltration. In 1306, when Edward I attempted the conquest of Scotland, he used the occasion of the knighting of his own son to issue a proclamation offering dubbing to all candidates who presented themselves at the ceremony, the king assuming the cost of the festivities and presenting the new knights with suits of clothing (not, however, armor). Two hundred and sixty-seven candidates appeared, of whom two were trampled to death in the crush at Westminster Abbey.[77]

The new knightly class consciousness was reflected in the now ostentatious dubbing ceremony. Raymond Lull's late-thirteenth-century *Libre del orde de cauayleria* described a ritual very different from that of the eleventh century or even the twelfth. Lull recommended that the rite be performed on a feast day, when many people would be assembled in church. The candidate must confess his sins and fast the day before and spend the night in solitary vigil in the church. Above all, he must not listen to "troubadours and storytellers who speak of rottenness and sin." In the morning, he must hear Mass, take an oath "to keep the honor of chivalry with all his power," and listen to a sermon setting forth the articles of the Christian faith, the Ten Commandments, the seven sacraments of the Church, and other pertinent matters. The sponsor, himself a man with "the virtue and order of chivalry," then stood forth. The candidate knelt before the altar and lifted his eyes and hands to heaven; his sponsor girded him with the sword, kissed him, and gave him "a palm *(colée* or *paumée)* in order that he remember that which he receives and promises, and the great charge in which he is obligated and bound, and the great honor which he receives by the order of chivalry." Then the new knight should "ride through the town and show himself to the people," so that everyone could see that he had been made a knight, and that night he must "make a great feast" and "give fair gifts and great dinners" and "joust and . . . sport and do other things which appertain to the order of chivalry." Maximum fanfare would impress onlookers with the worth and splendor of the knightly order.

Lull's work not only describes the formula for dubbing, but dwells at length on the religious significance of knighthood, in effect elaborating on the Vulgate *Lancelot*'s account of the Lady of the Lake's discourse. When wickedness came into the world, God chose one man out of each thousand, "most loyal, most strong, and of most noble spirit, and better educated and mannered than all the others." To serve this man, a beast was chosen, "most suitable, most fair, most courageous, and most strong to sustain exertion, and most able to serve man," the horse. The chosen man derived his title from the horse (*chevalier* in French). "Thus to the most noble man was given the most noble beast." Then "all the arms such as are most noble and suitable to battle" were chosen and given to the knight. The knight was given dominion over many men, and a squire and servant to take care of his horse. "And it behooves also that the common people labor in the lands in order to bring forth fruit and goods, whereof the knight and his beast have their living, and that the knight rest himself and stay at his abode according to his nobility, disporting himself upon his horse in order to hunt or in other manner . . . and that he take his ease and delight in things of which his men have pain and travail."

A knight's duties and responsibilities were threefold: he must "maintain and defend the holy Catholic faith," he must be a "governor," and he must "uphold and defend his worldly or earthly lord."

Lull even pedantically elucidated the moral-religious significance of each piece of armor and equipment that the knight assumed: the sword (in the form of the cross) showed that its owner must combat the enemies of Christianity and maintain justice; the spear signified truth; the helmet "dread of shame"; the hauberk resistance to "vices and faults"; the mail stockings were meant to keep him from straying; the spurs to endow him with diligence and swiftness in pursuit of duty; and on through gorget, mace, knife, shield, gauntlets, saddle, horse, bridle, horse armor, coat, coat of arms, and banner.[78]

Significantly, the girding on of the sword was no longer the crowning element of the dubbing ceremony. Knights no longer monopolized the profession of arms, and war was not the sole knightly business.

Knighthood was already becoming honorific rather than substantive.

the
knights templars:
soldiers, diplomats,
bankers

⊷§ WE HAVE HEARD THAT A NEW SORT OF CHIVALRY HAS APPEARED ON
EARTH, AND IN THAT REGION WHICH ONCE HE WHO CAME FROM ON HIGH
VISITED IN THE FLESH . . . A NEW SORT OF CHIVALRY THAT TIRELESSLY
WAGES . . . WAR BOTH AGAINST FLESH AND BLOOD AND AGAINST THE
SPIRITUAL FORCES OF EVIL.
—Bernard of Clairvaux, *In Praise of the New Chivalry*

⊷§ BY [THE TEMPLE], THE ORDER OF KNIGHTHOOD FLOURISHES AND IS
REVITALIZED [AND ENABLED TO DO WHAT IT SHOULD]: THAT IS, DEFEND
THE POOR, WIDOWS, ORPHANS, AND CHURCHES. . . .
—La Règle du Temple

⊷§ FOUL TEMPLARS, WICKED HOSPITALERS, EACH FULL OF ZEAL AND
WITHOUT WEAKNESS, LIKE A NEST OF VIPERS, SERPENTS UNDER THEIR
VARIEGATED SKINS, RED-HAIRED MEN WITH BLUE EYES, ON THEIR BLACK
HORSES. . . .   —Imad-ad-Din, *Conquest of Syria and Palestine by Saladin*

AFTER THE First Crusade, the bulk of the responsibility for maintaining the Christian presence in the Holy Land was borne by members of the Military Orders.[1] In the eyes of the Church, the brother knights of these institutions were par excellence "soldiers of Christ," the epitome of chivalry.

The Orders' original mission was the protection of pilgrims visiting the shrines of the Holy Land. To this duty was soon added what became their chief purpose: garrisoning the conquered land against a persistent and numerous enemy. The Order of the Temple was founded in about 1119 by two knights, Hugues de Payns, from Champagne, and Geoffrey de St. Omer, from Artois. The two men swore poverty, chastity, and obedience before the patriarch of Jerusalem and announced their mission of protecting and aiding pilgrims. First known as "the poor knights of the Temple of Solomon," from its location in Jerusalem, the Order was supported by two great Crusading lords, Hugues, count of Champagne, and Fulk, count of Anjou, and it was recognized by the Church at the Council of Troyes in 1128, which commissioned Bernard of Clairvaux, founder of the Cistercian Order, to draw up a Rule for it. After the Council, a group of Templars led by the two founders toured France and England soliciting recruits and grants of land. Bernard's Rule, adapted from that of the Cistercians, proved exceptionally appropriate for a military order. The Templars' discipline on the march and in battle quickly marked them as the elite troops in any Crusading army.

Largely thanks to the support of Bernard of Clairvaux, the Order soon enjoyed a popularity in Europe beyond its founders' dreams. At the request of Hugues de Payns in the early 1130s, St. Bernard wrote a tract, *In Praise of the New Chivalry*, acclaiming the concept of a fighting brotherhood dedicated to Christ. The worldly chivalry of the past was sinful—"*non dico militiae, sed malitiae*," "I do not call it a militia but an evil." He drew a vivid picture: worldly knights covered themselves with ornaments like women—silk cloths for their horses; tunics for their hauberks; painted lances, shields, and saddles; and reins and spurs decorated with gold, silver, and precious stones.

"Clad in such pomp, in shameless fury and thoughtless stupidity you hasten to your deaths," and all for a cause "so light and frivolous that it terrifies the conscience." In contrast, the Templars risked no sin in killing since their enemies were enemies of Christ; their killing was "not homicide but malicide." Their lives were governed by discipline that Bernard himself had prescribed; they owned no private possessions, avoided all excess in food and clothing, and lived "as a single community in a single house, eager to preserve unity of spirit in a bond of peace." Besides shunning such vanities and follies as gaming, hunting, storytelling, and worldly entertainment, they scorned the care for personal appearance that other knights affected, wearing their hair cut short, leaving their beards uncombed, and riding to battle shaggy, dusty, darkened by sunburn, to "seek not glory but victory . . . meeker than lambs and fiercer than lions." At once monks and knights, "they vigilantly and faithfully guard . . . the Holy Sepulchre."[2]

TEMPLE CHURCH, LAON, WITH CHARACTERISTIC ROTUNDA AND DOME, IN IMITATION OF THE CHURCH OF THE HOLY SEPULCHRE IN JERUSALEM.

The Temple won a succession of exemptions and privileges, financial, spiritual, and administrative, that freed it of numerous taxes and eventually made it independent of all ecclesiastical authority except that of the pope, indeed, immune from all jurisdiction other than papal. Its increasing privilege followed and accompanied its growing wealth. Individual Templars owned nothing, but gifts and bequests of every description poured in to the Order in Europe and the Holy Land: lands, serfs, cattle, mills, winepresses, money, and goods. "Temples," establishments in the form of fortified structures, often of masonry, were founded throughout France, England, Spain, Germany, and Italy. Major facilities were built in the cities, smaller centers in the countryside. All were organized into provinces, each with its Master and Commander. The purpose of these European establishments was to supply the Temple in the Holy Land with two things: money and soldiers.

Most of the rural establishments were headed by two or three members of the Order, who were not knights but minor officials called *frères casaliers*, and who administered the local estates and supervised the agricultural laborers. The urban centers were manned by knights, sergeants, and priests, as well as servants. The largest and most important in Europe was the commandery in Paris, a strong masonry keep with towers, located on the Right Bank. Its spacious walls enclosed a chapel built with a rotunda in imitation of the Church of the Holy Sepulchre in Jerusalem. Besides the Temple Enclosure, the Paris commandery owned entire streets in the city.[3] In London the Templars built a commandery and a church with a rotunda in Holborn, then in the middle of the twelfth century moved south to the bank of the Thames, where they constructed the New Temple in the form of a large church in Gothic style but, like other Templar churches, distinctively round in form. The establishment eventually included several small chapels and two large halls, one, a "hall of priests" used for meetings of the chapter, connected to the church by a cloister, the other a "hall of knights," where the knights lived; across the Thames was a fifteen-acre field used by the Templars for military exercises. Most towns, in England as in Europe, had a Templar commandery, usually with a round church about which clustered the Templar community.[4]

But the vital center of the vast network remained the house in Jerusalem, near the Golden Gate and the Dome of the Rock. A German pilgrim of 1165, John of Würzburg, was impressed by the

GROTESQUE HEADS DECORATE TEMPLE CHURCH, LAON.

great stables that could lodge "more than two thousand horses or a thousand five hundred camels," and the "new and magnificent church which was not finished when I visited it"—St. Mary Lateran. The refectory, which the Templars called the "palace," was a huge Gothic structure, its vaulted roof supported by columns, its walls covered with trophies taken from the enemy: swords, helmets, painted shields, and gilded coats of mail. At mealtimes trestle tables were set up and spread with linen cloths; the flagstone floor was covered with rushes. Between the palace and the church stood the dormitories, corridors of monkish cells furnished with a chair or stool, a chest, and a bed with mattress, bolster, sheet, and blanket. The sergeants slept in a common room. The complex included an infirmary; individual houses for the officers; a "marshalsy" or armory where weapons, armor, and harness were kept and where mail and helmets were forged and horses shod; the draper's establishment, where cloth was stored and clothing and shoes made; and the kitchens. Excavated into the rock were deep wells, and there were vast cellars for the storage of grain and fodder. Outside the city the Temple maintained cattle, horse, and sheep farms.[5]

The Templar organization created an incessant traffic between Europe and the Holy Land, shipping gold, silver, cloth, armor, and horses to the East, whence returned brothers on missions to the West,

RUINS OF ROUND TEMPLE CHURCH, LANLEFF, BRITTANY.

HOSPITALER CASTLE, LE POËT-LAVAL, PROVENCE.

sick or elderly knights on leave, visiting officers on tours of inspection. A stream of messengers traveled in both directions.

The total number of Knights Templars in the Holy Land at any one time was never large. Figures in the thousands given by the chroniclers for battles were typically exaggerated and included sergeants, vassals, mercenaries, and native auxiliaries called Turcopoles. The number of knights engaged in a single battle rarely exceeded four hundred. The total of Templars in Europe also was numbered in the hundreds, at most one or two thousand.[6]

The extraordinary success of the Templars and St. Bernard's promotion of the Order soon led to imitations. The Hospital of St. John of Jerusalem, founded before the First Crusade by merchants from Amalfi as a hospice for pilgrims, staffed by Benedictine monks, began during the Second Crusade (1146–1149) to take part in fighting. By the mid-twelfth century it had become a Military Order, while retaining its philanthropic character, and the dual role was formalized in 1206. Between 1164 and 1170 the Orders of Calatrava, Santiago, and Alcantara were established to fight the Moors in Spain and Portugal. A hospital set up in Acre by German merchants from Lübeck and Bremen in 1190, during the Third Crusade, adopted the Rule of the Hospitalers and was recognized as an independent order. In 1198 it was transformed into the Order of Teutonic Knights, which, however, did most of its fighting in Europe, in the Baltic region.

For a century and a half the defense of the Christian European bridgehead in Asia Minor was primarily in the hands of the garrisons of Templars, Hospitalers, and Teutonic Knights. But whenever a new Crusade was undertaken, the knights of the Orders were obliged to submit to the leadership, usually royal or imperial, of the expedition's head. The arrangement did not always work smoothly. Men who spent their lives in the Holy Land often had a different perception of the military and political situation from the leaders of the Crusade and therefore favored a different strategy. More, their self-interest might diverge from that of Crusaders bent on achieving an immediate and perhaps chimerical objective. An ill-conceived Crusading operation might end by leaving the permanent garrison of the country worse off than it had been to start with. Crusaders returned home, but the Military Orders remained, a small Christian island in a stormy Muslim sea. Often, however, the superior experience of the Orders was recognized and deferred to. In 1148, in the Second Cru-

ENTRANCE GATE TO
TEMPLAR COMMUNITY,
RICHERENCHES, PROVENCE.

sade, Louis VII of France prevailed upon his knights to place themselves under the orders of the Templar officers, who divided them
into squadrons and trained them to endure attack without being
drawn into pursuit, to attack only under orders, to rally to the main
body of the army on signal, and to maintain a fixed order of march.[7]

The Orders were prominent in the Christian resistance against Saladin, the great sultan who united the Muslims in the last quarter of the twelfth century for a major Islamic offensive. Checked at Ascalon in 1177 and a year later at Jacob's Ford on the northern frontier of the Kingdom of Jerusalem, Saladin gained a decisive victory at Hattin in 1187. Some two hundred Templar and Hospitaler prisoners, including the Masters of both Orders, were executed at Saladin's command because they were "the firebrands of the Franks," and "these more than all the other Franks destroy the Arab religion and slaughter us."[8] Jerusalem fell at once, and the Third Crusade was organized in Europe in an attempt to recover it. When the Crusaders arrived, the Military Orders placed themselves formally under the command of Richard Lionheart, but actually they served as the Eng-

VAULTED CHAMBER, PART OF THE INTERIOR OF THE TEMPLAR CASTLE OF CHASTEL BLANC. (*FROM* A HISTORY OF THE CRUSADES, *EDITED BY KENNETH M. SETTON, UNIVERSITY OF WISCONSIN PRESS*)

lish king's chief advisers. Though the Crusade failed to recover Jerusalem, it established the Military Orders as major powers in Syria. Once again, the Crusaders, French, English, and German, went home, and the Templars and Hospitalers remained.

But unlike most of the handful of European settlers, with the exception of the Italian merchant colonies on the coast, they were backed by important resources in Europe, and Saladin and his successors had no easy time dislodging them. The most significant contribution the three great Orders made to the defense of the Holy Land was to build (or rebuild), maintain, and garrison the frontier castles.[9] These massive masonry fortresses represented the full development of medieval military science. Only the Military Orders were rich and powerful enough to keep them constantly manned and in fighting trim. At most strategic points, strongholds, perhaps in ruins, already existed. These were taken over, enlarged, and given the most up-to-date elaboration. Where necessary, castles were built from scratch. The Templars' largest fortress, the castle of Tortosa, in the county of Tripoli, was part of the defenses of the city of Tortosa, its concentric curtain walls overlooking the Mediterranean. It withstood Saladin's attack in 1188. Second in importance, Chateau Pélérin (Pilgrim Castle) was built in 1218 with the aid of the Teutonic Knights on a rocky promontory south of Acre. Surrounded on three sides by the sea, it was protected toward the mainland by three lines of defense, a moat with a low wall, a second wall with three rectangular towers, and a bailey (courtyard) defended by two towers 110 feet high in a massive curtain wall. Chateau Pélérin was never taken by the Muslims. Other Templar castles included Safad, east of Acre, Belfort, Chastel Rouge, Chastel Blanc, Baghras, and La Roche Guillaume.

The most famous of all the Crusader castles was the Krak des Chevaliers, northeast of Tripoli. An Arab castle on the site was captured by the Crusaders in 1110. A vassal of the count of Tripoli occupied it until 1142, when the count ceded it to the Hospitalers, who built a huge concentric fortress, its two rings of massive walls dominated by great towers and separated by a wide moat. The Hospitalers' other important castle, Margat, between Latakia and Tripoli, ceded to them by its baronial owner in 1186, was built on a mountain spur, with a double line of fortifications and a great circular tower that a thirteenth-century pilgrim described as seeming "to support the heavens, rather than exist for defense."[10] Saladin found both the Krak des Chevaliers and Margat too strong to attack.

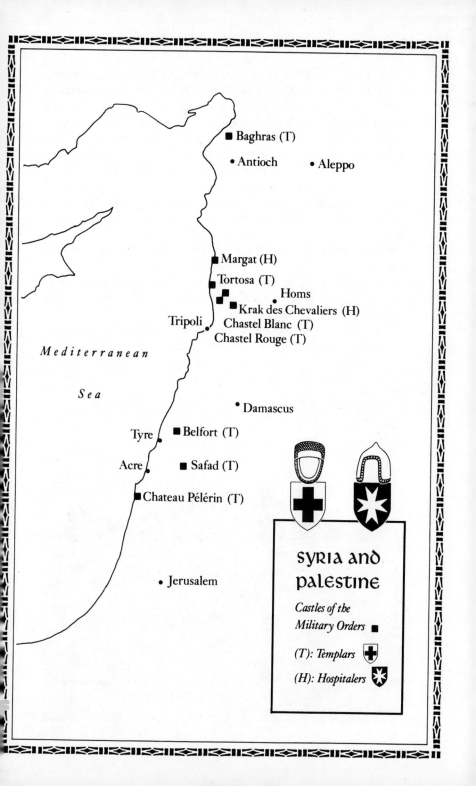

Baghras (T)

• Antioch   • Aleppo

Margat (H)
Tortosa (T)
        Homs
    Krak des Chevaliers (H)
Tripoli
Chastel Blanc (T)
Chastel Rouge (T)

Mediterranean

Sea

• Damascus

Tyre   Belfort (T)

Acre   ■ Safad (T)

Chateau Pélérin (T)

• Jerusalem

syria and palestine

Castles of the
Military Orders ■

(T): Templars

(H): Hospitalers

The Orders' military power inevitably involved them in the politics of the Crusader states. They took sides in the successional disputes of the Holy Land and in political conflicts imported from Europe. Usually the Hospitalers and Templars were ranged on opposite sides. In the early thirteenth century, when the Guelf-Ghibelline (papal-imperial) quarrel manifested itself in Syria, the Templars were Guelf, the Hospitalers Ghibelline. Sometimes the quarrel went beyond words, as in the 1240s when the Orders battled alongside members of the Italian merchant communes, the Templars on the side of the Guelf Genoese and Venetians, the Hospitalers on that of the Ghibelline Pisans.

The Templars' fund-raising activities led them into an incongruous enterprise: banking.[11] They began by lending money to finance pilgrims and Crusaders. The first record of a Templar loan is in 1135, to a couple who turned over their property in Saragossa, "houses, lands, vineyards, gardens, and all that we possess," against a loan that would allow them to make their pilgrimage to the Holy Sepulchre. The land was to be returned when the debt was repaid, the Templars

THE KRAK DES CHEVALIERS, MOST FAMOUS OF THE CRUSADER CASTLES, GARRISONED BY THE HOSPITALERS. (*FROM* A HISTORY OF THE CRUSADES, *EDITED BY KENNETH M. SETTON, UNIVERSITY OF WISCONSIN PRESS*)

realizing the revenues of the property in the meantime.[12] Thus despite the Church's prohibition of usury, the Order received disguised interest. From this modest beginning, it was only a decade to a huge loan to Louis VII for the Second Crusade. Besides lending money to clients, the Templars guarded and transported money and valuables. Monasteries had traditionally filled these roles of moneylender and safety deposit, but the Templars, with their estates and alms, their commandery-fortresses and military strength, soon preempted the business, contributing, in the view of some historians, to the development of modern credit practices.

In Europe, both Templars and Hospitalers served as advisers, messengers, envoys, and sometimes arbiters for the kings of France, England, and Germany. In the Holy Land they practiced diplomacy not only among the Christian states, but with the Muslim powers, for others and on their own behalf. As permanent residents in Asia Minor, the Military Orders had an interest in the balance-of-power politics of strong Muslim states such as Damascus and Egypt, and did not scruple to form alliances with one or another. Consequently, despite their undisputed military skill and valor, they were often regarded with suspicion in Europe. A chronicler reported French prince Robert of Artois exclaiming, "See the ancient treachery of the Templars! The long-known sedition of the Hospitalers!"[13] The Orders' advice in councils of war often conflicted with the very aims of the Crusaders. In the Third Crusade they actually dissuaded Richard Lionheart from attempting to retake Jerusalem, and when German emperor Frederick II successfully treatied with Egypt in 1229 for the peaceful return of the Holy City, Templars and Hospitalers opposed the move. The recovery of Jerusalem was actually undesirable to them because the city, no longer fortified, was difficult to defend. Their position was somewhat vindicated when on the expiration of a truce in 1239 the Muslims easily took back the city, but in Europe the Orders were widely perceived as having "gone native."

Some Templars and Hospitalers indeed had learned Arabic, and both Orders maintained friendly relations with Arab informants. The Syrian writer Usama (1095–1188) recounted an incident: "Whenever I went into [the al-Aqsa Mosque], which was in the hands of Templars who were friends of mine, they would put [a little chapel] at my disposal, so that I could say my prayers there. One day I had gone in, said the Allah akhbar, and risen to begin my prayers, when a Frank [Crusader] threw himself on me from behind, lifted me up, and turned me so that I was facing east. 'That is the way to pray!'

he said. Some Templars at once intervened, seized the man, and took him out of my way, while I resumed my prayer. But the moment they stopped watching him he seized me again and forced me to face east, repeating that this was the way to pray. Again the Templars intervened and took him away. They apologized to me and said: 'He is a foreigner who has just arrived today from his homeland in the north, and he has never seen anyone pray facing any other direction than east.' 'I have finished my prayers,' I said, and left, stupefied by the fanatic who had been so perturbed and upset to see someone praying facing [Mecca]!'"[14]

Individual members of the Military Orders passed their lives in obscurity if not anonymity. The Orders absorbed their personalities and in many cases even their names. The names of masters and many other officers of both Templars and Hospitalers, however, have been preserved, and chronicles and other records give us glimpses of their careers and sometimes of their characters. Where the family origins of Masters and other important officers can be identified, they are typically of high status, sometimes connected to royalty. Occasionally a single family produced several officers. The Milly family, from Picardy, lords of territories in the Holy Land, numbered among its members Masters of both Temple and Hospital. Another family, the Montaigus, from the Auvergne, also contributed Masters of both Orders as well as many magnates of the Church.[15] In some cases it is possible to trace a career from simple brother-knight, either in Europe or Syria, to preceptor (commander) of a local unit, to more important officer—governor of one of the Order's castles or Master of a province—to one of the major officials in the Holy Land, Seneschal, Marshal, Commander of the Kingdom of Jerusalem, or Commander of Tripoli and Antioch, and finally to Master of the Order.

As an outlet for surplus sons of knightly families, the Military Orders combined the attraction of knight-errantry with the advantages of membership in the clergy. Just as Crusading gave knights the opportunity of simultaneously exercising their profession and earning salvation, the Temple, Hospital, and Teutonic Order offered the spiritual advantages of the monastery together with the pleasures of warfare, the promise of adventure, and the charm of foreign travel. Unlike a single Crusade, the Order provided a lifelong career, with membership in an institution of great prestige.

Though originally the rules of the Orders merely stipulated that a candidate had to be a free man and legitimate, as the class system hardened during the thirteenth century, enlistments came to be limited to the sons of knights or descendants of knights on the father's side.[16] An initiation ceremony, that of Gerard de Caux, a candidate for membership in the Knights Templars at the end of the thirteenth century, has been preserved in the records of the Templars' trial. Gerard, along with two others, was received into the Order in "the house of the Temple at Cahors, in the morning, after high mass." The preceptor of the province, Brother Guigo Adhémar, was supported by the preceptor of a neighboring commandery, Raymond Robert; the preceptor of Cahors, Brother Pierre; a brother priest, Raymond de la Costa; and two knights of the Order, names not given. The three young men had been knighted together five days before. As the candidates waited in a room next to the chapel of the Temple, Raymond Robert and another knight approached them and asked, "Do you seek the company of the Order of the Temple and the participation in the spiritual and temporal goods which are in it?" The three replied that they did.

"You seek what is a great thing," the brother knights continued, "but you do not know the strong precepts of the Order; for you see us from the outside, well dressed, well mounted, and well equipped, but you cannot know the austerities of the Order . . . for when you wish to be on this side of the sea, you will be beyond it, and vice versa, and when you wish to sleep you must be awake, and when you wish to eat you must go hungry. Can you bear these things for the honor of God and the safety of your souls?"

When the young men assented, the Templars asked a series of questions: Did they believe in the Catholic faith? Were they in holy orders or married or promised to another Order, were they of the knightly class and legitimate, had they bribed anyone to gain entrance, did they have any secret infirmity that would inhibit their service, were they in debt? Their answers being satisfactory, the Templars instructed them to turn toward the chapel and pray that with God's will their petition be granted; then the two Templars withdrew to make their report to Brother Guigo.

After a time the Templars returned, bade the candidates take off their "caps and coifs," and led them into the presence of Brother Guigo. They knelt before the preceptor and with clasped hands asked him "for the companionship of the Order and participation in the spiritual and temporal goods which are in it," promising to be "serving slaves" of the Order and "to put aside our will for that of another." Brother Guigo administered the oath: they swore obedience to the Master of the Temple and to their other superiors in the Order, promised to "preserve chastity, the good usages, and the good customs of the Order," to live without property, to help preserve the Kingdom of Jerusalem and conquer what was not yet acquired, never to allow "any Christian man or woman to be killed, or disinherited unjustly," to give a good account of any property of the Temple that might be entrusted to them, and never to leave the Order without permission of their superiors.

Brother Guigo accepted them into the Order, invested them with their mantles, blessed them, raised them to their feet, and kissed them on the mouth. The other Templars also kissed them. Brother Guigo then seated himself, invited the new brothers to sit at his feet, and delivered a lengthy instruction, explaining the discipline and routine of conventual life, closing with the words: "Go, God make you worthy men."[17]

The new knights were furnished with clothing and equipment. Each received two shirts, a narrow-sleeved tunic to be worn over them, two pairs each of shoes and underdrawers, a long jerkin divided below the waist, a long straight cape tied or hooked at the neck, a light summer mantle, a winter mantle lined with sheeps- or lambswool, a broad leather belt, a cotton cap, and a felt hat. They were furnished with two towels, one for the table, the other for washing, and with bedding, including a heavy blanket, white, black, or black-and-white striped, the Templar colors. The knight sometimes wrapped himself in the blanket while riding or used it to cover his horse at night.

Their armor was also given them: mail coat and leggings, helmet, shoes, and the "coat of arms," a white surcoat with red crosses back and front to be worn over the armor. This garment, widely copied in Europe, was evidently a borrowing from the Saracens for protection against the sun, which on a sultry day could make chain mail or plate armor burning hot. Each new knight was given a sword, a lance, and a triangular shield of wood covered with leather, as well as three knives, one of them for eating. The Order supplied its members with horses, three for each brother knight, one for a sergeant, and specified numbers for the various officers.[18]

In the monastic tradition, the life of the brother knight was strictly regulated by the canonical offices. Exactly as in a monastery or convent, the bell rang at midnight for matins. The knight rose from his bed, put on a mantle over the shirt and underdrawers in which he slept, donned stockings, shoes, and a cap, and joined his brothers en route to the chapel. There the knights said thirteen Our Fathers. Leaving the service, they went to the stable to see that their horses were fed and watered, observing strict silence, then returned to their cells, saying another Our Father before going back to sleep. At prime (four A.M. in summer, six in winter), they rose once more, dressed, and returned to the chapel to hear Mass; the canonical services of prime, tierce, and sext were then said one after the other, "for this is the custom of the House."[19] After Mass the brothers busied themselves with individual tasks.

At dinner, the first meal of the day, knights and sergeants were served first, the squires and servants afterward; in the commanderies of the Holy Land, the native light horsemen known as Turcopoles ate at a separate table. On the ringing of a bell, the knights took their places; a second bell rang and the sergeants were seated. Unlike some monastic establishments where two men shared a bowl, each knight was given a bowl and cup. He provided his own knife and spoon. The meal was not spartan; there was often a choice of meats, so that a brother who did not like beef could eat mutton; when supplies were abundant three kinds of meat might be served. If a brother did not like the appearance or aroma of the meat, he could ask for a substitute. Portions were distributed equally, and those who chanced to receive better helpings were expected to share them. The Master had the privilege of sending dishes to any of the brothers, even those who were doing penance. The leftovers were given to the poor. During the meal, the brothers preserved silence while a priest read aloud. No one left until dinner was ended "unless he had a nosebleed, and then he must return when the bleeding was staunched."[20]

The afternoon services of nones and vespers were said at two or three and five or six. The only brothers excused were "the brother of the bakery, if he had his hands in the dough, and the brother of the great forge, if he had boiling iron on the fire . . . and the brother of the smithy if he was shoeing a horse . . . or a brother who was washing his hair," and these must come to say their prayers when they were able.[21]

After vespers, supper was served, with the same ceremony as dinner. During fast days only one meal was eaten, but one adequate for fighting men who needed to stay in top condition. The celebrated Paris preacher Jacques de Vitry, who became bishop of Acre in 1216, preached a sermon to the Templars in which he told a story to emphasize this point:

"Once there were certain brother-knights of your House who were so fervent in fasts and austerities that they easily succumbed to the Saracens through the weakness of their bodies. I heard about one of them, a very pious knight, but without prowess, who fell from his horse at the first lance blow that he received in a skirmish with the infidels. One of his brothers helped him back into the saddle, with great danger to his own person, and our knight rode again toward the Saracens, who unhorsed him again. The other knight, having twice raised and saved him, said, 'Look out for yourself henceforth, Sir Bread-and-Water, for if you are knocked off again, I won't be the one to pick you up!' "[22]

At nine, when compline was rung, the brothers assembled to drink diluted wine and receive their orders for the following day. Each then tended again to his horses and harness, "and if he has anything to say to his squire, he must say it pleasantly and softly, and then he may go to bed. And when he is in bed, he must say an Our Father so that if he has committed any sin since compline God may pardon him. And each brother must keep silence from compline to prime, except for a necessity."[23] Silence was maintained at night even when on the march.[24]

To sustain discipline, the severest penalties were dismissal, temporary exile from the Order, or temporary loss of the habit. Many of the prohibitions were concerned with ordinary crimes or misdemeanors: simony, in this case giving or accepting a bribe to secure admission to the Order; killing or injuring Christians; theft, embezzlement; carnal intercourse with a woman; sodomy; false witness; unbelief; refusing hospitality to a traveling brother; giving away or wasting the Order's property. Brothers could not possess money of their own, or carry it without permission. Fighting among the brothers was condemned—they must not "maliciously thrust at or strike a brother . . . and if shedding of blood should result, they may be imprisoned."[25]

Strict obedience was stressed above all. The brothers could do nothing without permission—"bathe, or be bled, or take medicine, or go to town, or gallop a horse."[26] In battle they were not to attack without the leader's command "except that they should do this to help any Christian being pursued by a Turk intending to kill him." During a *chevauchée*, they must maintain their line of march, although a knight could take a quick turn to try his horse and harness. In combat, disobedience was severely punished. A knight who separated himself from his squadron was sent back to camp in disgrace, on foot, to stand trial by "the justice of the House."[27] Even the Commander of Acre, Brother Jacques de Ravane, was put in irons for making an unauthorized raid that ended in disaster.[28] Likewise, Brother Baldwin de Borrages, commander at Chateau Pélérin, escaped judgment of the Order after a similar incident only by fleeing the country.[29]

The worst conceivable crime for a member of a Military Order was apostasy, denying the Cross, even to save his life. Roger l'Aleman, a Templar knight with powerful connections, was expelled from the Order for reciting from the Koran while a prisoner, despite his protest that he had been tricked.[30]

In the Crusade of St. Louis (Louis IX of France), the last full-scale Crusade of the Middle Ages (1249–1252), the Military Orders can be seen in all their typical roles: as soldiers, diplomats, and bankers.

Both the Templars and the Hospitalers took part in the decision-making that preceded the Crusade. The Orders were represented at the council of war that chose Egypt as the target of attack. They did not, however, agree with the decision. The Master of the Temple, Guillaume de Sonnac, and the Marshal of the Hospitalers, Guillaume de Corceles, both wrote Louis warning him that Egypt and Damascus, traditional rivals, were negotiating an alliance that would upset the balance of power and threaten the weak Christian coastal settlements of Jaffa and Caesarea. De Sonnac reported that he had been approached by an Egyptian emir who wanted a treaty with the Crusaders and offered to put the king in touch with him. It was rumored among the Crusaders that De Sonnac had himself initiated the détente—in the picturesque expression of a chronicler, that he and the sultan had "concluded such a fine peace that they had had themselves bled in the same basin."[31] Louis wrote the Master forbidding such unauthorized relations with the enemy.[32]

A Templar officer, Renaud de Vichiers, former Master of the Temple in France, now serving as Marshal in the Holy Land, accompanied the king on his journey to the East. The Templar contingent was led by Guillaume de Sonnac. The current Master of the Hospitalers, captured at the battle of Gaza five years before, was still a prisoner in Cairo, and the Marshal of the Hospital commanded in his place.

Mediterranean Sea

Alexandria

Damietta

Mansourah

egypt-
the crusade
of st louis

EGYPT

Cairo

Nile River

Contrasted with the troops of the French king, who were arrayed in the usual motley variety of garments and armor, the Orders presented the uniform appearance of a modern army. Each Templar knight wore over his mail hood a rigid helmet that left only the face uncovered, and over his hauberk his white coat of arms sewn back and front with red crosses. Templar sergeants wore black tunics, also adorned with crosses.[33] The Hospitalers, who had previously worn black monastic robes over their armor, had recently adopted tunics with crosses similar to those of the Templars (which a decade later they changed for scarlet tunics with white crosses).[34] Besides the brother knights and sergeants of the Orders, both Templars and

Hospitalers employed troops from outside their membership, lay knights who were their vassals, mercenary knights, and Turcopoles.

The two Orders had recently been involved on opposite sides of one of the intermittent civil wars of the Latin states, but in preparation for his expedition St. Louis had taken care to get them reconciled. The Crusade began well, with a successful landing on June 4, 1249, at the mouth of the Nile across from Damietta. After several hours' assault, Damietta was evacuated by the Muslims, and the Crusaders streamed into the city. The leaders of the army were billeted in mosques and palaces, while the Templars, Hospitalers, and other troops pitched their tents on the island in the Nile where they had disembarked. The Templars placed the tent that served as chapel in the middle of their camp, the round tent of the Master next to it, then the tents of the Marshal and Commander and of the commissariat, the tents of the knights in a circle around the chapel. When firewood and fodder for the horses had been brought by the squires, food was distributed and the knights ate in their tents.[35]

The promising beginning was not followed up. One of the king's brothers, Alphonse of Poitiers, was late in arriving with his command, and it was not until five months later, in November, that the advance toward Cairo began.

In the march the Military Orders took the key positions of van- and rearguards. The knights rode in squadrons, their squires either in front, carrying their lances, or behind with their relief mounts. They never broke ranks on the march.[36] The king wished some of their discipline would rub off on his own men, one of whom, Gautier d'Autreche, during the fighting at Damietta had been mortally wounded in a single-handed foray, causing Louis to comment that "he would not care to have a thousand [such] men."[37]

The submarshal of the Templars rode at the Marshal's side carrying the banner. To give the signal for a charge, the Marshal took the banner, while other knights grouped themselves around him to protect it; if the Marshal was killed, a knight named by him in advance replaced him. It was strictly forbidden to lower the banner or to use it as a lance.[38]

South of Damietta the army halted and dammed a small tributary of the Nile to make a ford. As the Templar van started to cross, according to the eyewitness account of St. Louis's biographer and seneschal, Jean de Joinville, the Muslims suddenly attacked. At first the Templars held formation and refused to risk counterattack, but when a Turk brought a Templar to the ground directly in front of the Marshal, he exclaimed, "For God's sake, let's get at them! I can't stand it any longer!" and struck his spurs into his horse. The whole army followed the Templars and all the Turks, according to Joinville, were killed.[39]

When the French approached the main Egyptian defensive position at Mansourah, separated from them by a branch of the Nile, they came under severe fire of enemy missiles. The king ordered a causeway constructed across the river. Covered walkways (cats) were built to shelter the workers from stones hurled by Egyptian siege machines on the other side. Work on the causeway began a week before Christmas, but it was constantly frustrated by the Saracens, who dug new channels for the stream on their bank.

On Christmas day as Jean de Joinville and his knights sat at dinner in the tent of another French lord, the Saracens attacked and killed some knights strolling outside the camp. Joinville and his host hastily armed themselves and galloped out to fight, but would have been overpowered by numbers had not "the Templars, who on hearing the alarm had come up, covered our retreat well and valiantly."[40]

The Saracens began to hurl missiles of Greek fire, setting the movable towers and catwalks ablaze. The situation seemed hopeless, when a native offered to sell crucial information: the location of a ford farther down the river. The crossing was planned for February 7. An advance guard composed of the king's brother Robert of Artois, the Templars, and an English contingent was to ford the river, secure the opposite bank, and wait for the others to cross; again the Templars were to form the vanguard, the count of Artois was to lead the second rank, and the king would follow with the rest of the army.

The crossing was achieved—with some difficulty, for the water was deeper and swifter than the native had said. Once across, Artois and his men ignored their orders and set off in impetuous pursuit of the enemy. Brother Gilles, the Commander of the Temple, admonished the count to stop and wait for the king and the rest of the army, appealing to his pride as a knight by assuring him that in making the crossing he had already accomplished "one of the greatest knightly deeds that had been done in a long time in the East." If they allowed themselves to be scattered and divided, the Saracens would rally and overpower them. One of the count's knights accused the Templars of being wolves in sheep's clothing: "If the Templars and the Hospitalers and the others in this country wanted it so, the land would have been conquered long ago!" The count told Brother Gilles to stay if he was afraid. Gilles replied, "Sire, neither I nor my brothers are afraid. . . . We will go with you, but truly we doubt if either we or you will return."[41]

The rash count and his men pressed on toward Mansourah, while the Templars, unable to dissuade, loyally supported. The army "struck spurs into their horses and rushed headlong in pursuit of the Turks, who fled before them, right through the town of Mansourah and on into the fields beyond towards Cairo." There they came face to face with a fresh enemy force, the Mameluk guard of the emir Baybars. Retreating into the narrow streets of the town, the French found themselves in a trap, as the enemy threw down from the rooftops "great beams and blocks of wood." The count of Artois was killed "and so many other knights that the number of dead was estimated at three hundred," wrote Joinville. "The Templars, as their Master told me later, lost on this occasion some two hundred and eighty men-at-arms." The Master himself, wounded in the face, lost an eye.[42]

Unable to rescue their comrades in Mansourah, by nightfall the French managed, by desperate fighting, to reach a point on the river opposite their old camp; here reinforcements arrived, and the Saracens again fell back to Mansourah. The Provost of the Hospitalers, Brother Henry de Ronnay, comforted the king for the loss of his brother by assuring him that by his deeds he had gained more honor than any other king of France, "For, in order to fight your enemies, you swam across a river, to rout them utterly and drive them from the field. Besides this, you have captured their machines, and also their tents, in which you will be sleeping tonight." The king replied, "May God be worshipped for all He has given me," but, Joinville reported, "big tears began to fall from his eyes."[43]

After the battle of Mansourah, Louis had the choice of retreating to Damietta or holding his position on the Nile. He chose to remain. The French army was harassed by constant raids, and at sunrise on February 11, the Saracens mounted a full-scale attack. The first assault was met by the king's brother Charles of Anjou, king of Sicily, and the barons of the Holy Land. "The enemy tackled him in the way that men play chess," Joinville reported, "for first of all they sent their foot soldiers forward to attack him, and these hurled Greek fire at his troops. Then all the Saracens, both mounted and unmounted, pressed so hard on our people that [Charles of Anjou], who was on foot among his knights, was quite overpowered." The king charged in person, sword in hand, "so far forward among the ranks of the Turks that they burnt his horse's crupper with Greek fire," and rescued his brother. Two more "battles," divisions of knights, met the onslaught, holding back the Turks.

"The next to meet the enemy's onset was Brother Guillaume de Sonnac, Master of the Temple, with the few members of his Order left to him after the battle on Shrove Tuesday. He had had a barricade erected in front of his men made up of the machines we had taken from the Saracens. When the enemy . . . hurled Greek fire at the defenses he had put up, these caught fire quickly. . . . The Turks did not wait for the fire to burn itself out, but rushed in and attacked the Templars amid the flames. . . . Behind the Templars there was a tract of land . . . which was so thickly covered with the Saracens' darts that you could not see the ground." The Master lost his other eye and died shortly after of his wounds.[44]

The Crusaders held out, but their losses were heavy. "The river was full of corpses," wrote Joinville, "from one bank to the other, and as far upstream as one could cast a small stone."[45] The Saracens dismantled boats, carried them around the Christian camp by camel, and launched them downstream, cutting off the Crusaders from their supply base at Damietta. Soon the army was racked by hunger and plagued by sickness. At the end of March the king ordered a withdrawal, but it was too late; halfway back to Damietta the French were forced to surrender.

The Templars sent the news of the catastrophe to their brothers in France: only three Templars and five Hospitalers of the Crusading army had survived.

Negotiations for a peace agreement began. The Saracen envoys suggested exchanging the prisoners for Templar or Hospitaler castles, but this was impossible because every castle governor had sworn an oath never to surrender his castle to procure a man's release from captivity. Louis IX himself endorsed the refusal, preferring to pay an enormous ransom, half of it immediately.

"It took the whole of that day [May 7] and the next day until night to count the money," Joinville wrote, "which was reckoned by weight in the scales." At about six on Sunday evening it became evident that the money was "a good thirty thousand pounds short of the sum required." Joinville advised the king to send for the Commander and the Marshal of the Temple, since the Master was dead, and ask them to lend him the money from that deposited for safekeeping.

Presented with the request by Joinville, however, the Commander, Etienne d'Otricourt, refused. "My lord of Joinville, . . . you know that all the money placed in our charge is left with us on condition of our swearing never to hand it over except to those who entrusted it to us." "On this," Joinville reported, "many hard and insulting words passed between us." Marshal Renaud de Vichiers found a way out of the dilemma. Joinville might simply "take the money if we will not lend it. . . . If you take what is ours here in Egypt, we have so much of what is yours in Acre that you can easily give us proper compensation."

The king accepted the suggestion and sent Joinville to take the money from the Templars' flagship. The Commander declined to accompany him, but the Marshal went along. They found the Temple Treasurer in the ship's hold, where the money on deposit was kept in chests, each labeled with the name of the Crusader-client. Joinville demanded the keys; the Treasurer refused—Joinville believed that the man was taking advantage of his condition, wasted as he was by dysentery. "I caught sight of a hatchet lying there; I picked it up and told him I would make it serve as His Majesty's key." The Marshal thereupon ordered the Treasurer to turn over the keys, and Joinville took enough money to complete the ransom.[46]

The Templars evidently approved of Renaud de Vichiers' handling of the affair, for when he returned to Acre they elected him Master—with the support of the king, according to Joinville.

Joinville had another experience with the Templars as bankers. Collecting his own back pay from the king, he deposited most of it with the Commander of Acre. Later he sent a messenger to withdraw cash, but "the Commander told him that he had no money of mine, and did not know me." Joinville had to appeal to Renaud de Vichiers, and after suffering "for four whole days . . . such anxiety as a man must feel when he has no money to meet expenses," received his funds. To his further satisfaction, the Commander was demoted.[47]

Joinville also had the opportunity to observe successful Templar and Hospitaler diplomacy. A sinister Islamic chieftain known to the Europeans as the Old Man of the Mountains ruled as Grand Master of the feared "Assassins" of Persia, who extorted tribute by threatening the lives of rulers, both Christian and Muslim. The Old Man sent emissaries to King Louis in Acre demanding payment. The representatives, splendidly dressed, postured and threatened: one held in his clenched fist "three knives, with blades that fitted each into the handle of another," which he was to present to the king if he refused the offer, "in token of defiance"; a second carried "a stout roll of linen wound round his arm, which he was to present to the king as a winding-sheet for his burial." But Joinville discovered that the Assassins themselves paid tribute to both Templars and Hospitalers, whose Masters refused to be terrorized, although "the Emperor of Germany, the King of Hungary, the Sultan of Cairo, and other rulers" had surrendered to the extortion. The envoy made an offer: Louis could fulfill his obligations toward the Old Man of the Mountains by arranging for the latter to be released from paying tribute to the Hospital and the Temple.

The king told the chief envoy to return in the afternoon, and summoned the Masters of the Temple and Hospital. The Assassin found them seated on either side of the king, who told him to repeat the message he had delivered that morning. The two Masters then had orders given him "in the Saracen tongue" to come to the headquarters of the Hospital the following day. When he appeared, they told him through an interpreter that he had "acted very rashly in daring to send such an insolent message to the king . . . [and] if the honor of the king . . . had not been involved they would have had [the emissaries] drowned in the filthy sea of Acre. . . ." The envoy was commanded to go back to his lord and return in a fortnight with "such a letter and such jewels as may appease His Majesty and make him graciously pleased with you." The crestfallen envoy obeyed, and on his return brought his lord's ring, engraved with his name, and other gifts, including his shirt, explaining that "as the shirt is closer to the body than any other garment, so did their lord hold His Majesty as closer to himself in love than any other king."[48]

In August, the king's brothers sailed for home, taking with them the bulk of the army; the king remained, and a quarrel between the Muslims of Syria and Egypt strengthened his position. He found himself holding the balance of power between Syrians and Egyptians, with both parties suing for his support. The Egyptians, heretofore slow in adhering to the terms of their treaty with Louis, began to send large groups of prisoners back, at the same time offering alliance, with the prospect of restoring Syria west of the Jordan to the Crusaders. Negotiations were proceeding when the king learned that the Templars had been carrying on diplomacy of their own with

Damascus. Renaud de Vichiers had sent his Marshal, Hugues de Jouy, to the sultan of Damascus to work out an agreement over some land held by the Temple. The contract was made, subject to the king's approval, and Brother Hugues returned, bringing with him a Damascene emir as the sultan's representative. The king was furious; the Master should not have negotiated an agreement without consulting him. Such insubordination must not go unpunished, and the king decided to exact reparation from the whole Order, in the form of a disciplinary session of one of its own chapters. "The king had the flaps of three of his pavilions raised," Joinville wrote, "and all the lower ranks of the army were given leave to come and see. . . . The Master of the Temple and all his knights advanced barefoot right through the camp. . . . The king made the Master of the Temple and the sultan's envoy sit in front of him, and addressed the former in a loud voice. 'Master,' he said, 'you will tell the sultan's envoy that you regret having made any treaty with his lord without first speaking to me. You will add that since you did not consult me you must hold the sultan released from the agreement he has made with you, and hand all relevant documents back to him.' Thereupon the Master of the Temple produced the written agreement and handed it to the emir, saying as he did so: 'I give you back the contract I have wrongly entered into, and express my regret for what I did.'

"Then the king told the Master and other Templars to rise, which they accordingly did. 'Now,' said His Majesty, 'kneel and make reparation to me for having thus approached the sultan against my will.' The Master knelt, and holding the hem of his mantle toward the king, surrendered to him everything his Order possessed, so that His Majesty might take from it whatever compensation he might choose. 'I declare . . . ,' said the king, 'that Brother Hugues, who made this agreement, shall be banished from the whole Kingdom of Jerusalem.' "[49]

Brother Hugues was banished, and the Order, angry at the public humiliation, soon after either deposed or demanded the resignation of Renaud de Vichiers.

The last Christian prisoners were returned, the remaining half of the ransom was canceled, and Louis made an alliance with the Egyptians in 1252, supporting their invasion of Syria in return for Jerusalem, Bethlehem, and most of the land west of the Jordan. But the allies were blocked from joining forces by the Syrian occupation of

Gaza, and a treaty was signed between the Syrians and Egyptians in April 1253 before Jerusalem could be regained.

Although Louis made one more attempt at a Crusade in the last year of his life, 1270, he drew little support in Europe. The age of Crusading was in fact over. The great rearguard of the Military Orders fought heroically to the end, their castles like the knights themselves falling one by one until in 1291 Templars and Hospitalers made their last stand in Acre. In the final battle, the Marshals of both Temple and Hospital were killed, the two Masters mortally wounded. The Master of the Hospitalers, dying in Cyprus, wrote to the Prior of the province of St. Gilles "in great sadness of heart, overcome with deep sorrow. . . ."[50]

A troubadour named Oliver the Templar penned a bitter requiem:

Anger and sadness have entered my heart
So that I hardly dare remain alive,
For they have lowered the Cross that we took
In honor of the One who was crucified.[51]

The spirit of 1095 had indeed vanished from Europe, its fanaticism and idealism replaced by a more rational and material outlook. Perhaps the spirit of 1291 was exemplified less by the Templars who perished sword in hand amid the flames of Acre than by a knight named Roger de Flor who fought bravely till the cause was lost and then executed a coolheaded escape, loading a ship with jewels, silks, church ornaments, and other valuables, and sailing out of the stricken harbor in a shower of missiles, to snatch a fortune from catastrophe.

With the end of the Christian European presence in the Holy Land, the Military Orders lost their reason for being but continued to exist on the strength of their wealth, power, and organization. A generation after the fall of Acre, the most prestigious of the three, the Knights Templars, fell victim to their very wealth when Philip IV of France hit on the liquidation of the Order as a financial expedient. The Templars were accused of a variety of crimes, chief among them heresy, idol worship, and sodomy; a number of confessions were obtained by torture; the Grand Master and several others were burned at the stake; and the Order was suppressed. The pope, who pronounced the dissolution, prevailed on Philip to concede the confiscated Templar lands to the Hospitalers, who thus gained a fresh lease on life. Philip himself profited from the sale of chattels and the cancellation of his own large debts.

The Hospitalers remained for a time based on Cyprus, then retreated first to Rhodes and finally to Malta, where they withstood a prolonged siege by the Ottoman Turks in 1565, and whence they were finally expelled by Napoleon's expedition of 1798.

The Teutonic Knights, never important in Asia Minor, played a historic role in northeast Europe, where they conducted "Crusades" against the pagan natives of Livonia (modern Lithuania, Latvia, and Estonia) and founded the state of Prussia. The Order reached the height of its power in the fourteenth century but declined rapidly following its defeat by Polish and Lithuanian forces at the battle of Grünwald in 1410. Its last branch was dissolved by Napoleon in 1809. In 1834 both Hospitalers and Teutonic Knights were revived: the Hospitalers by the establishment of a headquarters in Rome, where they remain to this day, a medieval relic with members around the world; the Knights converted into an honorary ecclesiastical institution with headquarters in Vienna.

For European knighthood, however, the real legacy of the Military Orders was not their anticlimactic later history but the conspicuous model they furnished of the Christian warrior, the knight who served God through the profession of arms.

BERTRAND
DU GUESCLIN:
A KNIGHT OF THE
FOURTEENTH
CENTURY

◄§ REGNAULT DU GUESCLIN WAS THE CHILD'S FATHER,
HIS MOTHER WAS A GENTLE LADY AND VERY FAIR.
BUT AS FOR THEIR CHILD, I MUST TELL YOU
THERE WAS NONE UGLIER BETWEEN RENNES AND DINANT.
—Jean Cuvelier, *Chronique de Bertrand du Guesclin*

◄§ "SIR BERTRAND," SAID THE KING, "I HAVE NEITHER BROTHER,
NOR COUSIN, NOR NEPHEW, NOR COUNT, NOR BARON IN MY KINGDOM
WHO WOULD REFUSE TO OBEY YOU. IF ANY DID, HE WOULD KNOW
MY ANGER." —Froissart, *Chroniques*

◄§ "IF THE KING WANTS TO MAKE ME CONSTABLE,
HE MUST PAY HIS SOLDIERS TO MAINTAIN THEM . . .
FOR SOLDIERS WANT THEIR PAY.
IF THEY AREN'T WELL PAID, THEY WON'T SERVE,
AND IF THEY GO UNPAID THEY'LL PILLAGE."
—Du Guesclin, quoted by Cuvelier

BERTRAND Du GUESCLIN

(pronounced Gecklin), the most famous knight of the fourteenth century, was born in Brittany in about 1320 and died July 13, 1380, while besieging a castle in Gascony.[1] In between he fought in a half-dozen large battles, in dozens of smaller battles, and in hundreds of sieges, in addition to uncounted and nameless skirmishes, raids, sorties, surprises, and ambushes. Besides the thousands of blows dealt and received in these with sword, axe, mace, and lance, he fought many duels and took part in numerous tournaments. By the time of his death at sixty, his body was covered with scars. Taken prisoner four times, he witnessed and indeed encouraged the rise in the price of his ransom to the princely figure of 100,000 gold florins. In his turn he profited from the ransoms of hundreds of noble and knightly captives and exacted levies from innumerable captured castles, towns, and cities, but, caring nothing for wealth, he died nearly as poor as when he was born. A popular hero of legendary proportions, he was accorded the lion's share of the credit for the reversal of the tide of the Hundred Years War that took place under Charles V in the 1360s and 1370s.[2] No great general in the modern sense, but a consummate leader, he owed his success to his reckless bravery, physical hardihood, and talent as a *guerroyeur,* a planner and manager of operations on the petty scale on which nine tenths of the warfare of his day was conducted.

In addition to his valor and skill, Du Guesclin was universally credited by his contemporaries with a recommended but rare knightly virtue, a solicitude for the poor and helpless. Nineteenth-century historians, regarding patriotism as a virtue necessary to a hero, credited him with contributing to the birth of national sentiment, though he himself claimed only the medieval and knightly virtue of loyalty.

As in the case of William Marshal, we owe information on Du Guesclin's personal life to the fact that he became famous. In addition to the *Chronicles* of Froissart, he figures prominently in the *Cronica*

As in the case of William Marshal, we owe information on Du Guesclin's personal life to the fact that he became famous. In addition to the *Chronicles* of Froissart, he figures prominently in the *Cronica*

STATUE OF BERTRAND DU GUESCLIN, DINAN, BRITTANY.

del rey don Pedro of Lopez de Ayala, an eyewitness to much of Du Guesclin's Spanish adventure, and in several other histories and chronicles of the era. But the sole source of information about his birth, boyhood, and youth, and about numerous details of his mature life, is the *Chronique de Bertrand du Guesclin,* by a Picard trouvère named Jean Cuvelier. A long (22,790 lines) poem, Cuvelier's work exhibits the colorfully unreliable character of an epic, yet its proximity in time—written within a year of its hero's death—gives it considerable credibility, supported by the agreement of other sources on many facts. Its popularity may lend added credence, since many of Du Guesclin's companions-in-arms, including the royal princes who served with and under him, owned copies, that of the duke of Burgundy reputed worn by much perusal. Nothing is known of Cuvelier himself or his sources, which may have included a lost journal kept by Du Guesclin's herald-at-arms. Like Froissart and chroniclers going back to Herodotus, Cuvelier freely reports speeches and dialogues that perhaps show only what the writer and his readers regarded as appropriate.

There is no reason to doubt Cuvelier's statement that Bertrand was born the oldest child of the large family of Regnault du Guesclin, a knight of modest fortune, in La Motte, near Dinan, Brittany.[3] Regnault was a younger son of a family whose elder branch held extensive lands on the little peninsula on which St. Malo stands. His fief of La Motte–Broons was only slightly augmented by the dowry of his wife, Jeanne Malemains, consisting of a piece of land and a mill. Jeanne was credited with bringing to the marriage beauty rather than wealth, which perhaps drew the more attention to a conspicuous lack of beauty on the part of her firstborn, who was named for his godfather, Bertrand de Saint-Perm, a knightly friend of the family. According to Cuvelier, the boy's mother was so repelled by his looks that she treated him with a coldness that provoked resentment expressed in savage outbursts against parents, siblings, and the world. What is well established by other sources is that as a grown man Du Guesclin was the reverse of handsome, and, at least in his younger manhood, subject to fits of furious anger.[4] There is no indication, however, that he retained any lasting resentment against his mother.

Perhaps his status as first child in a large family inclined him to leadership. He organized the boys of the neighborhood in tournaments in imitation of adult sport, much as a youthful leader of a later

age might organize football games. Bertrand always commanded one party in the melee, but when his side appeared to be winning too easily he switched to the other. The battle ended on his command, whereupon (says Cuvelier) he led the way to a local inn and stood treat. To pay for this extravagance he is said to have sold a horse of his father's, which led to a ban on his tournaments, doubly enforced by Regnault's order to his peasants to keep their sons from associating with Bertrand, and by locking Bertrand in his room. But the Du Guesclin manor house was hardly a donjon and one day Bertrand, who was fifteen or sixteen, seized the keys from the woman servant who brought him his food, locked her up in his place, commandeered a farm horse from a peasant, and rode thirty kilometers without saddle or bridle to Rennes, where he had an aunt and uncle. The aunt was shocked but the uncle indulgent and he was allowed to stay.[5]

Bertrand is described at this stage as of middle height (probably not much over five feet), with swarthy complexion, a flat nose, gray eyes, broad shoulders, long arms, and small hands.[6] One Sunday he accompanied his aunt to church but slipped away to join in a combat organized by the town youth of Rennes. He succeeded in overthrowing a young champion who had hurled a dozen others to earth, but injured his knee on a sharp stone and had to be helped home. His aunt reproached him, partly for fighting, more for fighting with lower-class boys, and extracted a promise to fight henceforth only in noble tournaments.

Time brought reconciliation with his father, and shortly afterward an opportunity to fulfill his promise to his aunt. The marriage of the duke of Brittany's niece to a nephew of the king was the occasion for a celebratory tournament in Rennes to which Bertrand's father repaired with the family's best horse. Bertrand took a nag from the stable, followed, and met with luck. Tournaments had undergone refinement since William Marshal's time, with the action limited to a single field, the "lists," and a fixed number of courses, or charges, assigned to each cavalier. A cousin of Bertrand's had completed his courses and was willing to lend horse and armor. Galloping into the lists, Bertrand unhorsed several combatants without revealing his identity. The only champion to rival him was his father, with whom he avoided combat. His helmet got knocked off by another adversary and the elder Du Guesclin, recovering from his astonishment, promised to treat him properly in the future, in other words, to provide him with suitable horse and armor.[7]

Armor was in the mid-fourteenth century slowly but definitely evolving from mail to plate. Breastplates were occasionally worn under or over the hauberk in the thirteenth century and perhaps earlier; by Du Guesclin's time the practice was common. In the earlier period the breastplate was typically of *cuir bouilli*, leather hardened by boiling with wax, whence the name cuirass, but by now it was nearly always of iron. More widely used, however, was the "coat of plates," a garment of leather or fabric armored with vertical rectangular iron plates, at first nearly knee length, later shortened. Reinforcing plates were also widely worn, on elbows, knees, and at the throat, and were becoming popular for thighs, shins, arms, and shoulders as the advantage of smooth plate in warding off glancing blows of point or blade became recognized.[8]

Arming either for tournament or battle, a well-equipped knight of the 1340s would have first donned a close-fitting shirt, short breeches, and hose. Over these would go mail leggings, heavy quilted thigh

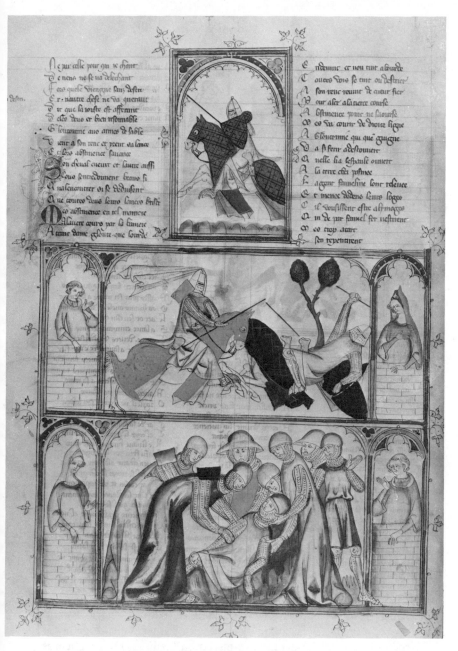

FOURTEENTH-CENTURY TOURNAMENT:
CENTER, BREAKING A LANCE; *BELOW,* SUCCORING THE WOUNDED.
(BIBLIOTHÈQUE NATIONALE, MS. FR. 146, F. 40V)

FOURTEENTH-CENTURY
BRASS RUBBING OF THE
TOMB OF SIR HUGH
HASTINGS SHOWS
REINFORCING PLATES ON
MAIL. *(BRITISH LIBRARY,
ADDIT. MS. 32490 B. 12)*

protectors (gamboised cuisses) with knee plates attached, greaves for
the shins, and iron shoes (sabatons). Next he put on the heavy fabric
acton, over which went his hauberk with shoulder and elbow plates
attached, and his coat of plates. The surcoat went over everything.
A narrow belt circled the waist; the broader sword belt hung more
loosely around the hips. Gauntlets of iron plates riveted to layers of
fabric, tinned or coppered against rusting, were drawn over the
hands. A new rounded or conical helmet (basinet) had a visor to
protect the face. Its crown was lined with leather pulled together at
the top by a cord; when it was placed on his head, the knight was
ready for combat. The shield had diminished in size, becoming a
downward-pointing triangle with curved sides, but it was still considered indispensable.[9]

In whatever form, armor was virtually indestructible (damage could be repaired by the blacksmith) and was handed down from grandfathers and fathers to sons and grandsons. The work of certain armorers and their centers—Milan, Nuremberg, Toledo—was especially esteemed, and later Du Guesclin took the opportunity of his stay in Spain to equip himself with Spanish mail.

While Du Guesclin was graduating from childish to adult tournaments, the quarrel between Edward III of England and Philip of Valois over the crown of France was slowly ripening into war. As maternal grandson of Philip IV, Edward had a stronger claim than his Valois rival, but Philip's lawyers exhumed the ancient Salic law and argued that royal descent had to be through the male line.[10] Edward was only sixteen at the time the question arose (1328) and lost out, but several years later a minor incident aggravated a problem more deep-seated than succession. The great principality of Aquitaine, comprising most of southwest France, inherited by marriage by the English crown, awkwardly owed feudal homage to the kings of France. Both the act of homage and Aquitaine's indeterminate borders created trouble. Edward, now a grown man, combined his immediate with his long-term grievances and put forward his claim to the French throne.

At nearly the same time (1341) a second, very similar successional quarrel broke out in Brittany, a quasi-independent province (like Aquitaine) whose duke left a niece and a half-brother as potential heirs. The half-brother, Jean de Montfort, claimed the crown on the basis of the Salic law, never heretofore applied in Brittany (or any other province). The niece, Jeanne de Penthièvre, was the lady whose marriage to Charles de Blois was celebrated in the tournament at Rennes where Bertrand du Guesclin and his father had met. She appealed to Philip of Valois, now Philip VI of France, uncle of her husband. Jean de Montfort on his side appealed to Edward III of England. As a result, the English and French monarchs were doubly arrayed against each other over the question of female succession, but ironically enough, on opposite sides in the two cases, Edward upholding female succession in France and rejecting it in Brittany while Philip defended it in Brittany without admitting it in France.

No one guessed that the Breton dynastic war would rage and smolder through twenty-three years, much less that the larger conflict would come to be known as the Hundred Years War and have, among other results, a large impact on the institution of knighthood. An augury came in the first great battle of the war, at Crécy in 1346,

BATTLE OF CRÉCY, 1346,
FROM THE *CHRONIQUES* OF
FROISSART. *(MUSÉE DE
L'ARSENAL, MS. 5187, F.
135V)*

in which Philip's old-fashioned army, whose principal element was the armored horseman, was routed by Edward III's slightly smaller but more modern force, which included a strong contingent of archers armed with the Welsh longbow. At one time much was made of the effectiveness of the longbow, but except for its more rapid rate of fire it had no advantage over the crossbow, which it never replaced in continental Europe. The English success with the longbow had its chief effect on military practice and consequently on knighthood by stimulating interest in the crossbow, a compact, easily fired weapon that owed its muzzle velocity and consequent range and accuracy to its use of horn, later metal, instead of wood as the power source.

More significant both for the future of warfare and the future of knighthood was the radically new organizational basis of Edward's army. Philip had assembled the ancient feudal host by the traditional summons to the royal vassals, who in turn called on their knights and retainers to perform their traditional military obligation, which they did with their traditional inefficiency. In England, however, a long history of argument over the feudal obligation with respect to service overseas, that is, in defense of the king's French lands, had prepared

ENGLAND

• Bruges

• Calais
X X Agincourt
Crécy • Arras

English Channel

Harfleur •
Rouen
Caen • Evreux • Mantes
NORMANDY X Paris
X Cocherel
Verneuil

• Compiègne
• Reims

• Dinan
BRITTANY
Rennes
LeMans • Patay X Orleans

Angers

FRANCE

X Poitiers

Atlantic

Ocean

La Rochelle

• Bordeaux
AQUITAINE

• LePuy

fRance in the hundred yeaRs waR

Battle X

the way for a new departure. Borrowing heavily from Italian bankers against the lucrative royal wool tax,[11] Edward appointed captains to enroll and train paid "retinues" of archers and men-at-arms, both captains and retinues secured by "indenture"—contract. The resulting professional army not only triumphed on the battlefield at Crécy, but achieved something considerably more difficult by capturing the important port city of Calais. Large battles were rare in the Middle Ages, and though often tactically decisive, that is, ending in the destruction of the losing army (typically 20 to 50 percent killed, according to a modern scholar),[12] they rarely had an equivalent strategic or political effect. Calais was taken only after a siege of nearly a year, an extraordinary medieval military effort. Its capture was of great economic value to Edward as a port for the wool trade with Flanders, but it also provided an easy entry into northern France for expeditionary forces from England.

A few months after Crécy, the English won a smaller battle in Brittany. At La Roche-Derrien casualties were very heavy on both sides, and Charles de Blois, commanding his army in person, and many times wounded, was taken prisoner. His stubbornly valiant wife, Jeanne, set about raising his ransom while continuing the war.

Bertrand du Guesclin, though not present at the battle, had already followed the example of his father and uncles in embracing the cause of Jeanne and Charles de Blois. Froissart lists him among the "good knights and squires" who repelled an English attack on Rennes in 1343,[13] but otherwise his early career in arms is obscure, with no further mention by Froissart or any other chronicler. Yet there is no reason to doubt Cuvelier's picture of young Du Guesclin at the head of a guerrilla band operating from the fastness of Broceliande, a forest southwest of Rennes whose mysterious enchantments are celebrated in the tales of the Round Table. Apparently he received no stipend from Charles de Blois, but depended for supply on the support of the local peasantry, from among whom he recruited his followers, and whom he equipped—horses, arms, armor—in part by purloining his mother's jewelry.[14] He made restitution thanks to an adventure more in the character of Pancho Villa than in that of Sir Lancelot. Ambushing three English soldiers carrying a chest of gold coins destined by Edward III for his garrison in the castle of Fougeray, he killed all three with his axe.[15] On a visit to his mother, he told her (according to Cuvelier), "Madame my mother, please pardon the thefts I've sometimes committed against you. . . ." And for each penny taken he returned twenty shillings.[16]

CASTLE OF MONTMURAN, NEAR RENNES, BRITTANY,
IN WHOSE CHAPEL DU GUESCLIN WAS KNIGHTED IN 1354.

Emboldened, the young guerrilla chief determined to attempt the capture of Fougeray itself. For his small band neither siege nor assault was practicable, and so he had recourse to a third classic method: ruse. Choosing a moment (summer of 1350) when a part of the garrison was on a combat mission elsewhere, he enlisted the aid of the local inhabitants to disguise half his troops as peasants bringing firewood to the castle. Some concealed their weapons under women's skirts and hid their beards in sunbonnets. When the drawbridge was lowered, Du Guesclin was the first to leap across it and attack the sentries. The gate was won, but the castle's defenders rallied and the attackers were themselves hard pressed when a fresh reinforcement of horsemen made a timely arrival.[17]

Du Guesclin was not strong enough to hold Fougeray, which was retaken in 1352 by Robert Knowles, a famous English captain and one of Du Guesclin's lifelong adversaries. Meantime, Du Guesclin profited from the news of his exploit in gathering fresh recruits, even including a few knights proud to serve under so redoubtable a squire. In 1354 Du Guesclin was himself tardily knighted. In the previous three years both his mother and father had died, giving him as oldest son a modest inheritance. To his success as guerrilla chief he had added laurels as a champion in tournaments in Pontorson, and in April 1354 a new feat of arms provided the occasion for his knighting. The Sire d'Audrehem, marshal of the king of France and royal lieutenant for the Breton-Norman frontier, was invited to dinner on Holy Thursday by the Lady of Tinteniac in her castle of Montmuran. Hugh of Calveley, an English captain famed for his giant stature, planned to ambush d'Audrehem and his party, but Du Guesclin, getting wind of the affair, organized a counterambush, and in the resulting fracas Calveley and a hundred others were captured. One of the lords present, Eslatre des Mares, castellan of Caux, conferred knighthood on the hero of the encounter.[18] By this time, mid-fourteenth century, the honor was perfunctorily accepted as their due by the few youths of the upper nobility, but for the numerous sons of the lesser nobility to which Du Guesclin belonged it was no such matter of course. Du Guesclin was thirty-four by the time he achieved it. Cost was more than ever an obstacle to many poor or landless squires. As a squire, a man had a good chance of having his needs taken care of, his horse and equipment furnished. As a knight, he would be expected to furnish himself with not one but three horses, and in addition to equip his own squire, with the total cost running into hundreds of pounds (livres).

In recompense, the title of knight offered some material benefits. The English system of hiring soldiers was gradually spreading, and a knight ordinarily commanded double the pay of a squire—about 15 shillings (sous) per day compared with seven and a half.[19] A knight was also entitled to a larger share of booty and ransoms. More important to Du Guesclin, the knightly title was still virtually indispensable to a leader.

Whatever these considerations weighed, Du Guesclin took the noneconomic aspect of knighthood seriously, donning the traditional white robe in the chapel of the Montmuran castle to swear the oath to serve God, defend the weak, and combat treachery. Grasping the triangular pennon that had become one of knighthood's symbols, he chose as his battle cry, "Notre Dame—Guesclin."

By the time he joined in the defense of Rennes in 1356, he had probably already made the transition from unpaid volunteer to paid professional soldier (in the service of Charles de Blois). The English military star was again in the ascendant, thanks to a brilliant victory won by Edward III's oldest son, the Black Prince, and his Anglo-Gascon captains at Poitiers. The battle probably would have had few

KNIGHTING ON THE BATTLEFIELD, FOURTEENTH CENTURY,
A RARE BUT OCCASIONAL OCCURRENCE.
(*BIBLIOTHÈQUE NATIONALE, MS. FR. 343, F. 79*)

consequences except that King John II of France, a doughty but empty-headed votary of knighthood's ideals, disdained a prudent retreat, fighting on foot until overpowered and made prisoner. The duke of Lancaster now sought to deliver a parallel blow in the Breton subwar by capturing Rennes, the capital and principal stronghold of Charles de Blois. The city's defense was commanded by a knight and an ex-peasant. The knight, Bertrand de St. Perm, was Du Guesclin's godfather; the former peasant, Penhouet, a self-made captain experienced in the ruses of warfare. He frustrated an enemy mining project by placing on the walls copper basins containing lead balls whose rattling pinpointed the excavation below and guided a successful countermine. When the duke of Lancaster caused a herd of pigs to be driven past the gate as a temptation to the hungry town to surrender, Penhouet had a squealing sow led out as the drawbridge was lowered. The hogs stampeded over the bridge, which was promptly raised after them.[20]

Du Guesclin joined a small relief force gathering at Dinan, northeast of Rennes. He was watching companions playing a game of tennis when he received word that his younger brother, Olivier, had been treacherously made prisoner during a truce. Flying into a fury, he rode the forty kilometers to Lancaster's camp, breaking in on a chess game the duke was playing with Sir John Chandos. The duke sent for Thomas of Canterbury, the English knight who had taken the prisoner. Canterbury demanded trial of the charge by judicial combat, to which Du Guesclin readily acceded. Before a large assemblage of both armies the two champions fought on horseback, with sword and dagger. Canterbury lost his sword, Du Guesclin leaped to the ground to retrieve it, Canterbury sought to ride him down, and Du Guesclin stabbed the Englishman's horse, causing it to collapse, pinning its rider. Du Guesclin had to be dragged off his adversary, for whom Chandos and Robert Knowles pleaded mercy. Du Guesclin cooled down, and there followed a feast with the ladies.[21]

Lancaster swore he would rather have five hundred archers enter Rennes in its relief than Du Guesclin, to whom he vainly offered bribes to change sides. Shortly after, Du Guesclin treated the duke to a ruse. While his own force hovered in concealment, a civilian allowing himself to be taken prisoner gave false information about the approach of a large relief army. When Lancaster took his army off to meet it, Du Guesclin plundered his camp and took the spoils into Rennes, sending word to the duke offering to return some of the wine for his dinner. Lancaster invited him to share it. Du Guesclin accepted and at dinner got involved in another duel when an English knight challenged him to break three lances. At the first shock Du Guesclin's lance passed through his adversary's mail, pierced his lung, and toppled him from the saddle. Such jousts—Du Guesclin fought still another before the siege was over—enlivened the monotony of siege warfare with the color of the tournament. It was doubtless a regret of Du Guesclin's life that he did not participate in the most famous such event, the Battle of the Thirty in 1351, in which thirty chosen French knights fought thirty English, Gascon, and Breton knights before a large audience. Empty of military significance, the French triumph was cheered by trouvères, chroniclers, and other devotees of the legendary past.

Lancaster made a final attempt to carry Rennes by assault with the aid of a great wooden siege tower. Repelled, he agreed to withdraw under a face-saving formula devised by Du Guesclin that allowed the duke to enter the town long enough to plant his banner on the wall.

For his successful defense, Du Guesclin was handsomely rewarded by Charles de Blois with the town and castellany of La Roche-Derrien.

While Brittany continued to suffer the depredations of war, next-door Normandy began to share them, with the outbreak of the "Navarrerie," a war waged against the king of France by his relative the king of Navarre, who was yet another Charles, known to history as Charles the Bad. His small realm of Navarre, astride the Pyrenees, presented no threat, but Charles the Bad was also lord of a substantial piece of Normandy, including towns on the Seine that controlled Paris's outlet to the sea. The dauphin Charles, the future Charles V (the Wise), wanted a commander for French royal forces based on Pontorson, in Brittany near the Norman border. Charles was wise enough to have fully adopted by now the English system of hiring soldiers by contract instead of relying on the old feudal levy of his father and grandfather. When Du Guesclin was recommended to him, Charles offered to put him at the head of sixty men-at-arms and archers. Du Guesclin countered by offering his own band of Bretons, who thus passed with their captain into the pay of the kingdom of France at 200 livres Tournois per year. Du Guesclin was invariably punctilious in collecting his company's pay, not shrinking from dunning the king personally for any tardy arrears.[22]

Through the next several years Du Guesclin's reputation grew with endless sieges, surprises, sallies, and raids, interspersed with tournaments and duels. At one siege, under the eyes of the dauphin, he fell fifty feet into the moat when his scaling ladder was overthrown. Dragged from the water by his heels and revived, he demanded, "Have we taken the fort?"[23] He surprised and captured William Windsor, envoy of Edward III; surprised in his turn by Robert Knowles, he was made prisoner and had to use Windsor's ransom to pay his own. He defeated a much larger English force (of about three hundred) and was again captured in a skirmish, this time by his former captive Hugh of Calveley. His ransom having risen to 30,000 pounds, he had recourse to the dauphin for help in paying it and ended up making a trip to London, where the duke of Orleans was prisoner, to get a needed signature. For another victory over the English he was made a knight-banneret, entitling him to double the pay of a simple knight, a larger suite, the right to recruit followers, and a prestigious square banner in place of the triangular pennon of knighthood.[24]

By 1363 Du Guesclin had cleared a large part of the Cotentin, the peninsular half of Normandy, of enemy—Navarrese, English, and plain brigands. One of the latter, a notorious chief named Roger David, personally surrendered to Du Guesclin to avoid lynching by the citizens and promised to serve Charles de Blois. This chivalrous prince had become a warm admirer of Du Guesclin, who strove, with mediocre success, to honor Charles's adjuration to "love the poor people and not allow them to be plundered and mistreated."[25] Toward the wealthy merchants and upper clergy Du Guesclin's attitude was quite different, his extraction of the traditional conqueror's levy habitually seasoned with raillery.

In 1363 Charles de Blois helped arrange Du Guesclin's marriage. The bride, many years younger than her husband, was Tiphaine Raguenel, a noble lady whose father had been one of the combatants in the Battle of the Thirty. She foretold destinies by the stars and was reputed as beautiful as she was learned, in double contrast to the bridegroom, who expended more labor writing his name than in delivering a sword thrust and was reputed as ignorant as he was ugly.[26]

From the beginning of 1364 Du Guesclin received a new, enlarged authority from the royal power. King John II had died in comfortable captivity in London, where his anachronistic devotion to the ideals of knighthood had commanded the respect even of pragmatic Edward III. The former dauphin, succeeding to the throne as Charles V, was the reverse of his physically strong, mentally weak father and had already demonstrated the capacity to govern his war-afflicted country. Well acquainted with Du Guesclin's worth, he made him "captain-general of the bailliage of Caen and the Cotentin" and also lieutenant for the duke of Orleans for the lands between the Seine and Brittany, territory comprising most of the militarily sensitive area west of Paris. Charles the Bad of Navarre, recently quiet, had again renewed his hostility to the royal power, which had frustrated his desire to add the splendid ducal crown of Burgundy to his titles. It became imperative for Paris's safety to break the Navarrese hold on the Seine basin, commanded by the towns of Mantes and Meulan.

On a Sunday morning (April 7, 1364), Du Guesclin seized Mantes by a ruse. One hundred of his men waited stealthily outside till the gate was opened to allow the first wagon of the day to depart. Seizing it to block the gate, they spread through the neighboring streets, creating panic. By the time Du Guesclin could enter with the main body of his army, terrified citizens were jumping from the ramparts or fleeing in boats in the Seine. The Breton intruders wasted no time.

According to a chronicler, Du Guesclin "had it proclaimed through the town that no one was to hurt woman or child, but the town was already pillaged."[27] When three days later Du Guesclin and another captain forced entry into Meulan, whither most of the refugees from Mantes had fled, a second sack followed.[28] The two events did much to credit the popular saying that Breton and brigand were two words for the same thing.* The looting included theft of jewels and money belonging to the dowager Queen Blanche, whom Charles V hastily indemnified as recorded in a document that mentions prisoners taken by "our beloved and loyal knight, Bertran du Claequin," elsewhere referred to as "our loyal knight and chamberlain Bertren de Gueskin."[29]

The offensive was a technical violation of a truce. Protesting that he was the victim of royal aggression, Charles the Bad planned a daring, and potentially devastating, counterstroke. Charles V was preparing his coronation journey to Rheims. Charles the Bad conceived the idea of assembling an army west of Paris, intercepting the procession as it returned to the capital, and capturing the king. To execute the coup he recruited the Captal (Gascon: "lord") de Buch, a famous and colorful Gascon captain who was one of the chief victors of the battle of Poitiers. The Captal concentrated his force of three to four thousand Gascons, Normans, English, and undefined "brigands" at Evreux, northwest of Paris. Du Guesclin blocked him at Cocherel, where a fierce combat took place. At one moment the two leaders met face to face. The Captal split Du Guesclin's helmet with a blow of his mace, but he was himself unhorsed and taken. His English lieutenant, John Jouel, was mortally wounded, and his army slaughtered or scattered. Du Guesclin followed up his victory by storming the fortress of Valognes, and Charles the Bad gave up the war, agreeing to trade his piece of Normandy for token compensation in the south.[30]

Later that same year (1364) Du Guesclin took part in another rare field battle, this time with less fortunate results. The king of France no longer needing him, his services were sought once more by Charles de Blois, still locked in his Breton war, now with the son of his original rival. When the two armies met at Auray on the south coast of Brittany, young Jean de Montfort had the benefit of English

---

*The word "brigand" itself originally carried no pejorative connotation, merely designating certain Italian mercenaries (from their brigandine armor).

and Gascon commanders as well as troops and profited from the advice of Sir John Chandos to husband his reserve and win the hard-fought battle. Du Guesclin, commanding Charles' left wing, was the last holdout and was once more taken prisoner, wounded and streaming with blood. More important, through accident or design, Charles de Blois was slain on the battlefield instead of being captured. This event, rather than the outcome of the battle, determined the outcome of the war, because, unlike his Montfort rival, Charles left no heir.[31]

Du Guesclin's ransom having risen to 40,000 florins, he again appealed to Charles V for help in paying it, temporarily relinquishing his county of Longueville, bestowed as a reward for the victory of Cocherel. Charles V was glad to help since he again needed his Breton war dog, this time for an unusual service. The general lull that had set in on all fronts had left an unpleasant and dangerous legacy in the form of dozens of "free companies" of unemployed soldier-brigands who roamed the countryside pillaging, or even seized castles and imposed their reign of terror on whole districts. Local authorities, instead of joining forces against them, bribed the intruders to go elsewhere, and the major military effort required to extirpate them was beyond Charles's financial means. A new dynastic civil war across the Pyrenees offered an attractive solution. Henry of Trastamare, an illegitimate son of the late king of Castile, was contesting the throne held by his unpopular half-brother Pedro the Cruel. Charles V foresaw a dividend in the acquisition of a Spanish ally, and the enterprise promised above all to get the companies out of France. The king thought that Du Guesclin's name might suffice to attract the brigand captains, and such proved to be the case. In the words of a chronicler, "the said companies, English, French, Norman, Picard, Breton, Gascon, Navarrese, and others, men who lived off war, left the kingdom of France."[32]

In the winter of 1365 Du Guesclin's strange army wound through southern France to the passes of the Pyrenees, its appearance made the stranger by the adoption of the Crusader cross, in honor of a scarcely serious intention of fighting the Moors. The pope at Avignon, who had had no success in trying to get rid of the brigands by excommunicating them, gave the expedition not only his blessing but a large sum in cash, though voicing to Du Guesclin the sarcastic complaint that normally sinners paid for their absolution rather than getting paid for it.[33]

Du Guesclin is credited with a speech to his recruits that mixed the penitential with the profit-sharing motive:

"If we search our hearts, we have done enough to damn our souls. . . . We have ravished women, burned houses, slain children, exacted ransom from everyone, eaten their cows, oxen, sheep, stolen their geese, pigs, capons, drunk their wines, violated churches. . . . For God's sake, let us march on the pagans! . . . I will make you all rich if you [follow me]!"[34]

Hugh of Calveley, the giant Englishman, is said to have replied, "Bertrand, fair brother and comrade, mirror of chivalry, because of your loyalty and your valor, I am yours, I and all these here."[35]

Notwithstanding the crosses, all the towns shut their gates as the army approached, the citizens prudently observing its passage from the ramparts.

The campaign proved easy. The long war in France had seasoned its combatants and tested their equipment. Companies were composed either of men-at-arms (*hommes d'armes*) or of bowmen. All were mounted.[36] The men-at-arms, typically a few knights and eighty to a hundred squires, were almost equally armed and armored, carrying lance, sword, dagger, and commonly axe or mace. Plate and mail were worn in combination, mail still predominating, with breastplate and the variety of smaller pieces reinforcing.

Unlike the men-at-arms, bowmen fought on foot, but they needed horses to march, since their equipment, though lighter than that of the knights and squires, was heavy to carry long distances on foot: open helmet or iron hat, short-sleeved mail shirt (brigandine or jack) of iron disks sewn on leather, sword, dagger, and either English longbow and arrows, or French crossbow and quarrels.

Confronted by the heavily armed invaders, the weakly garrisoned Castilian towns often surrendered on demand, preferring to take their chances on relatively peaceable looting to the threat of massacre and pillage. Pedro the Cruel fled his capital of Burgos and Henry of Trastamare had himself crowned. Du Guesclin was made count of Borja and Magallon.

Most of the companies drifted back to France, where they presently found a new paymaster. Taking a leaf from his brother's book, Pedro the Cruel sought foreign help in the person of the Black Prince, who governed the ancient English province of Aquitaine, recently enlarged by his own conquests. Pedro offered a valuable accretion in the form of the Spanish ports on the Bay of Biscay. He

THE BLACK PRINCE: EFFIGY
IN CANTERBURY
CATHEDRAL. BOTH PLATE
AND MAIL ARE VISIBLE.
*(DEPARTMENT OF THE
ENVIRONMENT)*

also glibly promised to pay all the costs of an expedition. The Prince accepted and in the spring of 1367 led a powerful army, made up in good part of the same companies that had crossed the Pyrenees two years before. Du Guesclin urged guerrilla resistance, but Henry of Trastamare overruled him in favor of a pitched battle, at Najera, which he lost. Du Guesclin once more led the last resistance, covering the escape of Henry and falling prisoner to the Black Prince. Some of the Prince's aides advised him to refuse ransom, warning, "Do not loose the mastiff of Brittany," but Hugh of Calveley, Sir John Chandos, and others insisted on honoring the chivalric tradition and the Prince told Du Guesclin to name his own ransom. Du Guesclin fixed it at 100,000 gold doubloons,[37] an unheard-of sum for a nonroyal personage. He counted on the help of his great patrons but boasted that if need be, "There is not a woman at her spinning wheel in France who will not earn money to get me out of your hands."[38]

Charles V and Jeanne, widow of Charles de Blois, came to the rescue, Du Guesclin again sold lands, and in January 1368 he was able to quit Bordeaux. Cuvelier tells a pleasing anecdote: A party of Du

Guesclin's Bretons, taken prisoner at Najera and sent to find ransoms for themselves and comrades, stopped at an inn. The innkeeper was at first hostile to his rough-looking customers, but hearing them talk of Du Guesclin, turned friendly, produced roast meat and wine, and cited their chief as "the least covetous, the most courteous, the least proud, the best spoken of all the knights of the good God." Just then Du Guesclin himself appeared and gave the men enough florins for their ransom money and for horses and equipment. The Black Prince, hearing of the incident, is credited with saying, "I believe he will make us curse the hour when I freed him."[39]

Indeed, from this point on, success never ceased to crown Du Guesclin's enterprises in both Spain and France. Henry of Trastamare had refused to abandon his hopes of the Castilian crown and saw them rise once more when Pedro the Cruel failed to make good his openhanded promises to the Black Prince. Du Guesclin recruited a fresh army, smaller than that of 1365, but sufficient, and recrossed the Pyrenees. Again the shameless ruffians wore crosses, this time on the grounds that Pedro the Cruel was under papal ban, and despite their own fresh excommunication for unseemly behavior while crossing papal territory. At Montiel, Du Guesclin defeated Pedro's army, and Henry of Trastamare either fortuitously or deliberately killed his half-brother in a scuffle during a parley. Du Guesclin, already awarded the grandly empty title of duke of Molina, received a grander, emptier one of "king of Granada," a land entirely in Moorish possession. In 1370 he returned to France, rich in Spanish titles but poor in property.[40]

Charles V had repeatedly summoned, or rather importuned, him. He was also sought by Pedro the Ceremonious of Aragon to lead an expedition to Sardinia, but decided in favor of France, telling his companions, "When the king sent me off with the Great Companies, he would doubtless have liked to see us all hanged, but times have changed.[41] . . . Let us go. I have a Spanish coat of mail but a French shirt, and my shirt is closer to me than my coat of mail."[42]

The Castilian adventure had itself supplied the cause for resumption of the Hundred Years War. Pedro the Cruel's default on his promises had created serious financial embarrassment for the Black Prince, who found no recourse but an extraordinary five-year tax levy on his Aquitaine subjects.[43] The count of Armagnac, one of the great Gascon lords and pro-French to begin with, forbade the collection of the tax in his domains and appealed to Edward III. Getting no satisfaction, he turned to Charles V. By the treaty of Bretigny of 1360, Charles's father had conceded full sovereignty over Aquitaine to Edward, but Charles now coolly reneged and agreed to hear the complaint as the count of Armagnac's overlord.

Both Edward III and the Black Prince were sick and willing to compromise, but Charles was ready for war. His father and grandfather had been knightly kings who donned armor and fought in person but had never prepared for or begun a war. Charles, too frail to wear armor, had prepared for a war and was eager to begin it. He had studied the past campaigns and had reached conclusions that ran very contrary to the chivalric concepts of his father and grandfather. Battles he perceived as chancy and little productive, except through such accident as the capture or killing of a principal. That costly outcome Charles avoided by keeping his own valuable person safely in Paris. Against the other possible loss resulting from battle, that of a large part of his army, Charles guarded by forbidding his commanders in the field to fight unless they had clear numerical superiority. This decision left the enemy free to pursue the favorite English tactic of the *chevauchée*, or large-scale raid through the countryside, but despite pillaged churches and burning villages, the *chevauchée* was an essentially sterile form of warfare. In the end, provided the castles and walled towns held out, the raiding army had to return to one of its coastal bases without any lasting gain. To ensure that castle and town held, Charles had carried out a reform in the royal tax system to produce a dependable stream of revenue and a reform in the military system to repair battlements and train soldiers (including plenty of crossbowmen).[44] Nor was the king's strategy purely defensive. He contemplated an offensive against both the enemy's recent conquests and his old inherited lands. Rather than a spectacular *chevauchée*, Charles's offensive would consist of a succession of sieges designed methodically to wrest one district after another from its Anglo-Gascon defenders and their local allies. Some of the precious financial resource was expended on costly gunpowder for the new bronze and brass cannon capable of hurling stone projectiles against enemy walls.

Thus the historic roles in the war were reversed. The English, who had begun with innovative military organization and concepts, were now wedded to a futile (and characteristically knightly) policy of transitory destruction, while the French, who had begun with the feudal levy and the cavalry charge, had now adopted the un-knightly and even anti-knightly policy of refusing battle and concentrating on permanent military gains.

Charles's strategy was immediately tested in 1369 when in response to the French invasion of Aquitaine a powerful English expedition under a new duke of Lancaster, Shakespeare's John of Gaunt, a younger son of Edward III, landed at Calais and swept inland through Artois and Picardy. It left the usual devastation in its wake but all towns and castles held and the duke was not even able to take Harfleur (medieval predecessor of Le Havre), which he had intended as his point of egress on the Norman coast. Instead he had to return to Calais, where the next year a new expedition landed under Du Guesclin's old antagonist Robert Knowles. Besides being a veteran brigand, Knowles was under extra pressure to plunder because Edward III, short of funds, paid his men only until their arrival in France. Knowles levied tribute on the villages and monasteries, pillaging and burning those that did not submit, up to within sight of Paris.

Charles stubbornly held out against the expostulations of his councillors, partly out of necessity, since his available revenues were already committed to the fighting in Aquitaine. To appease protest, however, he made a momentous decision: the appointment of Bertrand du Guesclin as constable of France (October 2, 1370).[45] This office, which had evolved from minor officialdom to supreme military command, was normally reserved for the high nobility. Du Guesclin, who had just captured the towns of St. Yrieix and Brantôme in Aquitaine, left his small army in command of his nephew Olivier de Mauny and hastened to Paris. There he demonstrated political shrewdness by at first protesting that he did not deserve the honor: "Dear sire and noble king . . . I am a poor man of low birth. The office of constable is so great and noble . . . and involves commanding even more the great than the small. And here are your brothers, your nephews, your cousins—how can I command over them?"[46] The royal dukes joined the king in providing the necessary reassurance on this point. Du Guesclin had one more stipulation: the king must promise to credit no hostile reports until the constable had the opportunity to reply in person.[47] Then he accepted the insignia of office, which consisted of the king's own gold-hilted sword, and which carried with it the constable's right to a valuable share of booty taken by the army. More important to Du Guesclin, according to a believable passage in Cuvelier, was that the pay of his men be assured.[48]

Knowles was slowly withdrawing westward toward Brittany. Du Guesclin obtained permission to pursue him with a small force raised by the expedient of a loan exacted from the citizens of Paris and nearby towns. Du Guesclin himself contributed a set of plate he had brought from Spain, to which Tiphaine added her jewels and silver, meeting her husband in Caen for a last dinner off the plate before he set out in pursuit of the English. Knowles had experienced some of the difficulties Du Guesclin had foreseen for himself in commanding subordinates of nobler status than his own, and as a result his army had separated into two parts, a van under Knowles and a rear under Thomas of Granson. Du Guesclin overtook and surprised Granson at Pontvallain, south of Le Mans, killing or capturing his whole force, and followed up the victory by taking two towns and a fortified abbey, whose capitulation was negotiated by Du Guesclin's old friend-and-enemy Hugh of Calveley. On New Year's Day he was back in Paris to present his prisoners to the king.[49]

Over the next several years Charles's tactic, applied by Du Guesclin, reaped remarkable results. Town after town, castle after castle, fell to siege, assault, mine, ruse, or merely to Du Guesclin's persuasive oratory, in which a mixture of threats, promises, and appeals to loyalty was bellowed up at the battlements. When in 1372 Edward III dispatched a large expedition under the earl of Pembroke to reinforce Aquitaine, the Castilian enterprise of the previous decade paid a handsome dividend. A fleet of galleys sent by Henry of Trastamare, making an early use of gunpowder at sea, routed the English ships off La Rochelle and took Pembroke prisoner. Du Guesclin traded his Spanish estates to Henry for the person of the earl, whose ransom of 130,000 pounds Edward III undertook to raise with the aid of the town council of Bruges, capital of his Flemish ally. A legal complication arose when Pembroke died in captivity and the councillors of Bruges stopped payment, and in the end Charles V paid the remainder of the sum owing Du Guesclin.[50]

The French offensive on land continued. At Moncontour, northwest of Poitiers, an English captain who claimed that Du Guesclin had defaulted on a debt contracted in Spain hung Du Guesclin's coat of arms upside down on a gibbet over the town gate. Du Guesclin furiously pressed the siege until the town surrendered and the captain could be hung in the same place.[51] Receiving news that a pro-French faction in Poitiers was ready to open the city gates, he raced thither just in time to forestall Sir Thomas Percy with an English relief army. Independent-minded La Rochelle, isolated on the sea coast by the English naval defeat, got rid of its English garrison by a ruse and agreed to liberal terms.

Edward III prepared another large expeditionary force "to reconquer all he had lost, or lose all that remained," but contrary winds foiled the king, and Surgères, the stronghold it was intended to relieve, surrendered to Du Guesclin. On December 11 the constable, with the royal princes and other captains, made another solemn entry into Paris with prisoners, who included, besides the earl of Pembroke, Sir Thomas Percy and the Captal de Buch, for whom Charles V refused to name a ransom and who languished in Paris until his death.

Back in Aquitaine in 1373 Du Guesclin besieged Chizé, southwest of Poitiers, trapped a relief army and forced its surrender, and followed up by capture of both Chizé and the larger town of Niort.[52]

Edward III again had recourse to the *chevauchée*. This one was led by the duke of Lancaster, accompanied by Jean de Montfort, the Breton duke who had again allied himself with the English. Lancaster pillaged and burned a broad path from Calais to the Loire. Once again castles and towns held out, and once again Charles vetoed the clamor to fight a battle. Du Guesclin stoutly seconded the king. Froissart reports that he told the Great Council, "I don't say we should never fight them, but I want [the situation] to be to our advantage."[53] King and constable were vindicated when Lancaster's army found itself stranded in the most barren part of France as winter set in, and limped into Bordeaux with half its men and three quarters of its horses missing, and nothing to show for its effort.

Du Guesclin's public glory was marred for him by private grief when Tiphaine died at the age of forty-four. Two years later (1374), at the entreaty of Charles, he married Jeanne de Laval-Tinteniac, who like Tiphaine was a Breton and a daughter of one of the champions of the Battle of the Thirty. His second marriage like his first remained childless. Reports of illegitimate children seem to be belied by his failure to include them in his will.[54]

In the later 1370s, while the liberation and conquest of lands in the southwest continued, Brittany and Normandy again became scenes of warfare. Charles the Bad of Navarre once more joined Jean de Montfort of Brittany in allying with the English, and Du Guesclin was ordered to deal with both. The campaigns proved easy, but that in Brittany had a bitter outcome. Perhaps misled by the welcome widely bestowed on Du Guesclin, Charles the Wise made his only unwise move when he decided to annex this historically autonomous province to the crown (December 1378). The Bretons, who liked the king of France as an ally, had no use for him as a sovereign. A confederation for the defense of Breton independence was formed at Rennes, and Jean de Montfort, until now unpopular, was invited back from England, whither Du Guesclin had driven him. Even Jeanne, the widow of Charles de Blois, gave Montfort her support. Du Guesclin and other loyal Bretons urged Charles to give in, but the king insisted on a march on Rennes. For once the constable was unable to carry out the king's command, as his Bretons deserted by the hundreds. He ended by returning to Pontorson to renew his pleas for peace. In Paris he became the object of abusive criticism from royal officials who had advocated the annexation. In angry reply he offered to surrender his constable's sword to the king and go back to Castile. Charles prevailed upon him to go instead to Languedoc, whither a number of brigand bands, loosed by a papal-negotiated truce in the Aquitaine fighting, had roamed. Charles pointedly excluded Bretons from the force placed under Du Guesclin's orders, stirring him to an eloquent protest:

"Sire, I have fought often in France, in Spain, in battles, assaults, encounters, and sieges of cities. . . . Many good captains . . . have greatly aided me. Now that you have sent them away, I feel that I am losing much of my strength. . . . I beseech you most humbly, sire, to make peace with the duke of Brittany, for the men of war of that country have helped you very ably in all your conquests."[55]

Joining the duke de Berry, he helped take the Anglo-Gascon brigand stronghold of Chaliers, after whose fall he besieged Château-neuf-de-Randon, between Mende and Le Puy. There he fell ill with the "fever" that commonly afflicted the medieval military camp. Feeling his life nearing its end he dictated his will, remembering numerous old servitors and providing for prayers for his soul. He requested that he be buried at the church of the Jacobins at Dinan, where Tiphaine lay. The next day he had his constable's sword brought, saying, "Others, perhaps, would have made better use of it. Tell the king I am grieved not to have served him longer, but more faithfully I could not have."[56]

On the morning of July 13, 1380, he summoned the knights from the siege lines to bid them farewell: "I am very sorry to go without having . . . told the king of the merits of each of you." He added a last injunction: "Remember that your business is only with those who bear arms. The churchmen, the poor, the women and children are not your enemies."[57]

Shortly after he had died, with the crucifix clasped in both hands, the English captain came to surrender the town, kneeling to place the keys to the fortress on the dead man's shroud.

Du Guesclin's body was embalmed at nearby Puy-en-Velay, where his entrails were preserved while the body was carried to Brittany. Cities along the route rendered homage, people falling to their knees as the catafalque passed. Rites were performed in hundreds of towns and villages, those in the great cathedrals of Le Mans and Chartres rivaling the obsequies of kings. Charles decreed that Dinan should have only the hero's heart, and the funeral journey was completed in Paris, where the body was buried at St. Denis with the kings of France. The epitaph reads: "Here lies the noble man, Messire Bertrand du Guesclin, count of Longueville and constable of France, who died at the castle of Randon in Givaudan, in the seneschalry of Beaucaire, on July 13 MCCCLXXX. Pray to God for him."[58]

Three months later Charles V also died. All the territory lost by his father and grandfather had been recovered save Calais, and in addition the ancient English provinces of Gascony and Guienne had been reduced to the enclaves of Bayonne and Bordeaux. Brittany again drew close to France, and though no official end was made to the war with England, Wat Tyler's rebellion, provoked by a heavy war tax, signaled a cessation of hostilities until the next century.

Bertrand du Guesclin was perhaps as true a knight as a real-life man of the fourteenth century could be. His extraordinary popularity attests to his reputation for being "the most courteous" and "the least covetous" knight as well as a terrific fighter and born leader. He himself is reputed to have offered this self-evaluation: "A poor man who had riches and provinces pass through his hands and kept nothing, but gave all to the cause which he served."

His long career illuminates important developments that altered both the character of warfare and the institution of knighthood in the fourteenth century. In marked contrast to earlier practice he was knighted only at the age of thirty-four, and only following conspicuous service on the battlefield. No longer serving in response to the traditional summons of lord to vassal, he drew regular pay, fixed by law and contract, as a professional soldier, and dispensed it as a captain of mercenaries. The bands of disciplined "brigands" he led were the forerunners of the professional standing armies of the following centuries.

Within the cohort of the "men-at-arms"—the armored, mounted

hand-to-hand fighters—the knights still held their elite status, but they were now heavily outnumbered by the squires, who were similarly equipped and cost half as much. In addition, the long-range fighters, the archers and crossbowmen, had become more serious competitors, now wearing their own, somewhat lighter armor, and while still fighting on foot, moving to battle and siege on horseback. Whereas at the beginning of the century the archer or foot soldier had been regarded as militarily worth only a tenth as much as a mounted knight (the popular saying was that a hundred knights were worth a thousand foot soldiers), the mounted crossbowmen of Du Guesclin's campaigns in Aquitaine drew pay amounting to a third or half that of a knight, and nearly equivalent to that of a squire. The true foot soldier was for the time eclipsed.[59]

The emergence of gunpowder artillery added a still small but potent new element of military and social change. The brass, bronze, and iron cannon were made by common craftsmen who also took charge of their operation, serving directly under royal authority and separating the new arm from the traditional military class of knights and nobles.

On the other side of the coin, Du Guesclin's career shows how the leveling forces that were depriving the knight of his once unique military role were opening the way for those of exceptional ability to rise to the highest military offices (and civilian offices as well).

Finally, in Du Guesclin's appeals to incipient patriotism, appeals echoed by his contemporaries, both English and French, may be seen the beginning of the national consciousness that provided the psychological foundation for the modern European state, a trend that pointed toward the inevitable sunset of the age of chivalry.

english knights
of the
fifteenth century:
sir john fastolf
and
the pastons

◦§ IN THESE DAYS WE SEE OPENLY HOW MANY POOR MEN THROUGH THEIR SERVICE IN THE FRENCH WARS HAVE BECOME NOBLE, SOME BY THEIR PRUDENCE, SOME BY THEIR ENERGY, SOME BY THEIR VALOUR, AND SOME BY OTHER VIRTUES WHICH . . . ENNOBLE MEN.

—Nicholas Upton, *De Studio Militari*

◦§ AND NOWADAYS . . . THE MAN WHO DOES NOT KNOW HOW TO SET PLACES ON FIRE, TO ROB CHURCHES AND USURP THEIR RIGHTS AND TO IMPRISON THE PRIESTS, IS NOT FIT TO CARRY ON WAR. AND FOR THESE REASONS THE KNIGHTS OF TODAY HAVE NOT THE GLORY AND THE PRAISE OF THE OLD CHAMPIONS OF FORMER TIMES, AND THEIR DEEDS CAN NEVER COME TO GREAT PERFECTION OF VIRTUE.

—Honoré Bouvet, *Tree of Battles*

◦§ SIR JOHN FASTOLF, WHO WAS CONSIDERED A VERY WISE AND VALIANT KNIGHT. . . .

—Jean Wavrin du Forestal, *Anciennes chroniques d'Angleterre*

THE NAME OF Sir John Fastolf is known to us for a number of disparate reasons: as the skillful commander in a minor English victory in the Hundred Years War known as the "Battle of the Herrings" and a captain in a major defeat, the battle of Patay; as the author of a famous report to his government outlining a "scorched earth" policy; as a correspondent and protagonist in the Paston letters; and as the caricatured prototype of Shakespeare's Falstaff. His career may be seen as a continuation of Du Guesclin's in illustrating the evolution of warfare toward the professional army and toward the eclipse of the medieval knight.

Although an able and courageous soldier, Fastolf lacked the romantic appeal of William Marshal or Du Guesclin to inspire poets and biographers, and a record of his "Acts" composed by his secretary has disappeared. Nevertheless, thanks to the growth in literacy and documentation of the later Middle Ages, much significant biographical information can be gleaned from legal documents, letters, and references in chronicles.

Fastolf differed from most earlier knights in that he evidently was of middle-class origin—not unheard of by the fifteenth century. His ancestors were wealthy merchants in the Norfolk port of Great Yarmouth; his grandfather, Alexander Fastolf, was a shipowner. His father, John Fastolf, married into the lesser nobility, taking as wife a woman who was the daughter of one country gentleman and the widow of another. The elder John Fastolf became a squire in the household of King Edward III; in other words, a second-level member of a retinue composed of knights, squires, and sergeants.[1] From his father, John Fastolf the elder inherited manors in Norfolk, notably that of Caister, forty miles east of Norwich.[2]

The younger John Fastolf was born at Caister in 1380.[3] After his father's death three years later, his mother married a third husband, a squire in the household of the grandmother of the duke of Norfolk.[4] The boy may have been educated in the duke's own household. Unlike Du Guesclin and most earlier knights, he could read and write fluently and by the time of his death had acquired a library of at least twenty-five manuscript books, including Livy, Caesar, and four other histories; an English translation of Vegetius' treatise on the art of war; and two verse romances.[5] He was also proficient with figures and a capable businessman.

When he came of age in 1401, his circumstances were modest. He drew a small yearly income (£46) from two manors at Caister and one at Repps, six miles northwest. He became a squire in the retinue of Thomas of Lancaster, second son of Henry IV, whom he accompanied to Ireland when Lancaster was named lord deputy. There he made a provident marriage in 1408 to Millicent Tiptoft, twelve years his senior but the daughter of a member of the lesser nobility, widow of Sir Stephen Scrope, and possessor of lands in Yorkshire and Wiltshire that gave Fastolf a lifetime income of £240 a year.[6]

Exactly when Fastolf entered the king's service in France is unknown. The few notes that survive of the biography written by William Worcester, who served for many years as Fastolf's secretary, are chiefly a list of offices held by Fastolf from 1412 until his retirement in 1440. From this source we know that in 1412, the last year of Henry IV's reign, Fastolf was deputy constable of the castle and city of Bordeaux, and in 1413 he became governor of another Gascon castle. In 1415, when Henry V invaded Normandy, opening the second great phase of the Hundred Years War, Fastolf, thirty-five years old but still a squire, contracted to serve as a captain with ten men-at-arms and thirty archers.[7]

By the time of Fastolf's contract, the "indenture" system adopted in England in the early years of the Hundred Years War was well established. Mercenaries—mostly foreign knights—had been used in England since the Norman Conquest, but the employment of paid native soldiers was a novelty introduced by Edward I for his Welsh wars of the late thirteenth century. It had proved a brilliant success, ending the crown's dependence on reluctantly performed feudal service, as well as on reluctantly paid scutage. The last English feudal levy was summoned in 1327 for a Scottish war of Edward II. After that the contract, or indenture, system became standard.[8]

The new system was financed via parliamentary acquiescence in taxes on movable property, and especially the export tax on English wool, paid by foreign importers. The first indenture contracts were apparently verbal, concluded with the king's chief barons, who then made subcontracts with recruits. The earliest surviving written subcontract, dating from 1287, between the Welsh marcher (border) lord

Edmund Mortimer of Wigmore and a Yorkshire tenant-in-chief, Peter Maulay, specified in minute detail the horses that Peter should bring and the compensation he should receive if they were lost ("one with black feet and having one white foot, price 60 marks* . . . one other black horse with two white feet, price 30 marks . . . one other bay horse, price 18 marks . . . one sorrel horse, price 18 marks . . . one piebald horse, price 14 marks . . . one rouncey [pack] horse, price 100 shillings . . .").[9] Later contracts established a pattern, spelling out the number of men in the contingent and their status, whether bannerets, knights, squires, mounted archers, or foot archers; the length and place of service; wages and bonuses; expenses; compensation for lost horses; and the disposition of the "advantages of war": lands and castles seized, prisoners taken, and booty such as jewelry, plate, and coin.

In 1415 the magnates of the kingdom contracted to provide forces for the new campaign in France in which Henry V sought to press his claim to the French crown. A promising occasion was furnished by the mental illness of French king Charles VI and the feud between the supporters of the rival dukes of Orleans and Burgundy. The largest English retinues were provided by the dukes and earls: Thomas, duke of Clarence, 240 men-at-arms and 720 archers; Humphrey, duke of Gloucester, 200 men-at-arms and 600 archers; Thomas, earl of Arundel, 100 and 300 respectively; and on down to the earl of Salisbury, with 40 men-at-arms and 80 archers. The lesser peers contracted for smaller numbers. Retinues containing twenty or more men-at-arms were "great companies," all of which in 1415 were commanded by men who ranked at least as knights. Fifty-two lesser captains, among them Fastolf, contracted for from three to nineteen men-at-arms, and a few individual soldiers served with an archer or two and perhaps one companion. Most of the secondary captains were knights, but sixteen, like Fastolf, were squires. The individual soldiers were almost all squires. Men-at-arms and archers were provided in a ratio of approximately one to three, and usually the entire force was mounted, though part of it fought on foot.[10]

Artillery, which had made its appearance in the fourteenth century, had its own organization. In England as in France, cannon were manned by specialists, artisans drawn from the ranks of the middle and lower classes. Kings employed a master of the artillery, who if

*A mark was two thirds of a pound.

FIFTEENTH–CENTURY PLATE ARMOR:
ST. GEORGE AND THE DRAGON.
(BODLEIAN LIBRARY, MS. AUCT. D. INF. 2. II, F. 44)

not already a knight was usually knighted, and who operated foundry and armory, concluded contracts with the gunners, and commanded them in the field.[11]

A muster of the army was made at the port of embarkation, where the king's officials, one the paymaster, wrote down the strength and composition of the retinues; similar musters were made during the campaign, with dates of attendance and absence from the army carefully noted.

The period of service for a military retinue might be a quarter of a year, half a year, three-quarters, a full year, two years, or of indefinite duration. The theater was specified: Brittany, Aquitaine, or Normandy, occasionally with provision for a change in destination. The scale of wages was graduated according to rank and usually specified as the "customary rates of war." A quarter of a year's wages were paid in advance, usually when the captain arrived with his men at the port of embarkation. Customarily a bonus, a "regard," was also specified: 100 marks for the service of thirty men-at-arms for a quarter of a year, paid quarterly. A specially trained king's clerk and a knight were stationed at the port of embarkation to appraise the retinue's horses so that restitution could be made in case of loss. Transportation overseas and back for men and horses at the king's expense was stipulated; an earl could take six horses, a banneret five, a knight four, a sergeant three, and a mounted archer one.

The contract also spelled out the division of the spoils of war. At first the king granted the "advantages of war" to the indenturing captains, reserving for himself only the most strategic castles and lands and the most eminent prisoners, whose captors were promised a "reasonable reward." Following ancient military custom, captains shared in the spoils of the men who subcontracted with them, usually taking one-third. From about the middle of the fourteenth century it became the practice for captains to pay a third of this third to the king, plus a third of their own personal spoils, giving the king "thirds and thirds of thirds" of all the spoils.*[12]

Over the course of Fastolf's military career, essentially the quarter century from 1415 to 1440, armor continued its evolution. A list of the armor Fastolf owned after his retirement includes three haubergeons,

---

*Economic historian M. M. Postan believes that "in spite of these rules most fruits of soldierly pillage stuck to the fingers of lesser folk, the men-at-arms and the common soldiers of every kind."[13]

SIEGE OF A TOWN, FROM THE
FIFTEENTH-CENTURY *CHRONIQUES D'ANGLETERRE*.
(BRITISH LIBRARY, MS. ROYAL 14 E IV)

six pairs of cuirasses (front and back plates), several pairs of brigandines, a half dozen pieces of mail, two dozen helmets with and without visors, and various thigh pieces, shoulder pieces, greaves, and other plate.[14] By the mid-fifteenth century the haubergeon, a short version of the old hauberk, was universally worn, over a wool or linen jupon, in turn a short version of the old acton, padded but sleeveless, close-fitting and fastened in back by laces or by the new style of fastening, buttons. In Milan, the leading manufacturing center, the complete suit of plate armor was now fixed as consisting of a rounded breastplate cut off at the waist but overlapped by a plackart, or lower plate, attached to it by straps and buckles; a similar compound covering for the back, attached to the breastplate by shoulder straps and waist belt; shoulder pieces; complete arm, thigh, and lower leg pieces, protecting back as well as front; gauntlets of either the old hourglass-glove or the new mitten style, articulated once over the wrist and twice over the fingers; and basinet with hinged visor. The shield had, by mid-fifteenth century, virtually disappeared for mounted combat.[15]

In the brief, brilliant campaign of 1415 Fastolf proved a skillful captain and respected administrator, in combat and in military government. He participated in the short siege of Harfleur, at the mouth of the Seine where the expeditionary force landed, and distinguished himself in the great victory of Agincourt, in which the well-disciplined English archers repeated their Crécy victory against an enemy that had foolishly reverted to the outdated feudal levy. Agincourt was a typical medieval battle, bloody and tactically decisive, with the young duke of Orleans and other notables taken prisoner or slain. Yet like most medieval battles it had little effect on the course of the war. Henry V withdrew to England, leaving a garrison in Harfleur, of which Fastolf shared the command. Two years later, when Henry returned to undertake the conquest of Normandy, Fastolf fought in the sieges of Caen and Rouen and served as military governor of Condé-sur-Noireau, south of Caen. That year, at the age of thirty-seven, he was finally knighted.[16]

In 1418, revolution in Paris placed the capital in Burgundian hands, and when the following year the duke of Burgundy, John the Fearless, was assassinated by the Orleanist-Armagnacs, the new duke converted a secret pact with the English into an open alliance. For a moment it appeared that the adherence of the powerful duke, head of a quasi-independent state as well as of a major Paris faction, would tip the scales decisively in Henry's favor. The treaty of Troyes, signed in 1420, established the basis for a "dual monarchy" whereby Henry V was to marry the daughter of Charles VI, their son to become king of England and France. The English were invited to garrison Paris's inner castle, the Bastille, and Sir John Fastolf was named governor. Two years later Henry V's death of dysentery (August 1422) left an infant heir, Henry VI, under a regency headed by Henry's able brother, John, duke of Bedford. For grand master of his household, Bedford chose Fastolf.

As the conquest of northern France proceeded, Fastolf served as seneschal (administrator) of Normandy and in 1423 was named "lieutenant" (governor) of Anjou and Maine, provinces in the front line of the war. Later that same year he was sent to recover strongholds in Valois, northeast of Paris, where he captured the castle of Passy-en-Valois and took prisoner its governor, Guillaume Remon, thereby setting in motion a series of events that illustrate both the complexities that the institution of ransom could create and knightly perseverance in its pursuit. Remon was taken to the castle of Rouen, where he was held at Fastolf's expense, while Fastolf continued on to Maine, where he took part in the capture of Beaumont-le-Vicomte, north of Le Mans. During his absence, the strategic town of Compiègne, north of Passy, was retaken by the French. Bedford assembled forces to recover it, but the town resisted siege. Bedford had recourse to a stratagem. Many of the men in the garrison had previously served under Remon's command; Bedford brought the prisoner from Rouen and had him paraded under the walls of Compiègne with a rope around his neck, threatening to hang him unless the town capitulated. The garrison yielded, and Remon was released and freed of the obligation to pay ransom. Fastolf demanded compensation. A further complication was that Remon had had in his own custody at the time of the capture of Passy a number of foreign merchants, who had passed from being Remon's prisoners to being Fastolf's. Two of the merchants agreed to serve as sureties for payment of the ransom of the entire group. One of them was held in the Bastille, commanded by Fastolf himself, the other in the Chatelet, the prison of the provost of Paris. The prisoners submitted appeals to the Parlement of Paris. Suit and countersuit and jurisdictional disputes consumed four years before Fastolf's claims were satisfied, and even then he felt that the loss of Guillaume Remon was never compensated. Thirty years later he was still petitioning the king for recompense.[17]

In 1424 Bedford prepared to finish the conquest of Maine, assembling troops at Rouen. Marching south in August, the English met the French army in an open field outside the town of Verneuil, on the Norman border northwest of Chartres. William Worcester tells us that Fastolf "was created a knight banneret at the battle of Verneuil by John, regent of the kingdom of France"; whether before or after the battle is not specified. At this "second Agincourt," according to Worcester, Fastolf "won by fortune of war about 20,000 marks."[18] Fastolf's great coup, executed with another captain, Lord Willoughby, was the capture of the young duke of Alençon, who lived to be a favorite companion-in-arms of Joan of Arc. Since he was of royal blood, Alençon had to be turned over to Regent Bedford, but Fastolf and Willoughby were promised in return a "reasonable reward" of 5,000 marks apiece. Each actually received a thousand marks. Alençon raised the ransom in three years but Bedford apparently kept the money; twenty-five years later Fastolf sued Bedford's estate and suggested that Willoughby's widow do likewise.[19]

Despite his collection problems, Fastolf did well out of the war. In November 1424 he signed an indenture with Bedford to serve as captain of "eighty mounted men-at-arms [including himself] and two hundred and forty archers, for one whole year," beginning at Michaelmas past (September 29), the troops to be employed in the conquest of the county of Maine and its border region "and anywhere else in the kingdom of France where it shall be the will of the said lord regent to ordain."

The wages were specified: "For a knight banneret, captain of men-at-arms, four shillings sterling a day in English money; for a knight bachelor, likewise a captain, two shillings sterling; for a mounted man-at-arms, twelve pence sterling a day, with the accustomed rewards; and for each archer, six pence a day of the said currency. . . . And these wages shall be paid as from the day of the first musters," after that in advance for two six-week periods, then in advance by quarter-years. "And the said lord regent shall have both a third part of the profits of war of the said grand master [Fastolf], and a third of the thirds which the men of his retinue shall be obliged to give him from their profits of war, whether prisoners, booty, or anything else taken. . . . And the said grand master shall have any prisoners who may be taken during the said period by him or by those in his retinue: with the exception of any kings or princes, whoever they may be, or sons of kings . . . or other captains and persons of the blood royal . . . each and all of whom belong to the said lord regent, and he shall pay a reasonable reward to him or those whose prisoners they shall be. . . ." Fastolf undertook in return to serve the king and the regent and to use his company "in the best manner and means known to him, or which the said lord regent shall command him."[20]

The success of the subsequent campaign owed much to Fastolf, and Fastolf's fortunes owed much to the campaign. In August 1425 Le Mans capitulated to him and he was made lieutenant of the town under the earl of Suffolk; in September he captured the castle of Sillé-le-Guillaume, west of Le Mans, and was named its baron. The following year he won a rare new honor, being installed Knight of the Garter.

The Order of the Garter, conceived by Edward III in 1344 in imitation of King Arthur's Round Table, was the first of many honorary "secular orders" of knighthood, some short-lived, some lasting for centuries, designed to reward valor and glorify knighthood and to create a bond between the patron of the order and those on whom he bestowed membership: the Order of the Star founded by King John II of France, the Porcupine of the duke of Orleans, the Ermine of John IV of Brittany, the Dragon of René of Anjou, the Golden Shield of Duke Louis of Bourbon, the Golden Fleece of the dukes of Burgundy. Membership in the Order of the Garter was limited to the king and twenty-five knights. Of the original members all but one had been captains in France (one was Du Guesclin's old adversary Henry, duke of Lancaster, another Sir John Chandos), all but two were English (one of the two was the Gascon Captal de Buch, another of Du Guesclin's foes).[21]

Fastolf continued to amass profits, which he forwarded through English intermediaries in Normandy or through Italian merchants in Paris to two agents in England, John Wells, an alderman and grocer of London originally from Norwich and evidently a relation of Fastolf's, and John Kirtling, his chaplain, who handled both the revenues from Fastolf's English manors and the proceeds of war. The two acted as Fastolf's bankers and brokers, and when Fastolf's money remained in their hands for a length of time, they paid him five percent yearly interest; other tradesmen of Paris, London, and Great Yarmouth were also trusted with his funds. Such investments were temporary. Like most of his fellow captains, Fastolf put his money permanently in land, furniture, jewels, and plate.[22]

After a stay in England to deal with domestic politics, Bedford returned to France in March 1427, bringing with him Sir John Talbot, a talented soldier, to serve as chief field commander in a fresh offensive designed to win the war by breaking the French defense line on the Loire and conquering central France.

In the critical campaign that followed, Fastolf earned his greatest military distinction but, immediately after, a lasting and probably undeserved opprobrium. In October 1428, the English began the fateful siege of Orleans, with an Anglo-Burgundian army under the command of Talbot and Sir Thomas Scales. On February 12, 1429, Fastolf led a large commissary train from Paris bringing "herring and Lenten stuff" to the besieging army. Near Janville, a fortified town twenty miles north of Orleans, Fastolf learned that a large French and Scottish force was on its way to intercept him. Halting at once, he deployed his wagons in a circle. The French and Scots arrived and set up small cannon, which bombarded the wagons with some effect; but when the French and Scottish knights insisted on attacking, they were driven off by the well-protected English archers. Fastolf ordered his men to mount and counterattack, and the "Battle of the Herrings" turned into a rout with heavy casualties. Dunois, the "Bastard of Orleans" and leading French captain, was wounded, and Sir John Stewart, constable of Scotland, killed.

A chronicle called the *Journal du siège d'Orléans* reported that Joan of Arc, in Vaucouleurs attempting to persuade Robert de Baudricourt to send her to the king, had a clairvoyant revelation of the French defeat and used it to convince Baudricourt of her powers. True or not, after Joan had arrived in Orleans, Fastolf was much in her thoughts. When Dunois told her that Fastolf was again approaching with reinforcements, she exclaimed, "Bastard, Bastard, in the name of God, I order you that as soon as you hear of the arrival of Fastolf you will let me know, for if he gets through without my knowing it, I promise that I'll have your head cut off."[23] Shortly after, the French assault was delivered that ended the siege. As the English retreated, the French prepared to attack Jargeau, east of Orleans. Again a report signaled the approach of a relief army commanded by Fastolf. The French captains hesitated but Joan declared that they should not fear any numbers, for God was conducting the campaign.[24]

At the moment, Fastolf was actually still in Paris. Chronicler Jean Wavrin, a Burgundian enrolled in Fastolf's service, gave an eyewitness account of his master's part in the ensuing campaign. Receiving news of the French threat to Jargeau from Talbot, Bedford ordered Fastolf south with "the company of . . . about 5,000 combatants. . . . In this brigade were Sir Thomas Rempston, an Englishman, and many other knights and squires native to the kingdom of England." The army halted three days in Etampes, then marched on to Janville, where they waited for reinforcements that Bedford had summoned from England and Normandy.

Fastolf was still in Janville when word came that Jargeau had fallen, Meung was threatened, and the French were besieging Beaugency. "This news gave them great distress, but they could do nothing at the moment," Wavrin wrote. "They met in council to determine what they should do." At that moment Talbot arrived, with a small force, not the expected reinforcements, but "about forty lances [a lance was a knight and three or four auxiliaries] and two hundred

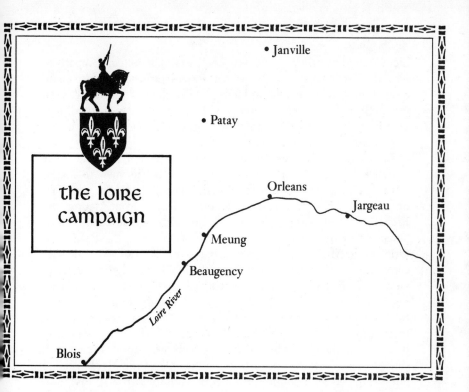

the loire
campaign

Janville

Patay

Orleans

Jargeau

Meung

Beaugency

Loire River

Blois

archers, and their arrival was very joyous for the English . . . for he was at that time regarded as the wisest and most valiant knight of the kingdom of England."

Fastolf, Thomas Rempston, and the other English knights dined in Talbot's lodgings. After dinner, the trestle tables cleared and removed, they resumed their council. Fastolf argued caution; English losses at Orleans and Jargeau had been heavy, their forces were weakened and exhausted; therefore he advised them to abandon Beaugency and "take the best treaty [truce] they could obtain" from the French, returning to their "castles and strong places" to recoup their strength. The advice was not welcome to the other captains, "especially Lord Talbot, who said that even if he only had his own people and those who wished to follow him, he would fight with the aid of God and *monseigneur* St. George." Fastolf, realizing that he was wasting his breath, left the council, "and the captains and chiefs of squadrons were ordered to be in the field the next morning."

When the army assembled, with standards, pennants, and banners flying, Fastolf again warned of the "dangerous perils that they might incur . . . and that they would only be a handful of men in comparison with the French, assuring them that if fortune turned against them, everything that the late King Henry had conquered in France, with great effort and over long time, would be on its way to perdition, wherefore he urged them to wait a little until their strength was reinforced."

When his advice was again ignored by Talbot and the other captains, Fastolf resigned himself and ordered his men to march toward Meung. The English, Wavrin writes, "rode in very fine order," but when they reached a point a league from Meung, the French, warned of their arrival, rode out with "about 6,000 combatants, led by Joan the Maid, the duke of Alençon, the Bastard of Orleans, the Marshal de La Fayette, Poton [de Xaintrailles], and other captains," ranging themselves for battle on a little ridge, for a better view of the English position. The English gave commands, "following the practice of King Henry [V] of England," to dismount and for the archers to drive pointed stakes into the ground, protecting their position. Two heralds were then sent to the French, suggesting that the issue be settled by combat between three knights from each side. To this chivalric suggestion the "people of the Maid" replied only: "Go and find lodgings, for it is late; but tomorrow, please God and Our Lady, we will see you from closer at hand."

The English continued on to Meung, where the town remained in English hands but where the French had captured the bridge over the Loire. There the English army spent the night, bombarding the bridge with their artillery in the hope of crossing the river to the southern bank and relieving Beaugency from that side.

In the morning they rose and heard Mass and were preparing to assault the bridge when a messenger arrived with word that Beaugency had surrendered and that the French were approaching. The assault was canceled, and the army assembled in the fields outside the city, where it formed in line of march to retreat to Paris: the vanguard, then the artillery and supply train, then the main contingent, led by Fastolf, Talbot, and the other captains, then the rearguard. "About a league" from the town of Patay the army halted, warned by the rearguard that they were being pursued. Scouts were sent out, and the army was ordered to deploy for battle, but the French attacked before the archers could plant their defensive stakes. Fastolf spurred toward the vanguard, intending to rally it to the main body, but its captain mistook his action for a signal for flight and galloped from the field, followed by his men. Realizing that the battle was already lost, Fastolf declared that "he would rather be dead or captured than to flee shamefully and abandon his men." But Talbot was taken prisoner, his men slaughtered, and "Sir John Fastolf left, with a very small company, uttering the greatest lament that I have ever heard a man make," recorded Wavrin.[25]

Another Burgundian chronicler, Enguerrand de Monstrelet, not an eyewitness, wrote an account of the battle that contained a hostile picture of "messire Jehan Fastocq" fleeing the battle "without striking a blow," and for his cowardice being stripped of the Order of the Garter by Bedford.[26] No source confirms the incident, and a historian of the Order believes that such an action would not have been within Bedford's power.[27] Talbot is known to have severely criticized Fastolf's behavior, and a decade later brought charges against him before the king and his council.[28] The charges were dismissed, but Monstrelet's account, which in making Fastolf a scapegoat probably reflected much current opinion, was adopted by English historians of the sixteenth century. These writers were in turn the sources for Shakespeare's *Henry VI, Part 1*, in which Fastolf's cowardice is blamed for the English defeat. In the folio edition, Fastolf's name is spelled "Falstaff," in later editions corrected to "Fastolfe." When Shakespeare later wrote *Henry IV*, he at first named the disreputable and cowardly old knight, friend of young Henry V's carousing days, after Sir John Oldcastle, a member of the pre-Protestant Lollard sect who was executed as a heretic in 1417. Oldcastle's descendants persuaded Shakespeare to change the name, and as a substitute he reverted to "Falstaff," the corrupted version of "Fastolf."[29] The character was so successful that he was given a final bravura appearance in *The Merry Wives of Windsor.* History has left no clues as to Fastolf's physical appearance, but his intelligence and ability are beyond question and there is little doubt of his courage. Shakespeare, however, fixed for posterity the image of "Falstaff" as a corpulent and cowardly buffoon.

That Fastolf was not long in disfavor with Bedford is demonstrated by the fact that his career continued as before. The year after the disaster of Patay (1430), he was named governor of Caen, and in 1433, when the Burgundians opened lengthy negotiations with Charles VII at Arras and the English were forced to join in, Fastolf was sent by Bedford as a plenipotentiary. On September 9, 1435 the English withdrew from the parleys; on the fourteenth Bedford, taken suddenly ill, died. Fastolf was an executor of his will. A few days later, the French and Burgundians concluded a treaty by which the duke of Burgundy recognized Charles VII as king of France and withdrew from the war. The English garrisons in the Paris region were left isolated. During the winter most of the lesser places fell, and in April 1436 Paris went over to Charles VII. Fastolf's old comrade-in-arms, Lord Willoughby, surrendered the Bastille and led the English garrison to Rouen.

While he was at Arras, Fastolf submitted a memorandum to Henry VI's council at Rouen giving his views as Bedford's chief lieutenant and military adviser.

He began by explaining the English decision to withdraw from the negotiations at Arras. Henry VI could not give up his claim to the French crown without admitting that his ancestors "had no right to the crown of France, and that all their wars and conquest hath been but usurpation and tyranny."* If their cause had been wrong, he asked plaintively, would God have given them so many victories? Furthermore, the French had never kept their treaties but had set them aside "by colored dissimulations and deceits." Therefore, the king must continue to press his claim, despite the opposition of the people of the occupied area of France, "who naturally love his adversary more than him."

He went on to propose that long sieges should be abandoned as wasteful of time, personnel, and money. No leader could conquer a great kingdom by continual sieges, considering the advanced character of the equipment and weapons of the day and the enemy's knowledge and experience of them. The king should therefore organize two armies of "about 750 lances" (3,000 men) led by "two notable chieftains, discreet and of one accord," to go on parallel expeditions, joining forces if necessary. These armies should land at a Channel port, either Calais or Le Crotoy, on the first day of June, and continue their campaign until the first of November, making their way "through Artois and Picardy, and so through Vermandois, Laonnais, Champagne, and Burgundy, burning and destroying all the land as they pass, both house, grain, vine, and all trees that bear fruit for man's sustenance, and all cattle that may not be driven to be de-

*Fastolf's memorandum is in English, here modernized, as are later quotations from the Paston letters.

stroyed; and those that may be well driven and spared in addition to the sustenance and victualling of the army, to be driven into Normandy, to Paris, and to other places in the king's obedience." Traitors and rebels (in other words, the population of the occupied area) must be treated to a "more sharp and cruel war" than ordinary enemies, or shortly no one would be afraid to rebel. The king might undertake "all this cruel war" without any accusation of tyranny, since he had offered his adversaries "as a good Christian prince" the opportunity of peace, "which offer the said adversaries have utterly refused."[30]

The report had two principal thrusts: first, it recommended a strategy in which the English concentrated on the defense and retention of Normandy, abandoning at least temporarily efforts to extend their conquests; second, it advocated clearing a wide band of territory of all that might be useful to the enemy and discouraging the inhabitants from aiding the French army.[31]

Fastolf's report has been cited as a statement of a policy created, in the words of a modern historian of the Hundred Years War, by "that old vulture Sir John Fastolf."[32] In reality the English had already been reduced to a defensive strategy before the treaty of Arras, while the "scorched earth" recommendation was no more than a candid description of the old English tactic of the *chevauchée* (which, contrary to Fastolf's conviction, had proved a failure). Indeed, it describes traditional medieval warfare in general, and is perhaps militarily most notable for its lack of appreciation of gunpowder artillery, which was on the point of revolutionizing siege warfare. On the expiration of the ten-year truce of Arras, the French rapidly reduced the English strongholds of Normandy and Gascony and won the war by the very siege methods Sir John Fastolf had condemned as futile.

On the philosophical plane, the Hundred Years War dramatized as never before the fundamental ambivalence of knightly attitudes. The glorification of knighthood continued to be the theme of Froissart and other chroniclers and poets as well as the object of the new secular military orders such as the Garter, while the elaborate tournaments staged by Edward III and others kept alive the pageantry of Arthurian romance. Even on the field of battle the archaic concept of war as sport was not totally dead. During the Christmas truce of 1428 at the siege of Orleans, English and Burgundian knights jousted with their French enemies, as in the previous century.[33] In the

French attack on the English redoubt at Orleans, a Spanish man-at-arms, Alfonso de Partada, called to a French knight to join him in guarding the rear of the assault column. The knight refused, saying that it was dishonorable to take a post in the rear. An argument ended with the two agreeing "to ride together side by side against the enemy, to prove which was the more valiant." Clasping hands, they galloped straight up to the English fortification.[34]

The other side of the coin was the perception of war as a free-enterprise business undertaking, its aim the capture of wealthy prisoners for ransom (but merciless slaughter of the less favored), pillage of churches and monasteries, and the robbery and torture of peasants.

An enlightening summation of the contemporary attitude is a book written by a cleric, Honoré Bouvet,* late in the fourteenth century.[35] Copied over and over, the *Tree of Battles* was widely read by the knightly class. Arthur de Richemont, constable of France in the final stage of the war, his adversary Sir John Talbot, and many other commanders on both sides owned copies. The book was often cited in military courts and by other writers.[36] The poet Christine de Pisan incorporated large extracts into her *Book of Feats of Arms and of Chivalry*, selections from which William Worcester translated into English for Fastolf.[37]

Bouvet adapted the *Tree of Battles* from a treatise by another cleric, John of Legnano, written in the context of fourteenth-century Italy, amid whose warring city republics the mercenary captains *(condottieri)* enjoyed even freer play than did their counterparts in France. Both authors drew on the unwritten "law of arms" that over centuries the knightly class had accumulated for division of booty and fixing of ransom, but their main discourse was pitched on a higher plane. Its concern was not the individual knight but the community.[38] In Bouvet's eyes, war was natural and inevitable, but its evils and injustices were largely the result of "false usage, as when a man-at-arms takes a woman and does her shame and injury, or sets fire to a church."[39] Wars should be conducted properly, ransoms should be "reasonable and not such as to disinherit [the captive's] wife, children, relations, and friends"; the man who exacted more was "no knight."[40] Civilian populations should be respected, for "the business of cultivating grain confers privileges on those who do it. . . . In all wars poor laborers should be left secure and in peace, for

*Or Bonet.

in these days all wars are directed against the poor laboring people and against their goods and chattels. I do not call that war, but it seems to me to be pillage and robbery. Further, that way of warfare does not follow the ordinances of worthy chivalry or of the ancient custom of noble warriors who upheld justice, the widow, the orphan, and the poor."[41]

Here Bouvet reiterated the adjurations of the Peace of God of four hundred years earlier, but elsewhere he laid down rules that reflected the needs of contemporary military commanders. A knight must accept discipline. He must not attack without orders, though it was a "plain and notorious fact that a young knight received more praise for attacking than for waiting."[42] Boldness might win "the vainglory of this world," but a knight should be bold only through "right knowledge and understanding."[43] A knight must be loyal first to the king, next to his lord, and next to the captain "who is acting in place of his lord as governor of the host."[44] He should not separate himself from the main battle to challenge a foe in single combat "to show [his] great courage."[45] In fact, he should "go nowhere at all" without his lord's permission.[46] He must remember precisely that he was not a knight-errant but a professional soldier, a man who "does all that he does as a deputy of the king or of the lord in whose pay he is."[47] Thus the popular vade mecum of the late medieval knight reinforced the old Christianizing ideals of the Round Table but to them added the iron demands of the modern army.

In 1440, after five more years in Normandy, Fastolf returned to England. He had made visits before, but this time he came to stay. He was sixty years old, and his military career was over, though he continued to serve the king as a member of the privy council.

He was rich. An evaluation of the receipts of his estates in 1445 brought the income from his English properties to an estimated £1,061, almost three-quarters of it from lands he had bought with his war profits. In addition, his properties in Normandy and Maine included ten castles, fifteen manors, and an inn at Rouen. Most had been granted by Henry V and Bedford, some in lieu of cash payment. Some had been purchased. Together they had at one time brought him an annual income of more than £675, but with the faltering English fortunes in France they now yielded only £401, a revenue that over the next few years dwindled and disappeared.[48]

He also engaged in commerce, reverting to his grandfather's métier. He owned several ships that plied between Great Yarmouth, London, and other east-coast ports and sometimes crossed to France, carrying wheat, barley, malt, raw wool, cloth, fish, and bricks. His manors produced wool, which he sold, and on at least one occasion he speculated in grain and made a killing.[49]

He owned fine houses not only in Norwich and Great Yarmouth but in Southwark, south of London Bridge, where presently he bought the Boar's Head Inn. His most impressive possession, however, was Caister Castle. While he was still engaged in the fighting in France, he had begun to build, on the site of the manor where he was born, a splendid structure containing twenty-six bedrooms, a chapel, a moat, and a great round tower ninety-eight feet high. The design was that of contemporary Dutch and German castles. Built of brick manufactured on the spot, Caister was embellished by stone from France, conveyed to the site by a canal that passed under an arch

CAISTER CASTLE, BUILT BY SIR JOHN FASTOLF OVER A PERIOD OF TWENTY-FIVE YEARS, WAS CONSTRUCTED OF NATIVE BRICK. DOMINATED BY A ROUND TOWER NINETY-EIGHT FEET HIGH, IT HAD TWENTY-SIX BEDROOMS. *(HALLAM ASHLEY)*

into the walled enclosure. Timber was brought from Fastolf's manor of Cotton, in Suffolk. On the wall of the Great Hall was carved the owner's coat of arms, a bush of feathers supported by two angels, each with four wings, the whole encircled by the Garter, with the motto, *"Me faut faire"*—"I must be doing." The castle was not completed until 1454, when Fastolf moved in, to remain until his death.[50]

The old soldier lived in style. An inventory of his clothing and furnishings at Caister in 1448 includes gowns of cloth of gold and satin, jackets of velvet, leather, and fine camlet wool, linen doublets and petticoats, silk bed canopies, fine horse trappings of scarlet cloth with red crosses and roses, silk surcoats embroidered with Fastolf's armorial bearings to be worn over armor, cushions of silk and velvet, numerous costly tapestries, featherbeds, silk coverlets, mattresses, candlesticks, bolts of cloth—damask, linen, embroidered silk and satin—silver dishes, some chased or with enameled or gilt decorations, silver saltcellars and basins, brass and copper pots and tubs. He owned gold and silver plate worth several thousand pounds.[51] He wore "daily about his neck" a gold cross and chain valued at £200, but his most valuable jewel was a "great pointed diamond set upon a rose enamelled white," incorporated in "a very rich collar called . . . a White Rose."[52] This ornament, worth the huge sum of 4,000 marks, had been given to Fastolf, along with other jewels, by Richard, duke of York, partly to repay a loan and partly to reward him for "the great labours and vexations sustained by the said knight for the said duke while he was the king's lieutenant in France and later in England."[53]

Fastolf's wife, Millicent, died in 1446 without giving him children[54] (an illegitimate son who became a monk predeceased him),[55] and he never remarried. As a result, the English properties bought with his war profits enriched another family, whose members became knights and finally joined the upper nobility. These were the Pastons, whose vast correspondence forms one of the most useful archives of late medieval social history. Their connection with Fastolf grew out of his legal and financial problems and personal vexations.

He was not popular in England. The unfair rumor of his behavior at Patay lingered, along with the general onus of being a king's councillor in a losing war. In 1450, during Jack Cade's rebellion, one of Fastolf's men was captured by Cade, who taxed him with his master's part in the war in France, where he had "diminished all the garrisons of Normandy and Le Mans and Maine, which was the cause of the losing of all the king's title and right of an inheritance that he had beyond the sea."[56]

In addition, the old soldier had gained a reputation for rapacity, the reverse of the knightly model of largesse. He heard of "scornful language of me" voiced at a dinner at Norwich, and begged one of his agents "that you give me knowledge by writing what gentlemen they be. . . . I shall keep your information secret, and with God's grace so purvey for them as they shall not [at] all be pleased. At such a time a man may know his friends and foes asunder."[57]

His estates caused him more substantive concerns. There were legal wrangles over the establishment of title, rents were difficult to collect, stewards were incompetent or dishonest. He wrote from London to Thomas Howes, his agent in Norfolk, demanding to be informed about those who infringed his rights. "If they will not dread nor obey [the law], then they shall be quit by Blackbeard or White-beard, that is to say, by God or the Devil. And therefore I charge you, send me word whether such as have been my adversaries before this time continue still in their wilfulness." He had heard "many strange reports of the governance of my place at Caister and other places," the sale of his wines on the sly, neglect of his possessions, trapping of his rabbits, and other misuse of his lands.[58] "Sir John Buck, parson of Stratford, fished my ponds at Dedham, broke my dam, destroyed my new mill," and "he and John Cole had by force this year and other years taken out of my waters at Dedham 24 swans and cyg-nets."[59] His sleepless suspicion did not endear him to his servitors. One of his agents wrote another that he had always been "cruel and vengeful . . . and for the most part without pity and mercy."[60]

Another of his agents, however, brought him comfort and reassur-ance. This was young John Paston, ambitious grandson of a "good plain husbandman"* who had managed to send his son to school to learn the law. The son rose to become a judge and to marry the daughter of a wealthy knight. Grandson John Paston, also educated in the law, likewise married an heiress, Margaret Mauteby, who was a distant relation of Fastolf's. In the early 1450s John became Fastolf's legal and financial counselor, just as the political disorders of the 1440s and 1450s were growing into the Wars of the Roses. A legacy

---

*Clement Paston was thus described by a hostile source, but this status seems to be confirmed by what documents have survived.[62]

of the military defeats in France, aggravated by Jack Cade's rebellion and abetted by the incompetence and later imbecility of Henry VI, the breakdown of authority opened a field to the private armies of the new "bastard feudalism" fostered by the military indenture system. Whereas military indentures between the king and his captains were for a year or less, the subcontracts of the captains with their men were usually for life. Joined to a lord's other attendants, indentured or merely hired, they formed bands of armed retainers capable of intimidating the king's justices and imposing their own local law.[61] Both Fastolf and the Pastons suffered depredations from such bands belonging to rapacious Norfolk neighbors. In 1451 a royal judicial commission was sent to Norwich to investigate the complaints of Fastolf and others, but the defendants corrupted one justice, who muzzled the plaintiffs' complaints (he "took them by the nose at every third word") and got the charges dropped.[63]

When Fastolf began his connection with John Paston, he was already in his seventies, in failing physical health and mental power, marshaling against the crown his still-outstanding claims amounting to about £11,000, stewing over the management of his affairs and the disposition of his inheritance. Stephen Scrope, Millicent Fastolf's son by her first marriage, had come to live with him at Caister, but Fastolf had no intention of making his stepson his heir. In fact, Scrope even accused his stepfather of improperly reducing Scrope's own estate. Fastolf had sold the wardship of his stepson for 500 marks, but when the new guardian proposed to marry the young man to his own daughter, had bought back the wardship. "He bought and sold me as a beast," Scrope wrote later, "against all right and law, to mine hurt more than 1,000 marks."[64]

As Fastolf's health deteriorated, John Paston assumed increasing control of his affairs. In a characteristic medieval effort to ensure his soul's salvation, the old knight had made up his mind to found a college at Caister where "seven priests and seven poor folk" would be maintained. Arrangements were still not complete in the spring of 1459 when he fell ill of asthma and a "hectic fever." In June he made a will providing for the college to be established, maintained by income from his estates. A lengthy document, the will also granted funds for prayers to be said for his soul and the souls of his father, mother, wife, and other relations and friends and for six months' wages of his servants. The vestments and ornaments of his chapel were to be given to "the monastery church of Saint Benet,

HERE AND ON FACING
PAGE: SPANDREL OF THE
MAIN GATEWAY OF ST.
BENET'S ABBEY, WHERE SIR
JOHN FASTOLF WAS
BURIED. *(HALLAM ASHLEY)*

where I shall be buried." Marble effigies were to be erected over the tomb of his father in the parish church of St. Nicholas at Yarmouth and over that of his mother in the parish church of Attilburgh, his father's effigy "with escutcheons of arms of him and his ancestors," his mother's with those of her three husbands.[65]

John Paston was in London when Friar Brackley, a Franciscan monk and friend of the Pastons who was in attendance on the sick man, wrote urging him to return to Caister. "It is high time; he draweth fast homeward, and is right low brought, and sore weakened and enfeebled. . . . Every day this five days he saith, 'God send me soon my good cousin Paston, for I hold him a faithful man, and ever one man.' *Cui ego* [to which I]: 'That is sooth.' *Et ille* [and he]: 'Show me not the meat, show me the man.' "[66]

John Paston arrived in time for the deathbed watch. Testimony at a hearing seven years later paints a picture reminiscent of a Molière

play—the coming and going to the sickroom where the master lay dying, while the household routine proceeded—horses shod in the stable, the servants chattering at breakfast, the laundress delivering clean linens, farmers arriving to collect money due for grain or capons or wagon hire to carry malt to Yarmouth. Every day a servant visited the sickroom to shave the old man. A distant relative, Richard Fastolf, came down from London to beg "help . . . so that he might marry," and found the dying man tottering about his chamber on the arms of two servants. To Richard's petition he replied that he had already made his will and that it provided for him (the will made in June, however, contained no such provision). John Monk, a smith of Norwich, said that he had been "frequently in Sir John's chamber" on the Friday and Saturday before his death and that "he was so weak for want of breath that he could not speak distinctly"; his attendants had to put their ears to his mouth, and "when people spoke to him to comfort him in his illness, he only answered by sighs." The chaplain came to say prayers with him, as was his daily wont, but said the service alone, "while Fastolf lay on his bed and said nothing."[67]

Despite what he had told Richard Fastolf, on November 3 a new, much shorter will was drawn up, making John Paston the chief heir, his inheritance limited only by provision for the college at Caister and a nominal payment to the other executors.[68] Two days later the old knight died. He was buried in the chapel of Saint Benet's (Benedict's) Holm, a monastery a few miles west of Caister.

Overnight, John Paston found himself a very rich man, possessor not only of Caister Castle but of three other houses, at Yarmouth, Norwich, and Southwark, ninety-four manors, a large sum in cash, and a fortune in jewels, plate, furnishings, and clothing. He also inherited all Fastolf's troubles, and more. Rumors circulated at once that he had unduly influenced his old master or even forged the new will. Outraged would-be beneficiaries raised their voices, among them William Worcester. The duke of Exeter laid claim to Fastolf's house in Southwark and presently seized it. The Pastons successfully took possession of most of Fastolf's manors in Norfolk and Suffolk, but in 1461 when the civil war broke out again the duke of Norfolk laid hands on Caister Castle. John Paston appealed to the new king, Edward IV, and eventually got the castle back, but lawsuits pursued him, and before his death in 1464 he served three brief terms in Fleet prison. In the fierce struggle for influence with those in authority, however, John Paston evidently held his own, bequeathing his family a position of wealth and power. He refused the honor of knighthood that was pressed upon him,[69] preferring to join the large number of landed gentry who paid cash to avoid military and other knightly service and were content to write "Esquire" after their names instead of "Sir" in front of them.[70] He did serve two terms as knight of the shire, or member of Parliament, an honor and duty that no longer required actual knighthood—in the words of a modern scholar, the knights of the shire had achieved a position in which the term "shire" had outrun in significance the term "knight," and although most of the men returned as shire-knights had sufficient property to be subject to distraint of knighthood, sometimes as few as half of them were actually knights.[72]

John Paston's son, also named John, growing up in a situation of affluence and elevated status, spent an apprenticeship at the court of Edward IV and at twenty-one was knighted. Yet even now the

GATEHOUSE, ST. BENET'S ABBEY,
WHERE SIR JOHN FASTOLF WAS BURIED. *(HALLAM ASHLEY)*

family did not escape its troubles with Fastolf's inheritance. Two of the other executors of Fastolf's will summarily sold Caister Castle to the duke of Norfolk, who sent armed men to take possession. Sir John Paston's younger brother, confusingly also named John, commanding the little castle garrison, withstood a siege for some days and finally surrendered on terms. After the duke's death in 1476 the

Pastons once more recovered Caister, and at long last settled with their rivals, sharing the properties, somewhat diminished in the course of the struggle, and transferring the bequest for a college from Caister to Oxford, where the hall of Magdalen College carries Fastolf's armorial bearings to this day.

Sir John Paston was a knight of a different stamp from the hard-bitten old warrior who was the source of the Pastons' fortune. A pleasure-loving courtier, he lived agreeably in London and answered his mother's pleas for thrift with recommendations for the sale of farms or the pawning of plate. More resembling Shakespeare's Falstaff than had the real-life Fastolf, he distinguished himself as a soldier only by participating on the losing side in the battle of Barnet in 1471, in which Edward IV defeated the Lancastrian army of the earl of Warwick.[73] Sir John died in 1479, and his younger brother John became head of the family. Active and energetic, this John Paston served as sheriff of Norfolk in 1485–1486, fought in the battle of Stoke in 1487, and was knighted on the field.[74]

The family flourished under the Tudors, increasing in wealth and importance. The sons were habitually knighted, managed their estates, and served the king. In the seventeenth-century Civil War, they took the Royalist side, lost most of the family fortune, and were forced to sell Caister. With the Restoration they returned to favor. Sir Robert Paston became earl of Yarmouth, and his eldest son, William, married one of Charles II's numerous illegitimate daughters. Accession to the upper ranks of the nobility made it appropriate for the family to prove its pedigree with a genealogy. Compiled in 1674 for Sir Robert Paston, it was evidently based on a family tradition current in the fifteenth century but not supported by any surviving documents. Copied on fine vellum and illustrated with 260 coats of arms, it traced the family to a reputed Norman ancestor, "Wulstan de Paston," a cousin of the earl of Glanville, and pictured his descendants as landed aristocrats; even John Paston's grandfather Clement, the "good plain husbandman," was given a coat of arms.[75]

Genealogies, however, could not repair the family's losses after the new political reversal of the revolution of 1688. The last Lord Yarmouth lived into the eighteenth century, a Tory survivor in a Norfolk dominated by great Whig families. He died without heirs in 1732, leaving nothing but debts.[76]

the long twilight
of chivalry

◄§ OH YE KNIGHTS OF ENGLAND, WHERE IS THE CUSTOM AND USAGE OF
NOBLE CHIVALRY THAT WAS USED IN THE DAYS OF KING ARTHUR? WHAT
DO YE NOW BUT GO TO THE BAGNIOS AND PLAY AT DICE. . . . LEAVE THIS,
LEAVE IT AND READ THE NOBLE VOLUMES OF THE HOLY GRAIL, OF
LAUNCELOT, OF GALAHAD, OF TRISTRAM, OF PERSEFOREST, OF PERCIVAL,
OF GAWAIN AND MANY MORE. THERE SHALL YE SEE MANHOOD, COUR-
TESY, AND GENTLENESS. AND LOOK IN LATER DAYS OF THE NOBLE ACTS
SINCE THE CONQUEST. . . . READ FROISSART. AND ALSO BEHOLD THAT
VICTORIOUS AND NOBLE KING HARRY THE FIFTH, AND THE CAPTAINS
UNDER HIM . . . AND MANY OTHERS WHOSE NAMES SHINE GLORIOUSLY
BY THEIR VIRTUOUS NOBLESSE AND ACTS THAT THEY DID IN HONOR OF
THE ORDER OF CHIVALRY.   —Conclusion of William Caxton's
                    translation of *The Book of the Ordre of Chyvalry* (1484)

◄§ IN OUR FOREFATHERS' TIME, WHEN PAPISTRY, AS A STANDING POOLE,
COVERED AND OVERFLOWED ALL ENGLAND, FEW BOOKS WERE READ IN
OUR TONGUE, SAVING CERTAIN BOOKS OF CHIVALRY . . . WHICH, AS SOME
SAY, WERE MADE IN MONASTERIES, BY IDLE MONKS, OR WANTON CAN-
ONS: AS ONE FOR EXAMPLE, *MORTE ARTHURE:* THE WHOLE PLEASURE OF
WHICH BOOK STANDETH IN TWO SPECIAL POINTS, IN OPEN MANSLAUGH-
TER, AND BOLD BAWDRY: IN WHICH BOOK THOSE HE COUNTED THE
NOBLEST KNIGHTS, THAT DO KILL MOST MEN WITHOUT ANY QUARREL,
AND COMMIT FOULEST ADULTERIES BY SUBTLEST SHIFTS. . . .
                    —Roger Ascham, *The Scholemaster* (1570)

◄§ AT A VILLAGE OF LA MANCHA, WHOSE NAME I DO NOT WISH TO
REMEMBER, THERE LIVED A LITTLE WHILE AGO ONE OF THOSE GENTLE-
MEN WHO ARE WONT TO KEEP A LANCE IN THE RACK, AN OLD BUCKLER,
A LEAN HORSE, AND A SWIFT GREYHOUND. . . . THE ABOVE-MENTIONED
GENTLEMAN IN HIS LEISURE MOMENTS (WHICH WAS MOST OF THE YEAR)
GAVE HIMSELF UP WITH SO MUCH DELIGHT AND GUSTO TO READING
BOOKS OF CHIVALRY THAT HE ALMOST ENTIRELY NEGLECTED THE EXER-
CISE OF THE CHASE AND EVEN THE MANAGEMENT OF HIS DOMESTIC
AFFAIRS.   —Miguel de Cervantes, *Don Quixote* (1605)

IN THE final centuries of the Middle Ages, knighthood reached its highest pinnacle of prestige but showed unmistakable signs of decay. In the thirteenth century the numbers of knights had dwindled and their function in society had ceased to be exclusively military. The ceremony of dubbing had become merely honorific, no longer a necessary prerequisite for the career of a fighting man, and many fighting men had ceased to seek the honor. In the fourteenth century the knights' monopoly of elite status in the army was challenged by these "squires," who equally with them became indentured captains. In England in the following century, knights, squires, and simple "gentlemen"* similarly shared the political functions of the community. Simultaneously, the money fees of "bastard feudalism" replaced the old links of lord and vassal: land, homage, and feudal loyalty.

The indenture system, which had served as the instrument of recruitment almost throughout the Hundred Years' War, began to be replaced in the middle of the fifteenth century by new military arrangements. Already foreshadowed by earlier French army reforms, a system of permanent *"compagnies de grande ordonnance"* was established in 1445 by Charles VII, each company of a hundred lances (600 men), headed by captains appointed by the king, the companies stationed in designated towns and paid and supplied by their respective provinces. To reinforce this mounted force in time of crisis, Charles formed the *francs-archers* (free bowmen), some 8,000 strong, infantry reservists who lived at home, were exempt from royal taxes, were equipped if necessary at the expense of their parishes, practiced their skills regularly and underwent periodic inspection, and could be summoned at the will of the king. To this cavalry and infantry were added royal companies of artillery, the whole forming a permanent professional army.

*An English antiquarian of the early twentieth century reported that in his researches he had discovered the earliest use of the word "gentleman" to have occurred in 1413 when one Robert Erdeswyke of Stafford so described himself in defending himself against an indictment for housebreaking, wounding with intent to kill, and procuring murder.[1]

In 1473 Charles the Rash, duke of Burgundy, reorganized his army into companies of cavalry, archers, and foot soldiers, the companies divided into squadrons subdivided into smaller units, each with a commander, forming the echeloned structure characteristic of the modern army.

Other European countries copied France and Burgundy, and the army raised by private contract was gradually replaced by armies under the direct command of the ruling authority and financed by the state. In these new national armies, knights served but were indistinguishable from nonknightly men-at-arms who wore the same armor, rode the same horses, and came to earn the same pay.[2]

The maturing of the artillery arm contributed to the trend. Artillery had played a small role in Du Guesclin's war, a larger one in Fastolf's, and finally a crucial one in the French siege and field operations of the last stage of the Hundred Years' War. The knight was no more vulnerable to gunfire than anyone else, but expensive cannon and gunpowder strongly reinforced the trend toward national professional armies.

The knight Jean de Bueil (1405–1478), who fought under Joan of Arc at Orleans and was one of Charles VII's counselors, in his late years penned an autobiographical prose romance* that provides a realistic picture of contemporary war and its demands on the soldier: the privations that "all men who wish to acquire honor and glory through war must bear and endure patiently."[3] Modern war, said De Bueil, was a profession, not a sport. Knights who had spent their lives at court were not fitted for it, either in hardihood or skill.[4] Discipline, sound tactics, and rational strategy were required, not impulsive heroics. "The good and valiant knights, captains, and mercenaries should not plan and direct the difficult enterprises of battle by force of arms and number of men alone, but also by subtlety and good prudence."[5] As for the role of cannon, De Bueil described no fewer than 240 different kinds, giving the quantity of powder for the discharge of each, the number of horses needed to haul it, and the number of cannonballs necessary for a siege.[6] In his account, ransoms are disposed of by prior contract, as is the booty gained by raids frankly designed to obtain it.[7] When the enemy suggests a sort of Battle of the Thirty, De Bueil's hero (and alter ego), the Jouvençel,

---

*Fastolf was a character in this *roman à clef* under the name of "Messire Jehan Helphy, a notable knight, and wise and rich" (II, p. 236); Bedford and Joan of Arc's companion-in-arms La Hire are also represented.

refuses: "We have come to drive [the enemy] out and to wage war against them on our terms, not on theirs."[8] Jousting he treats with contempt; the man who indulges in it does so only out of vainglory. "He spends his money, he exposes his body to take life or honor from the one he fights, which brings him little profit; while he is thus occupied, he abandons war, the service of his king, and the public good; and no one should expose his body except in meritorious deeds."[9]

In words more expressive of the patriotism and esprit de corps of the modern soldier than of the individualism of the medieval knight, he explains that in war, love of comrades, hatred of tyranny, and loyalty to a good cause bring "a joy that can only be described by the man who has experienced it." A man strengthened by these emotions is "truly afraid of nothing." The man who serves in the profession of arms, even for a secular cause, is "blessed in this world and the next, and a true servant of God."[10]

But while military progress was stifling the old knightly spirit of individual glory, the age nevertheless celebrated the fame of individual knights whose deeds, thanks to the improved state of communications, were widely reported. The most famous was Pierre Terrail, the "Chevalier Bayard" (c. 1473–1524), who fought in the Italian wars of Charles VIII and Francis I of France and distinguished himself not only by his feats of arms and skillful generalship but by his character: he was reputed to be the perfect knight, *"sans peur et sans reproche."* Mortally wounded, fittingly enough by a musket ball, he rebuffed the comfort offered him by his enemy, the rebel Constable de Bourbon: "Sir, there is no need to pity me, for I die in good state. But I pity you, who fight against your prince, and your country, and your oath."[11]

The Chevalier Bayard's biography, like those of William Marshal and Bertrand du Guesclin, records its hero's accomplishments not only on the battlefield but in the tournament, where he won all the prizes but often chivalrously yielded them to the runners-up. Bayard's tournaments were fought "at the barriers," with combatants approaching each other on either side of a wooden fence. Although Bayard sometimes killed opponents, the tournaments by now were designed as spectacles and athletic competitions, in contrast to the earlier rough and tumble. They might still end with a melee, but always an orderly and well-regulated one.

The fifteenth- and sixteenth-century revival of the old chivalric customs, known mainly from the romantic depictions of Froissart

FIFTEENTH-CENTURY TOURNAMENT:
KNIGHTS JOUST AT THE BARRIERS,
WHILE LADIES WATCH.
(*BRITISH LIBRARY, MS. NERO D IX, F. 32B*)

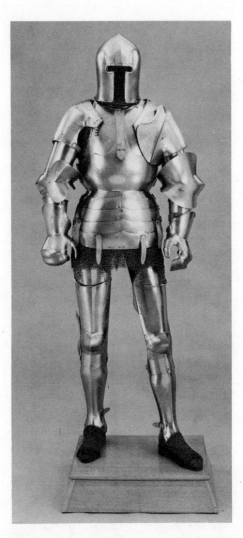

MILANESE ARMOR, C. 1450:
OVER HIS HAUBERK THE
KNIGHT IS CLAD IN PLATE
FROM HEAD TO TOE, WITH
MITTEN GAUNTLETS AND
ELABORATE SHOULDER AND
ELBOW REINFORCEMENT.
*(GLASGOW MUSEUMS AND
ART GALLERIES)*

and the Arthurian legend, resulted in what one modern historian has termed an "Indian summer" of knighthood, or at least its external forms.[12] The tournament, held on the occasion of a marriage, a diplomatic mission, or accession to a throne, was an adjunct of theatrical productions and partook of their character. The jousting, usually with blunted weapons, was done by the book, its proclamations, challenges, and individual contests conducted in accordance with rules laid down in manuals and adjudged by a Court of Chivalry. The art of heraldry blossomed into maturity. Tunics blazed with coats of arms over gleaming suits of armor whose plates were sometimes intricately incised, canceling the defensive advantage of a smooth surface. The completeness of the plate also cost something in military practicality through the accretion of weight. A suit of armor for the joust made in Augsburg in about 1500 weighed ninety pounds (41 kilograms).[13] Often pageantry took precedence over fighting. An instance of the elaboration the tournament could receive occurred in 1468 in Bruges on the occasion of the marriage of the duke of Burgundy to Princess Margaret of England. Lasting ten days, the tournament was designed around the conceit of a captive giant and the princess of an unknown isle. The champion who freed the giant would win the princess. A dwarf dressed in crimson and white satin led the giant into the lists by a chain, tied him to a gilded tree, and sounded a trumpet, summoning the "Knight of the Golden Tree," attired in velvet and ermine. Each day of the tournament was marked by different kinds of jousts, ending with a melee on the last day, twenty-five knights to a side. At the final banquet a female dwarf in cloth of gold rode into the banquet hall mounted on a mechanical lion to present a marguerite (daisy) to the new Duchess Margaret, and a sixty-foot mechanical whale was hauled in, its tail and fins working, its mouth emitting music.[14]

In England printer and translator William Caxton contributed to the revival with two publications: a translation (c. 1484) of Raymond Lull's manual for knights, now two centuries old, under the title *The Book of the Ordre of Chyvalry,* and Sir Thomas Malory's *Morte d'Arthur* (1485). Malory's treatment of the "matter of Britain" restored Arthur to the central role he had lost in the French romances. The mysticism of the Grail legend, the rigmarole of courtly love, and the nuances of satire found little favor with Malory, who, like Caxton, looked back on the age of chivalry with the blind eye of nostalgia. Both Malory and Caxton fitted their view of chivalry into the more modern sentiment of nationalism, Caxton urging Englishmen to "read Froissart,"[15] in whose pages Edward III and his marauding captains took on the glamour of Lancelot and Arthur. Froissart was translated into English in 1523 by John Bourchier, Lord Berners, who explained that his intention was to make available to the "noble gentlemen of England . . . the high enterprises, famous acts, and glorious deeds done and achieved by their valiant ancestors."[16]

Lord Berners's translation was "commanded" by Henry VIII, an enthusiastic practitioner of knightly exercises, whose accession to the throne was celebrated with splendid jousts in which the king himself took part, wearing tilting armor of his own design. Later Henry arranged with German emperor Maximilian, another devotee, to import German armorers to man his "Almain [German] Armouries" at Greenwich. Henry maintained permanent tilting areas at Westminster, Greenwich, and Hampton Court,[17] but the climax of his tourneying occurred when he met Francis I of France in the "Field of Cloth of Gold" near Calais in 1520. Both kings jousted, Francis's horse in purple satin trappings trimmed with gold and embroidered with raven's plumes, Henry's in cloth of gold fringed with damask. French knights wore doublets of cloth of silver and purple velvet, English of cloth of gold and russet velvet. Archery, now displaced by gunpowder small arms, was also a nostalgic feature of the tournament, Henry proving himself "a marvelously good archer." Wrestling was added extemporaneously to the program. A chronicler reported that after the jousts the two kings "retired to a pavilion . . . and drank together, and then the king of England took the king of France by the collar and said to him, 'My brother, I want to wrestle with you,' and gave him one or two falls. And the king of France, who is strong and a good wrestler, gave him a 'Breton turn' and threw him on the ground. . . . And the king of England wanted to go on wrestling, but it was broken off and they had to go to supper. . . ."[18]

In the reign of Queen Elizabeth, elaborate tournaments continued, but the actual jousting became secondary to masques and allegories and displays of horsemanship (manège). Tournaments were now irrelevant to the careers of knights and gentry, whose functions were those of a governing class, a transformation reminiscent of that of the Roman *equites*, and whose military role, though it continued, was no longer the clash of shock combat. The education of the knight as set forth in a plan that Sir Humphrey Gilbert (c. 1537–1583) conceived for an academy in London to train "the youth of nobility and gentlemen" is indicative of the changes. The young gentlemen should study Latin language and literature, philosophy, law, contemporary history, oratory, heraldry, and courtly protocol. They should learn the art of war, but instead of lance and sword they must master mathematics, engineering, ballistics, and military theory.[19]

To Caxton and Malory, chivalry was a practical mode of conduct fallen into disuse but susceptible to revival. A hundred years later, in Edmund Spenser's *Faerie Queene* (published 1590–1596), it had faded to a romantic memory of "those antique times / In which the sword was servant unto right."[20] Spenser drew his inspiration in part from the Italian poet Ariosto (1474–1533), whose intentions, however, were very different. Ariosto belonged to an Italian tradition developed in the fifteenth and sixteenth centuries combining the epic material of the *chansons de geste* with elements of the romances. Matteo Boiardo's *Orlando Innamorato* (*Roland in Love*, 1483) mingled Charlemagne legend and Arthurian romance in a lively combination of heroic deeds, magic, and love. In his satiric *Orlando Furioso* (*Roland Mad*), Ariosto pictured knights and ladies living by the old codes of chivalry and courtly love in a sixteenth-century world in which "the cruel art" of artillery had eclipsed the sword, and "martial glory [is] lost."[21] Where the epic Roland was the model of loyalty to his lord, Ariosto's Orlando forsakes Charlemagne for the love of a lady, only to be driven mad when she runs off with a Saracen foot soldier.

Ariosto was neither the first poet nor the last to treat chivalry satirically. Both an English verse written by an unknown author around the middle of the fifteenth century, *The Turnament of Totenham*, and the slightly earlier Swiss comic poem, Heinrich Wittenweiler's *Ring*, describe tournaments in which peasants joust in a burlesque of the courtly spectacle. In the English verse, village youths vie for the hand of Tyb, the reeve's daughter; in the *Ring* the peasant Bertschi Triefnas celebrates his marriage to his hunchbacked, flatfooted, goitered sweetheart Metzli Ruerenzumph by a joust on the village green. In both poems, the combatants' mounts are mares, asses, and workhorses; their helmets baskets, bowls, and buckets; their shields winnowing baskets; their weapons rakes, hoes, and flails. While the "ladies" watch, the rustics at first punctiliously follow the rules of the tournament, but break into a wild free-for-all. The feasts that follow are drunken brawls, the whole effect parodying the clichés of courtly romances as well as the practices of tournaments.[22]

The chivalric mystique was rebuffed not only by Renaissance humanism but by Protestantism. Elizabethan moralist Roger Ascham identified the Middle Ages with Catholicism and regarded chivalric literature as the creation of "idle monks or wanton canons." He lamented the day when "God's Bible was banished [from] the Court, and *Morte Arthure* [Morte d'Arthur] received into the Prince's chamber."[23]

The most devastating blow to decaying chivalry was struck by a man who was himself a professional soldier. Miguel de Cervantes's

Don Quixote (1605) has been called "the first modern novel." The gaunt old Knight of the Sorrowful Countenance, his brain addled by reading too much chivalric literature, rides through the countryside on his spavined horse, in rusty armor and pasteboard helmet, fighting muleteers, windmills, and flocks of sheep in the name of his "lady," in reality nothing more than a "good-looking country wench." After a long succession of disillusioning experiences, he forswears on his deathbed "all profane stories of knight-errantry . . . those foolish tales that up to now have been my bane," and sets down as a condition in his will that his niece should marry only a man who "shall be found never to have read a book of knight-errantry in his life." Cervantes concludes, "My sole aim has been to arouse men's scorn for the false and absurd stories of knight-errantry, whose prestige has been shaken by this tale of my true Don Quixote, and which will, without any doubt, soon crumble in ruin. *Vale.* "[24] Such is the power of Cervantes's ironic but compassionate pen, however, that the reader is in danger of concluding that the rest of the world is mad and the noble old man sane.

In the eighteenth century two distinct currents of thought emerged in respect to chivalry. The rationalist philosophers scorned all things medieval as barbarism, superstition, and ignorance. But a body of conservative scholars, the most famous of them J.-B. de la Curne de Sainte-Palaye (1697–1781), studied the art, subjected the history to critical examination, and edited the literature of the Middle Ages. Sainte-Palaye's *Mémoires sur l'ancienne chevalerie* (1759), with its description of dubbings and tournaments and account of the code of chivalry, exerted a powerful influence on European intellectuals, including Gibbon, Sir Walter Scott, and Robert Southey. His critique revived the popularity of Froissart, who had fallen into neglect, and his *Histoire littéraire des troubadours* (1774), widely circulated and translated, won a permanent place on library shelves. Many of the printed editions of medieval chronicles, literary works, and documents used today were prepared by scholars of the eighteenth century.[25]

The industrial age in Britain, however, produced the most spectacular revival of interest in the medieval knight, his milieu, military practices, armor, and above all code of behavior.[26] In the early 1800s Sir Walter Scott re-created in *Ivanhoe* and other novels and poems a world of castles, knight-errantry, and chivalric virtues. It was a world of the distant past, whose defects he acknowledged in his essay

DANTE GABRIEL ROSSETTI, *SIR GALAHAD*. (*THE TATE GALLERY, LONDON*)

on chivalry written for the *Encyclopaedia Britannica* in 1818*—fanaticism and superstition, the immorality of "courtly love," the extravagance of knightly enterprises. But "nothing could be more beautiful and praiseworthy than the theory on which it was grounded." The best elements of the chivalric code had produced the system of manners of the "gentleman."[27] Scott himself was such a believer in the code that when a publishing firm in which he was partner went broke, he refused to go into bankruptcy, assumed the entire debt, and spent the rest of his life writing to pay it—indeed, the debt was finally paid off by his posthumous royalties.

Later writers took up the chivalric theme. Malory, who like Froissart had undergone a long period of neglect, was resurrected in a new edition that inspired Tennyson to a series of poems culminating in *The Idylls of the King.* Tennyson's knights of the Round Table swear

> To break the heathen and uphold the Christ,
> To ride abroad redressing human wrongs,
> To speak no slander, no, nor listen to it,
> To honour his own word as if his God's,

*Scott's article appeared in one of the half-volumes of the *Supplement to the Sixth Edition* issued from 1815 to 1820.

> To lead sweet lives in purest chastity,
> To love one maiden only, cleave to her
> And worship her by years of noble deeds,
> Until they won her. . . .[28]

The code of chivalry was primly summed up by Tennyson as: "Live pure, speak true, right wrong, follow the King."[29]

Other Victorian writers and artists joined the Poet Laureate. The Pre-Raphaelites fell in love with Galahad, Lancelot, Arthur, and Guinevere. The enthusiasm infected architecture, not only in the form of castle restoration but in an outburst of "Gothic" style, in which battlements and towers festooned country houses enclosing all the peaceful Victorian comforts. Armor came down from the attic, and antique dealers prospered. The most eminent Victorians, including Prince Albert, had their portraits done wearing plate armor or had themselves represented in effigy as knights on their marble tombs. Above all, the heroes of the Round Table were offered as examples to boys in school, in sport, and finally (1908) in the founding of the Boy Scouts.

The most memorable single expression of Victorian enthusiasm was the Eglinton Tournament, organized in 1839 by a rich young Tory lord, the earl of Eglinton, and described by Disraeli in *Endymion*. Samuel Pratt's showrooms in London furnished armor, horse trappings, pavilions, shields, banners, lances, swords, and medieval costumes. The setting was Lord Eglinton's castle, in Ayrshire, Scotland, near the English border, anachronistically built in 1797. The tournament drew an enormous throng, even though its sponsor sought to limit the gathering to members of the Conservative party, which was represented by numerous peers, baronets, knights, and ladies. Foreign guests included Prince Louis Napoleon.

The day dawned brightly, but by the time the grand procession to the lists was organized, clouds were gathering, and a thunder clap heralded a torrential downpour. Umbrellas went up, and the procession plodded through the mud, its leader, Lord Londonderry, the "paladin of the chivalric life and gallant bearing," under a large green umbrella, the Queen of Beauty and her maids of honor in closed carriages. The knights bravely tilted in a sea of slippery mud, and the tournament ended in chaos with bogged-down carriages and collapsing temporary buildings. Lord Eglinton and his guests stuck it out, and two days later the tournament was reenacted in sunshine, slightly marred only when in the closing melee two knights lost their tempers and had to be separated by the Knight Marshal. A medieval banquet at which each knight was attended by a page carrying his banner was followed by a ball in medieval dress.[30] But the fiasco in the mud was the image that lingered. "The Knights threw down their lances, and put up their umbrellas," Edward FitzGerald wrote,[31] and the knight-with-the-umbrella became a derisive symbol.

Eglinton and Tennyson were doing what Henry VIII and Francis I, Caxton and Malory had done, evoking an illusive and beguiling past, and finding in it a code of behavior for their own time. But the past had grown far more remote, not only with the passage of centuries but through the vast metamorphosis of Western society. The spirit of Eglinton survived into the twentieth century in a variety of forms, and traces of the chivalric code are preserved in details of latter-day etiquette. Such is the superficial legacy of the age of knighthood, now vanished beyond the reach of the irony of an Ariosto or a Cervantes.

Yet something more serious has endured. The ideals that Scott admired still command respect, at least in part because many men in the Middle Ages embraced them and tried to live by them: honor, unselfish service, dedication to justice, and the protest against war's brutalities embodied in the Peace of God. A nineteenth-century admirer of the chivalric code and critic of the Middle Ages, Eton master Johnson Cory, observed: "Bayard, instead of being the last of the true knights, was the first."[32] A shrewd comment, but if Bayard surpassed the real-life knights of the medieval period in knightliness, he did so by adhering to the model they had created.

Of the three elements of chivalry, the military, the courtly, and the religious, the medieval knight found the first the easiest to practice. Many successfully imitated the heroes of the *chansons de geste* in their loyalty and courage, and too many in their rashness and vainglory. The second element, the courtesy and liberality of the troubadour tradition, also fitted broadly into knightly life-style, though real-life behavior toward women often fell short of the prescribed ideal. It was the third set of virtues, set forth in the codes of chivalry and celebrated in the Arthurian romances, that was the most neglected. Knights fought for profit and killed without mercy, robbed those whom they should have defended, and violated those whom they should have respected.

Many medieval knights were Rolands, few were Galahads.

notes

1 / WHAT IS A KNIGHT?

1. Although much has been written about particular aspects of knighthood, surprisingly few general studies have been done by modern writers. The most recent are: Maurice Keen, *Chivalry*, New Haven, Conn., 1984; Richard Barber, *The Knight and Chivalry*, London, 1970; Sidney Painter, *French Chivalry*, Ithaca, N.Y., 1957 (first published in 1940 by the Johns Hopkins Press). Leon Gautier's *Chivalry*, published in French in 1884, was translated into English by D. C. Dunning, London, 1965.

2 / THE FIRST KNIGHTS

1. Michael Grant, *The Army of the Caesars*, London, 1974, pp. 21–22, 70–72, 93–94, 140–142; Grant, *The World of Rome*, New York, 1960, pp. 23, 39–40, 51, 52; Jérôme Carcopino, *Daily Life in Ancient Rome*, New Haven, Conn., 1970, pp. 60, 74–75.

2. Surveys of theories about the emergence of the knight and its connection with the beginnings of feudalism and the rise of the medieval nobility include: Carl Stephenson, "The Origin and Significance of Feudalism," *American Historical Review* 46 (1941), pp. 788–801; Leopold Génicot, "Recent Research on the Medieval Nobility," in *The Medieval Nobility*, ed. and trans. by Timothy Reuter, Amsterdam, 1978, pp. 17–35; E. Warlop, *The Flemish Nobility Before 1300*, trans. by J. B. Ross, 4 vols., Kortrijk, Belgium, 1975–1976, Vol. I, pp. 11–17; David Herlihy, ed., *The History of Feudalism*, New York, 1970, pp. xxii–xxvii.

3. Heinrich Brunner, *Deutsche Rechtsgeschichte*, second edition, 2 vols., Leipzig, 1906, 1928.

4. Marc Bloch, *Feudal Society*, trans. by L. A. Manyon, 2 vols., Chicago, 1964, Vol. II, pp. 283–286, 290–291.

5. Lynn White, Jr., *Medieval Technology and Social Change*, Oxford, 1962, pp. 1–41.

6. Georges Duby, "The Nobility in Medieval France," in *The Chivalrous Society*, trans. by Cynthia Poston, Berkeley, Calif., 1977, pp. 94–109; Karl Schmid, "The Structure of the Nobility in the Earlier Middle Ages," in Reuter, *The Medieval Nobility*, pp. 37–59; Franz Irsigler, "On the Aristocratic Character of Early Frankish Society," in Reuter, *The Medieval Nobility*, pp. 105–124; Leopold Génicot, "La noblesse au moyen âge dans l'ancienne 'Francie': continuité, rupture ou évolution?", *Comparative Studies in Society and History* 5 (1962–1963), pp. 52–59; Joan Martindale, "The French Aristocracy in the Early Middle Ages: A Reappraisal," *Past and Present* 75 (1977), pp. 5–45; Constance B. Bouchard, "The Origins of the French Nobility: A Reassessment," *American Historical Review* 86, No. 3 (June 1981), pp. 501–532.

7. D. H. Bullough, "Early Medieval Social Groupings: The Terminology of Kinship," *Past and Present* 45 (1969), pp. 16–18; Constance B. Bouchard, "The Structure of a Twelfth-Century French Family: The Lords of Seignelay," *Viator* 10 (1978), pp. 41–44; Martindale, "The French Aristocracy," pp. 38–43.

8. K. Leyser, "Maternal Kin in Early Medieval Germany: A Reply," *Past and Present* 49 (1970), p. 126. See also Bouchard, "Origins of the French Nobility," p. 504.

9. Herlihy, *History of Feudalism*, pp. 69–77; F. L. Ganshof, *Feudalism*, trans. by Philip Grierson, New York, 1961, pp. 3–12.

10. Bernard S. Bachrach, "Military Organization in Aquitaine under the Early Carolingians," *Speculum* 49 (January 1974), pp. 1–33; Bachrach, "Charles Martel, Mounted Shock Combat, the Stirrup and Feudal Origins," *Studies in Medieval and Renaissance History* 7 (1970), pp. 47–76; Bachrach, *Merovingian Military Organization 481–751*, Minneapolis, 1972, pp. 113–128; P. H. Sawyer, review of White, *Medieval Technology and Social Change*, *Past and Present* 24 (1963), pp. 90–95.

11. A. D. H. Bivar, "Cavalry Equipment and Tactics on the Euphrates Frontier," *Dumbarton Oaks Papers* 26 (1972), pp. 273–291; Bivar, "The Stirrup and Its Origins," *Oriental Art* N.S., I (1955) pp. 61–65.

12. David C. Douglas, *William the Conqueror*, Berkeley, Calif., 1967, p. 202.

13. Georges Duby, "The Origins of Knighthood," in *The Chivalrous Society*, p. 159.

14. Sally Harvey, "The Knight and the Knight's Fee in England," *Past and Present* 49 (1970), p. 15.

15. Karl Bosl, " 'Noble Unfreedom.' The Rise of the *Ministeriales* in Germany," in Reuter, *The Medieval Nobility*, pp. 291–311; John B. Freed, "The Origins of the European Nobility: The Problem of the Ministerials," *Viator* 7 (1976), pp. 213–241.

16. Georges Duby, *La Société aux XIe et XIIe siècles dans la région mâconnaise,* Paris, 1955, pp. 47, 70–71, 291–292.

17. Joseph and Frances Gies, *Life in a Medieval Castle,* New York, 1974, pp. 9–13, 21.

18. James Mann, *An Outline of Arms and Armour in England,* London, 1969, pp. 5–8; Mann, "Arms and Armour," in *The Bayeux Tapestry,* ed. by Sir Frank Stenton, London, 1965, pp. 56–69; Claude Blair, *European Armour circa 1066 to circa 1700,* Batsford, Eng., 1958, pp. 23–26.

19. Georges Duby, "The Evolution of Judicial Institutions," in *The Chivalrous Society,* p. 58.

20. Georges Duby, "The History and Sociology of the Medieval West," p. 86, and "Laity and the Peace of God," pp. 123–133, both in *The Chivalrous Society;* H. E. J. Cowdrey, "The Peace and Truce of God in the Eleventh Century," *Past and Present* 46 (1970), pp. 42–67; Roger Bonnaud-Delamare, "Fondement des institutions de paix au XI siècle," in *Mélanges d'histoire du moyen âge dédiés à la mémoire de Louis Halphen,* Paris, 1951, pp. 19–26; Bonnaud-Delamare, "Les institutions de paix en Aquitaine au XIme siècle," pp. 415–487, Egied I. Strubbe, "La paix de Dieu dans le nord de la France," pp. 490–501, and François-L. Ganshof, "La 'paix' au très haut moyen âge," pp. 397–413, all in *Recueils de la Société Jean Bodin,* Vol. 14, *La Paix,* 1961.

21. Duby, *Société,* pp. 155–160.

22. G. D. Mansi, *Sacrorum conciliorum nova et amplissima collectio,* Florence, 1759–1798, XIX, c. 267 (the Council of Poitiers).

23. Duby, "Laity and the Peace of God," pp. 125–127; Bonnaud-Delamare, "La paix en Aquitaine," pp. 422–423.

24. Cowdrey, "The Peace and the Truce of God," pp. 43, 45–46.

25. Ralph Glaber, *Historiarum libri quinque,* extract trans. by G. G. Coulton in *Life in the Middle Ages,* Cambridge, 1930, p. 6.

26. Adhémar of Chabannes, *Chronique,* ed. by J. Chavanon, Paris, 1897, quoted in Cowdrey, "The Peace and the Truce of God," p. 49.

27. Duby, "Laity and the Peace of God," pp. 130–132; Cowdrey, "The Peace and the Truce of God," pp. 52–53.

28. "The Peace and Truce of God at the Council of Toulouges," in F. A. Ogg, ed., *A Source Book of Medieval History,* New York, 1907, pp. 229–230.

29. Mansi, *Sacrorum conciliorum,* Canon 1, c. 827 (Council of Narbonne).

30. Bloch, *Feudal Society,* Vol. II, pp. 312–316, cites a pontifical (book of ceremonies) of Mainz c. 950 that describes the blessing of the sword and

eleventh-century pontificals of Besançon and Rheims in which the sword is not only blessed but girded on by an officiating priest.

3 / KNIGHTS OF THE FIRST CRUSADE

1. Baldric of Dol, *Historia Jerosilimitana*, in *The First Crusade, the Chronicle of Fulcher of Chartres and Other Source Materials*, ed. by Edward Peters, Philadelphia, 1971, p. 10 (reprinted from A. C. Krey, *The First Crusade: The Accounts of Eyewitnesses and Participants*, Princeton, N.J., 1921).

2. Robert the Monk, *Historia Hierosolymitana*, in Peters, *First Crusade*, p. 4 (reprinted from D. C. Munro, *Urban and the Crusaders*, Philadelphia, 1895).

3. Baldric of Dol, *Historia*, in Peters, *First Crusade*, p. 10.

4. Guibert of Nogent, *Historia quae dicitur gesta Dei per Francos*, in Peters, *First Crusade*, p. 15.

5. General works on the First Crusade include: Hans Eberhardt Mayer, *The Crusades*, trans. by John Gillingham, Oxford, 1972; Kenneth M. Setton, *A History of the Crusades*, 4 vols., Madison, Wis., 1969–1971, Vol. I, *The First Hundred Years*, ed. by Marshall W. Baldwin; Steven Runciman, *A History of the Crusades*, 3 vols., Cambridge, 1951–1954, Vol. I; Jonathan Riley-Smith, *What Were the Crusades?*, London, 1977.

6. Duby, *Société*, p. 361; Mayer, *The Crusades*, p. 24.

7. Duby, *Société*, pp. 52–63.

8. David Herlihy, "The Agrarian Revolution in Southern France and Italy, 801–1150," *Speculum* 33 (1958), pp. 23–41.

9. Duby, *Société*, pp. 266–272.

10. Ibid., pp. 52–53, 269–270, 272–281.

11. Ibid., pp. 240–241.

12. Ibid., pp. 243–244.

13. Ibid., pp. 185–191.

14. Ibid., p. 192.

15. Ibid., p. 441.

16. Ibid., pp. 192–193, 447–448. See also Sidney Painter, "Castle Guard," *American Historical Review* 40 (1935), pp. 450–459.

17. Duby, *Société*, pp. 192–193.

18. Ibid., p. 193.

19. Ibid., pp. 292–293, 295–296.

20. Ibid., p. 415.

21. Ibid., p. 411.

22. Marshall W. Baldwin, writing in *Encyclopaedia Britannica* (15th edition, "Crusades," Macropaedia, Vol. V, p. 297), estimates the Crusading army at 4,000 knights, 25,000 infantry; David C. Douglas, in *William the Conqueror*, pp. 198–199, assesses the English army at Hastings at "some 7,000 men," that of William the Conqueror as "slightly less numerous," both estimates including knights and infantry. P. Van Luyn, in "Les *milites* du XIe siècle," *Le Moyen Age* 77 (1971), p. 34, points out that in the chronicles of the Crusades no more than 1,500 knights are ever reported as actually assembled on a battlefield.

23. Van Luyn, "Les *milites*," pp. 217–220.

24. A. T. Hatto, "Archery and Chivalry: A Noble Prejudice," *Modern Language Review* 35 (1940), pp. 40–54.

25. Duby, *Société*, p. 239n.

26. *Gesta francorum et aliorum Hierosolymytanorum*, in Peters, *First Crusade*, p. 188 (reprinted from Krey, *The First Crusade*).

27. Ibid., p. 209.

28. Fulcher of Chartres, *Historia Hierosolymitana*, in Peters, *First Crusade*, p. 82 (trans. by Martha E. McGinty).

29. Ibid., p. 168.

30. Van Luyn, "Les *milites*," p. 30.

31. Duby, *Société*, pp. 177–178.

32. J. Boussard, "Henri Plantagenet et les origines de l'armée de métier," *Bibliothèque de l'École des Chartes*, 1945–1946, p. 193.

33. J. O. Prestwich, "War and Finance in the Anglo-Norman State," *Transactions of the Royal Historical Society*, V, 4 (1954), pp. 24–32.

34. William of Malmesbury, *Gesta Regum*, ed. by W. Stubbs, 2 vols., London, 1887–1889, Vol. II, p. 368.

35. Suger, *Vie de Louis VI le Gros*, in *Oeuvres Complètes de Suger*, ed. by A. Lecoy de la Marche, Paris, 1887, p. 11.

36. I. S. Robinson, "Gregory VII and the Soldiers of Christ," *History* 58 (1973), pp. 169–192; H. E. J. Cowdrey, "The Genesis of the Crusades," in *The Holy War*, ed. by T. P. Murphy, Columbus, Ohio, 1974; Carl Erdmann, *The*

Origin of the Idea of Crusade, trans. by Marshall W. Baldwin and Walter Goffart, Princeton, N.J., 1982.

37. Bryce D. Lyon, *From Fief to Indenture, the Transition from Feudal to Non-Feudal Contract in Western Europe,* Cambridge, Mass., 1957.

38. Wenrich of Trier, *Epistola Hilthebrando papae,* cap. 4, quoted in Robinson, "Gregory VII," pp. 173–174.

39. Archbishop Wibert of Ravenna, quoted in Robinson, "Gregory VII," p. 175.

40. *Registrum Gregorii VII,* quoted in Robinson, "Gregory VII," p. 174.

41. *Anonymi Gesta francorum et aliorum Hierosolymitanorum,* ed. and trans. by Rosalind Hill, London, 1962, p. 1 (henceforth, *Gesta*).

42. Ibid., p. 41.

43. *Revelations,* XXI:23.

44. *Revelations,* XXII:2.

45. Fulcher of Chartres, in Peters, *First Crusade,* p. 31.

46. Duby, *Société,* p. 361.

47. Fulcher of Chartres, in Peters, *First Crusade,* pp. 37–38.

48. Robert the Monk, in Peters, *First Crusade,* p. 4.

49. Mayer, *The Crusades,* pp. 40–41.

50. *The Chronicle of Matthew of Edessa,* trans. by A. Dostourian, University Microfilms, 1972, p. 294.

51. Raymond d'Aguilers, *Historia Francorum qui ceperunt Iberusalem,* trans. by John Hugh Hill and Laurita L. Hill, Philadelphia, 1968, pp. 79–80.

52. Alexandre Bruel, ed., *Recueil des chartes de l'abbaye de Cluny,* 6 vols., Paris, 1876–1903, Vol. V, pp. 51–53.

53. C. W. David, *Robert Curthose,* Cambridge, Mass., 1920, pp. 91–92.

54. Duby, *Société,* pp. 496–497.

55. Van Luyn, "Les *milites,*" p. 31.

56. Raymond d'Aguilers, *Historia,* pp. 36–37.

57. Ibid., p. 84.

58. *Gesta,* p. 27.

59. Raymond d'Aguilers, cited in Van Luyn, "Les *milites,*" p. 31.

60. Raymond d'Aguilers, *Historia*, pp. 17–18.

61. *Gesta*, p. 8.

62. Raymond d'Aguilers, *Historia*, p. 113.

63. Fulcher of Chartres, in Peters, *First Crusade*, p. 70.

64. On Crusading tactics and technology: R. C. Smail, *Crusading Warfare 1097–1193*, in *Cambridge Studies in Medieval Life and Thought*, Vol. III, N.S., Cambridge, Eng., 1956. On medieval warfare in general: C. W. Oman, *The Art of War in the Middle Ages* (revised edition), Ithaca, N.Y., 1953; John Beeler, *Warfare in Feudal Europe 730–1200*, Ithaca, N.Y., 1971; Philippe Contamine, *La Guerre au Moyen Age*, Paris, 1980.

65. *Gesta*, pp. 186–187; Raymond d'Aguilers, *Historia*, p. 61.

66. Fulcher of Chartres, in Peters, *First Crusade*, p. 46.

67. Raymond d'Aguilers, *Historia*, p. 35.

68. *Gesta*, p. 2.

69. Fulcher of Chartres, in Peters, *First Crusade*, pp. 54–55.

70. Ibid., p. 69.

71. Raymond d'Aguilers, *Historia*, pp. 118–119.

72. Fulcher of Chartres, in Peters, *First Crusade*, pp. 43–44.

73. *Gesta*, in Peters, *First Crusade*, p. 145.

74. Fulcher of Chartres, in Peters, *First Crusade*, p. 57.

75. *Gesta*, in Peters, *First Crusade*, pp. 164–165.

76. Raymond d'Aguilers, *Historia*, p. 78.

77. Ibid., pp. 124–125.

78. Ibid., p. 127.

79. *Gesta*, pp. 90–91.

80. Raymond d'Aguilers, *Historia*, pp. 127–128; Raymond is paraphrasing *Revelations*, XIV:20.

81. Fulcher of Chartres, in Peters, *First Crusade*, p. 77.

82. William of Tyre, *A History of Deeds Done Beyond the Sea*, trans. by Emily Atwater Babcock and A. C. Krey, 2 vols., New York, 1943, Vol. I, p. 371.

83. Raymond d'Aguilers, *Historia*, p. 128.

84. Ibid., p. 17.

85. Ibid., p. 79.

86. Ibid., p. 85.

87. *Gesta*, p. 15.

88. Ibid., p. 80.

89. Raymond d'Aguilers, *Historia*, p. 39.

90. Fulcher of Chartres, in Peters, *First Crusade*, p. 61.

91. Raymond d'Aguilers, *Historia*, p. 116.

4 / THE TROUBADOURS AND THE LITERATURE OF KNIGHTHOOD

1. *Biographies des Troubadours*, ed. by Jean Boutière and A.-H. Schutz, Toulouse and Paris, 1950, pp. 14–15.

2. Raymond of Durfort, as quoted in L. T. Topsfield, *Troubadours and Love*, Cambridge, Eng., 1976, p. 195.

3. *Les Poésies d'Arnaut Daniel*, ed. by René Lavaud, Toulouse, 1910, p. 28, verse IV, line 49.

4. Ibid., p. 80, verse XII, lines 57–58.

5. *Biographies*, pp. 15–16.

6. Dante, *Purgatorio*, XXVI, line 119. When Dante makes Arnaut speak, he does so in Provençal (lines 140–147). Modern critic and translator James Wilhelm calls Arnaut "a poet's poet."

7. On early medieval poetry: Reto R. Bezzola, *Les Origines et la formation de la littérature courtoise en Occident (500–1200)*, 3 vols., Paris, 1944–1963, Vol. I; Peter Dronke, *The Medieval Lyric*, London, 1968, and *Medieval Latin and the Rise of the European Love Lyric*, Oxford, 1965; Helen Waddell, *Mediaeval Latin Lyrics*, London, 1929.

8. A. Jeanroy, *La Poésie lyrique des troubadours*, 2 vols., Toulouse, 1934, Vol. I, pp. 321–325.

9. *Biographie.*, pp. 210–211.

10. Ibid., p. 23.

11. Ibid., pp. 408–409.

12. Meg Bogin, *The Women Troubadours*, New York, 1976.

13. Topsfield, *Troubadours and Love*, p. 3. General works on troubadour poetry also include: Jeanroy, *La Poésie lyrique des troubadours;* James Wil-

helm, *Seven Troubadours, the Creators of Modern Verse*, University Park, Pa., 1970; Linda M. Paterson, *Troubadours and Eloquence*, Oxford, 1975; Hendrik Van der Werf, *The Chansons of the Troubadours and Trouvères, A Study of the Melodies and Their Relation to the Poems*, Utrecht, 1972. An anthology of troubadour poetry that includes a vocabulary and basic grammar of the *langue d'oc* is: Raymond T. Hill and Thomas G. Bergin, *Anthology of the Provençal Troubadours*, 2 vols., New Haven, Conn., 1973. A small selection of troubadour verse is translated in: Anthony Bonner, *Songs of the Troubadours*, New York, 1972.

14. Christopher Dawson, *Medieval Essays*, New York, 1952, p. 230. See also: Julian Ribera y Tarrago, *Music in Ancient Arabia and Spain*, trans. by Eleanor Hague and Marion Leffingwell, New York, 1970, pp. 113–114; A. R. Nykl, *Hispano-Arabic Poetry and Its Relations with the Old Provençal Troubadours*, Baltimore, 1946; A. J. Denomy, "Concerning the Accessibility of Arabic Influence to the Earliest Provençal Troubadours," *Medieval Studies* 15 (1953), pp. 147–158.

15. Ordericus Vitalis, *The Ecclesiastical History of England and Normandy*, trans. by Marjorie Chibnall, 4 vols., Oxford, 1975, pp. 342–343.

16. *Biographies*, p. 7.

17. William of Malmesbury, *Gesta Regum Anglorum*, V, as translated in Topsfield, *Troubadours*, p. 12.

18. A recent edition of Guillem's work, with English translations, is: *The Poetry of William VII, Count of Poitiers, IX Duke of Aquitaine*, ed. and trans. by Gerald A. Bond, New York, 1982.

19. Ibid., pp. 10–13.

20. Provençal original, ibid., pp. 36–38 (translation by author).

21. Gaston Paris, "Lancelot du Lac: 2, Le conte de la charette," *Romania* 12 (1883), p. 519.

22. Ibid., pp. 459–534.

23. John F. Benton, "Clio and Venus: An Historical View of Medieval Love," in F. X. Newman, ed., *The Meaning of Courtly Love*, Albany, N.Y., 1968, pp. 19–42.

24. Lambert of Ardres, *Historia comitum Ghisnensium*, quoted in Georges Duby, *Medieval Marriage*, trans. by Elborg Forster, Baltimore, 1978, pp. 93–94. (An expanded version of this book has recently been published under the title *The Knight, the Lady, and the Priest*, trans. by Barbara Bray, New York, 1983).

25. Bogin, *The Women Troubadours*, p. 55.

26. Duby, "Youth in Aristocratic Society," in *The Chivalrous Society,* pp. 112–122.

27. *Biographies,* p. 167.

28. Ibid., p. 142.

29. Ibid., p. 231.

30. Ibid., p. 267.

31. Ibid., pp. 149–150.

32. Ibid., p. 199.

33. Ibid., pp. 285–306.

34. Ibid., pp. 530–533.

35. Joan M. Ferrante, *Woman as Image in Medieval Literature from the Twelfth Century to Dante,* New York, 1975.

36. Ezra Pound, *Personae,* New York, 1926, pp. 105–107.

37. Arnaut Daniel's works are available in four editions: U. A. Canello, *La vita e le opere del trovatore Arnaldo Daniello,* Halle, 1883; Lavaud, *Arnaut Daniel;* G. Toja, *Arnaut Daniel, Canzoni,* Florence, 1960; James Wilhelm, ed. and trans., *The Poetry of Arnaut Daniel,* New York, 1981.

38. Wilhelm, *Arnaut Daniel,* pp. 74–77.

39. Ibid., pp. 34–39.

40. Petrarch, *Trionfi,* in *Rime, canzoniere, trionfi, estravaganti,* ed. Attilio Nulli, Milan, 1956, p. 266 ("Triumphus cupidinis," IV, lines 40–43).

41. Provençal text from Lavaud, *Arnaut Daniel,* pp. 58–69; translation from Bonner, *Songs of the Troubadours,* pp. 162–163.

42. Dante, *De vulgari eloquentia,* ed. Pier Vincenzo Mengaldo, Padua, 1968, pp. 43–44 (II vi).

43. Provençal text from Lavaud, *Arnaut Daniel,* pp. 92–96; translation from Ezra Pound, *Translations,* London, 1953, pp. 178–181.

44. Hill and Bergin, *Anthology of the Provençal Troubadours,* Vol. I, p. 34.

45. Provençal text from Wilhelm, *Poetry of Arnaut Daniel,* pp. 2–4; translation from Bonner, *Songs of the Troubadours,* 161–162.

46. Dante, *Purgatorio,* XXVI, line 117.

47. Raimon de Miraval, *Du jeu subtil à l'amour fou,* ed. by René Nelli, Paris, 1979, p. 186.

48. Ronald J. Taylor, *The Art of the Minnesinger*, 2 vols., Cardiff, Wales, 1968; Margaret F. Richey, *Essays on the Medieval German Love Lyric*, Oxford, 1943; Richey, ed., *Selected Poems of Walther von der Vogelweide*, Oxford, 1948; P. B. Salmon, *Literature in Medieval Germany*, London, 1967, pp. 60–114.

49. *Le Chanson de Roland*, ed. by T. Atkinson Jenkins, Boston, 1924, pp. 171–172.

50. An account of the historiography of King Arthur is: Robert H. Fletcher, *The Arthurian Material in the Chronicles, Especially Those of Great Britain and France*, New York, 1965 (reprint of 1905 edition).

51. William of Malmesbury, *Chronicle of the Kings of England*, ed. and trans. by J. A. Giles, New York, 1968 (reprint of 1847 edition).

52. Geoffrey of Monmouth, *The History of the Kings of Britain*, trans. by Lewis Thorpe, Harmondsworth, Eng., 1980 (first published in 1966).

53. Ibid., p. 222.

54. Ibid., p. 229.

55. Ibid., p. 230.

56. *Wace and Layamon, Arthurian Chronicles*, ed. and trans. by Eugene Mason, London, 1962.

57. Ibid., p. 55.

58. Ibid., p. 43.

59. Ibid., p. 264.

60. R. S. Loomis, *Arthurian Literature in the Middle Ages*, Oxford, 1959.

61. R. S. Loomis, *Arthurian Tradition and Chrétien de Troyes*, New York, 1949; Jean Frappier, *Chrétien de Troyes, the Man and His Work*, trans. by Raymond J. Cormier, Athens, Ohio, 1982; Urban Tigner Holmes and Sister M. Amelia Klenke, *Chrétien, Troyes, and the Grail*, Chapel Hill, N.C., 1959; L. T. Topsfield, *Chrétien de Troyes, a Study of the Arthurian Romances*, Cambridge, Eng., 1981; John F. Benton, "The Court of Champagne as a Literary Center," *Speculum* 36 (1961), pp. 560–563, 585–591.

62. Margaret F. Richey, *Studies of Wolfram von Eschenbach, with Translations*, Edinburgh, 1957.

63. H. Oskar Sommer, ed., *The Vulgate Version of the Arthurian Romances, Edited from Manuscripts in the British Museum*, 6 vols., New York, 1969, Vols. II to V, *Lancelot*.

64. Chrétien de Troyes, *Le Roman de Perceval ou le conte du Graal*, ed. by William Roach, Geneva, 1956, pp. 16–17, lines 1725–1766.

65. Ibid., p. 48, lines 2827–2830.

66. Ibid., p. 49, lines 2848–2862.

67. Sommer, ed., *Lancelot*, Vol. III, pp. 113–118.

68. *L'Ordene de chevalerie*, ed. by Roy Temple House, Chicago, 1918.

69. Raymond Lull, *The Book of the Ordre of Chivalry*, ed. by Alfred T. P. Byles, London, 1926.

70. Ruth Huff Cline, "The Influences of Romances on Tournaments of the Middle Ages," *Speculum* 20 (1945), pp. 204–211; R. S. Loomis, "Edward I, Arthurian Enthusiast," *Speculum* 28 (1953); Loomis, "Arthurian Influence on Sport and Spectacle," in *Arthurian Literature in the Middle Ages*, pp. 553–559; Loomis, "Chivalric and Dramatic Imitations of Arthurian Romance," in *Medieval Studies in Memory of A. K. Porter*, Cambridge, Mass., 1939, pp. 79–97.

5 / WILLIAM MARSHAL: KNIGHTHOOD AT ITS ZENITH

1. *L'Histoire de Guillaume Maréchal*, ed. by Paul Meyer, 3 vols., Paris, 1901 (henceforth referred to as *H.G.M.*). Sidney Painter's biography, *William Marshal, Knight-Errant, Baron, and Regent of England*, Baltimore, 1971 (first published in 1933), is based largely on Meyer's edition of *H.G.M.*

2. Painter, *William Marshal*, pp. 3–4.

3. Ibid., pp. 4–10.

4. *H.G.M.*, Vol. I, pp. 15–20, lines 400–538.

5. Ibid., Vol. I, p. 22, lines 592–594.

6. Ibid., Vol. I, pp. 22–24, lines 595–650.

7. Painter, *William Marshal*, pp. 16–17.

8. *H.G.M.*, Vol. I, pp. 26–28, lines 703–749.

9. Ibid., Vol. I, p. 28, lines 750–762.

10. Ibid., Vol. I, p. 30, lines 805–820.

11. *L'Ordene de chevalerie*, pp. 46–50 (lines 110–248).

12. Ibid., Vol. III, pp. xxv–xxviii.

13. *H.G.M.*, Vol. I, p. 31, lines 821–822.

14. Ibid., Vol. I, pp. 31–37, lines 827–1106.

15. Ibid., Vol. I, pp. 42–43, lines 1142–1160.

16. Ibid., Vol. I, pp. 43–44, lines 1179–1200.

17. Ibid., Vol. I, pp. 44–48, lines 1201–1302.

18. On the tournament: Francis Henry Cripps-Day, *The History of the Tournament in England and in France*, London, 1982 (reprint of 1918 edition); R. Coltman Clephan, *The Tournament: Its Periods and Phases*, London, 1919; N. Denholm-Young, "The Tournament in the Thirteenth Century," in *Studies in Mediaeval History Presented to F. M. Powicke*, Oxford, 1948, pp. 240–268.

19. Blair, *European Armour*, pp. 191–192.

20. *H.G.M.*, Vol. I, pp. 48–51, lines 1303–1380.

21. Ibid., Vol. I, pp. 51–55, lines 1381–1503.

22. Ibid., Vol. I, pp. 260–261, lines 7203–7232.

23. Anthony R. Wagner, *Heralds and Heraldry in the Middle Ages, an Inquiry into the Growth of the Armorial Function of Heralds*, Oxford, 1956.

24. Blair, *European Armour*, pp. 29–31.

25. Painter, *William Marshal*, pp. 25–27.

26. *H.G.M.*, Vol. I, pp. 71–72, lines 1939–1948.

27. Ibid., Vol. I, p. 72, lines 1956–1958.

28. W. L. Warren, *Henry II*, Berkeley, Calif., 1973, pp. 580–584; Olin H. Moore, "The Young Henry Plantagenet in History, Literature, and Tradition," *Ohio State University Studies*, Vol. II, No. 12, Columbus, Ohio, 1925.

29. Painter, *William Marshal*, pp. 34–35; *H.G.M.*, Vol. I, p. 86, lines 2035–2142.

30. Painter, *William Marshal*, pp. 35–36; Warren, *Henry II*, pp. 117–139.

31. Painter, *William Marshal*, pp. 36–37.

32. *H.G.M.*, Vol. I, p. 88, lines 2391–2403.

33. Ibid., Vol. I, pp. 90–101, lines 2443–2772.

34. Ibid., Vol. I, pp. 123–125, lines 3381–3424.

35. Ibid., Vol. I, pp. 124–128, lines 3426–3520.

36. Ibid., Vol. I, pp. 141–155, lines 3888–4274.

37. Ibid., Vol. I, pp. 161–173, lines 4457–4796.

38. Ibid., Vol. I, pp. 184–211, lines 5095–5848.

39. Ibid., Vol. I, pp. 214–223, lines 5923–6192.

40. Warren, *Henry II*, pp. 591–593.

41. *H.G.M.*, Vol. I, pp. 235–236, lines 6525–6552.

42. Ibid., Vol. I, pp. 241–247, lines 6677–6864.

43. Ibid., Vol. I, pp. 247–252, lines 6865–6984.

44. Ibid., Vol. I, pp. 258–259, lines 7173–7184.

45. Bertran de Born, *"Planh,"* in *Anthology of the Provençal Troubadours,* Vol. I, pp. 109–110.

46. *H.G.M.,* Vol. I, pp. 262–263, lines 7259–7295.

47. Ibid., Vol. I, p. 263, line 7302.

48. Painter, *William Marshal,* pp. 61–67.

49. *H.G.M.,* Vol. I, p. 344, lines 9537–9550.

50. Painter, *William Marshal,* pp. 77–78.

51. Ibid., pp. 102–104.

52. Ibid., p. 122.

53. Ibid., pp. 180–182.

54. Ibid., pp. 192–227.

55. *H.G.M.,* Vol. II, pp. 300–302, lines 18351–18406.

56. Bosl, " 'Noble Unfreedom,' " pp. 307–311; Freed, "The Origins of the European Nobility," pp. 226–232.

57. Duby, *Société,* pp. 584–590; Duby, "The Transformation of the Aristocracy," in *The Chivalrous Society,* pp. 178–185.

58. Duby, *Société,* pp. 494–497.

59. Ibid., pp. 559–564; Duby, "The Transformation of the Aristocracy," pp. 179–180.

60. Peter Spufford, ed., *Origins of the English Parliament,* New York, 1967, pp. 5–8, 59–63; D. Pasquet, *An Essay on the Origins of the House of Commons,* trans. by R. G. D. Laffan, Exeter, Eng., 1964 (reprint of 1925 edition); Frank M. Stenton, "The Changing Feudalism of the Middle Ages," *History* n.s. 19 (1935), pp. 289–301; N. Denholm-Young, "Feudal Society in the Thirteenth Century: The Knights," *History* n.s. 29 (1944), pp. 107–119; R. F. Treharne, "The Knights in the Period of Reform and Rebellion, 1255–67: A Critical Phase in the Rise of a New Class," *Bulletin of the Institute of Historical Research* 21 (1946), pp. 1–12.

61. Warren, *Henry II,* pp. 352–354.

62. Pasquet, *Origins of the House of Commons,* pp. 13–23.

63. Spufford, *Origins of the English Parliament,* pp. 62–63; Treharne, "The Knights in the Period of Reform," pp. 2–4; N. Denholm-Young, *Seignorial*

Administration in England, London, 1937, pp. 66–85; Helen Cam, *The Hundred and the Hundred Rolls*, London, 1930, pp. 59–67; W. A. Morris, *The Medieval English Sheriff to 1300*, Manchester, Eng., 1927, pp. 167–185.

64. *Chronicon Monasterii de Bello*, London, 1846, p. 108.

65. Joseph R. Strayer, *Feudalism*, Princeton, N.J., 1965, p. 52; Warren, *Henry II*, p. 124.

66. W. Stubbs, ed., *Select Charters*, Oxford, 1921, p. 218.

67. *H.G.M.*, Vol. I, pp. 28–29, lines 761–768.

68. Denholm-Young, "Feudal Society," p. 115.

69. Blair, *European Armour*, p. 29.

70. Philippe Contamine, *La Guerre au moyen âge*, Paris, 1980, p. 199.

71. Denholm-Young, "Feudal Society," p. 117.

72. Harvey, "The Knight and the Knight's Fee in England," pp. 39–41.

73. Denholm-Young, "Feudal Society," p. 113.

74. Duby, *Société*, pp. 627–631; Duby, "The Transformation of the Aristocracy," pp. 182–183; Philippe Contamine, "The French Nobility and the War," in Kenneth Fowler, ed., *The Hundred Years War*, New York, 1971, p. 145.

75. Michael R. Powicke, "Distraint of Knighthood and Military Obligation under Henry III," *Speculum* 25 (1950), pp. 457–470; Powicke, *Military Obligation in Medieval England, a Study in Liberty and Duty*, Oxford, 1962.

76. Duby, *Société*, pp. 631–633; Duby, "The Transformation of the Aristocracy," pp. 182–185; Robert H. Lucas, "Ennoblement in Late Medieval France," *Medieval Studies* 39 (1977), pp. 240–242.

77. Denholm-Young, "Feudal Society," p. 118.

78. Lull, *The Book of the Ordre of Chyvalry*, pp. 77–89.

6 / THE KNIGHTS TEMPLARS: SOLDIERS, DIPLOMATS, BANKERS

1. General works on the Military Orders include: Marion Melville, *La Vie des Templiers*, Paris, 1951; Thomas W. Parker, *The Knights Templars in England*, Tucson, Ariz., 1963; Malcolm Barber, *The Trial of the Templars*, Cambridge, Eng., 1978; Georges Bordonove, *La Vie quotidienne des Templiers au xiii siècle*, Paris, 1975; Edith Simon, *The Piebald Standard: A Biography of the Knights Templars*, London, 1959; Jonathan Riley-Smith, *The Knights of St. John in Jerusalem and Cyprus, c. 1050–1310*, New York, 1967; Joseph O'Callaghan, *The Spanish Military Order of Calatrava and Its Affiliates*, London, 1975; Francis Gutton, *L'Ordre de Santiago*, Paris, 1972; Gutton, *L'Ordre d'Alcan-*

tara, Paris, 1975; Friedrich Benninghoven, *Der Orden der Schwertbrüder: Fratres Milicie Christi de Livonia*, Graz and Köln, 1965; P. Marion Tumler, *Der Deutsche Orden im Werden, Wachsen und Wirken bis 1400*, Vienna, 1955; A. S. Barnes, "The Teutonic Knights and the Kingdom of Prussia," *Dublin Review*, October 1915, pp. 272–283; Indrikis Sterns, "Crime and Punishment among the Teutonic Knights," *Speculum* 57 (1982), pp. 84–111.

2. Bernard of Clairvaux, *De laude novae militiae*, in *Sancti Bernardi opera*, Vol. III, ed. by J. Leclercq and H. M. Rochais, Rome, 1963, pp. 213–239.

3. Henri de Curzon, *La Maison du Temple de Paris*, Paris, 1888.

4. Parker, *The Knights Templars in England*, pp. 24–25.

5. Melville, *La Vie des Templiers*, pp. 69–73.

6. Barber, *Trial of the Templars*, p. 245; Parker, *The Knights Templars in England*, pp. 17, 135–136.

7. Virginia G. Berry, "The Second Crusade," in Setton, ed., *A History of the Crusades*, Vol. I, p. 500.

8. Ibn al-Athir, quoted in Riley-Smith, *The Knights of St. John*, p. 75.

9. Robin R. Fedden and John Thomson, *Crusader Castles*, London, 1957; T. S. R. Boase, "Military Architecture in the Crusader States in Palestine and Syria," in Setton, ed., *A History of the Crusades*, Vol. IV, pp. 140–164; Riley-Smith, *The Knights of St. John*, pp. 134–139; Melville, *La Vie des Templiers*, pp. 158–172.

10. Wilbrand of Oldenburg, quoted in Boase, "Military Architecture," p. 152.

11. Jules Piquet, *Des Banquiers au moyen âge: les Templiers*, Paris, 1939; Leopold Delisle, *Mémoire sur les opérations financières des Templiers*, Paris, 1889.

12. Melville, *La Vie des Templiers*, pp. 87–88.

13. *Matthew Paris's English History from the Year 1234 to 1273 (Chronica Majora)*, trans. by J. A. Giles, 3 vols., London, 1854, Vol. II, pp. 368–369.

14. Francesco Gabrielli, ed., *Arab Historians of the Crusades*, trans. from the Italian by E. J. Costello, Berkeley, Calif., 1969, pp. 79–80.

15. Melville, *La Vie des Templiers*, pp. 117, 147; Riley-Smith, *The Knights of St. John*, pp. 107–108, 155–156.

16. Riley-Smith, *The Knights of St. John*, pp. 236–237.

17. Barber, *Trial of the Templars*, pp. 253–257.

18. Melville, *La Vie des Templiers*, pp. 109–111; Bordonove, *La Vie quotidienne des Templiers*, pp. 79–81.

19. Henri de Curzon, *La Règle du Temple*, Paris, 1886, p. 172.

20. Ibid., p. 114.

21. Ibid., p. 115.

22. *The Exempla of Jacques de Vitry*, ed. Thomas Frederick Crane, London, 1890, LXXXV, pp. 38–39.

23. Curzon, *La Règle du Temple*, p. 171.

24. On the conventual life of the Templars: Melville, *La Vie des Templiers*, pp. 212–221; Bordonove, *La Vie quotidienne des Templiers*, pp. 82–92.

25. Barber, *Trial of the Templars*, p. 255.

26. Curzon, *La Règle du Temple*, p. 114.

27. Ibid., p. 124.

28. Ibid., p. 315.

29. Ibid., p. 329.

30. Ibid., pp. 296–297.

31. Melville, *La Vie des Templiers*, p. 239.

32. Ibid., pp. 288–289.

33. Ibid., pp. 109–111.

34. Riley-Smith, *The Knights of St. John*, p. 323.

35. Melville, *La Vie des Templiers*, pp. 113–115.

36. Ibid., p. 115; Bordonove, *La Vie quotidienne des Templiers*, pp. 170–173.

37. Jean de Joinville, *Vie de St. Louis*, in *Joinville and Villehardouin, Chronicles of the Crusades*, trans. by M. R. B. Shaw, Harmondsworth, Eng., 1963, pp. 308–309.

38. Curzon, *La Règle du Temple*, pp. 125–126.

39. Joinville, *Vie de St. Louis*, p. 211.

40. Ibid., p. 214.

41. *Recueil des historiens des Croisades: Historiens occidentaux*, Vol. II, Paris, 1859, *Continuation de Guillaume de Tyr (MS de Rothelin)*, pp. 604–605.

42. Joinville, *Vie de St. Louis*, pp. 218–219.

43. Ibid., p. 226.

44. Ibid., pp. 231–232.

45. Ibid., p. 236.

46. Ibid., pp. 258–259.

47. Ibid., p. 267.

48. Ibid., pp. 277–278.

49. Ibid., pp. 293–294.

50. Riley-Smith, *The Knights of St. John*, p. 197.

51. Olivier the Templar, quoted in Melville, *La Vie des Templiers*, pp. 260–261.

7 / BERTRAND DU GUESCLIN: A KNIGHT OF THE FOURTEENTH CENTURY

1. Simeon Luce, *Histoire de Bertrand du Guesclin et de son époque, La jeunesse de Bertrand (1320–1364)*, Paris, 1876. Other modern biographers include D. F. Jamison, *Bertrand du Guesclin et son époque*, trans. from the English by J. Baissac, Paris, 1866; Roger Vercel, *Du Guesclin*, trans. as *Bertrand of Brittany*, London, 1934; Rene Maran, *Bertrand du Guesclin, l'epée du roi*, Paris, 1960.

2. On the Hundred Years War in the fourteenth century: Edouard Perroy, *The Hundred Years' War*, trans. by W. B. Wells, London, 1962; K. A. Fowler, ed., *The Hundred Years War*, New York, 1971; A. H. Burne, *The Crécy War*, London, 1955; Philippe Contamine, *Guerre, état, et société à la fin du Moyen Age*, Paris, 1972; Contamine, *La Guerre de Cent Ans*, Paris, 1968.

3. On the French nobility of the fourteenth century: Edouard Perroy, "Social Mobility among the French *Noblesse* in the Later Middle Ages," *Past and Present* 21 (1962), pp. 25–38; Philippe Contamine, "The French Nobility and the War," in Fowler, ed., *The Hundred Years War*; P. S. Lewis, *Later Medieval France, the Polity*, London, 1968.

4. *Chronique de Bertrand du Guesclin, par* [Jean] *Cuvelier, trouvère du XIVe siècle*, ed. by E. Charrière, 2 vols., Paris, 1839, Vol. I, beginning p. 6, line 75, with variants given in footnote.

5. Cuvelier, *Chronique*, Vol. I, pp. 10–13, lines 154–272.

6. *Chronique (anonynyme) de sire Bertrand du Guesclin*, Paris, 1842, p. 2, cited in Jamison, *Du Guesclin*, p. 11.

7. Cuvelier, *Chronique*, Vol. I, pp. 20–24, lines 420–540.

8. Blair, *European Armour*, pp. 38–39, 54–55.

9. Ibid., pp. 40–41, 53.

10. Perroy, *The Hundred Years' War*, pp. 69–76; Perroy considers the quarrel over Aquitaine more substantive than the dynastic question in causing the war.

11. E. Russell, "The Societies of the Bardi and Peruzzi and Their Dealings with Edward III 1327–45," in *Finance and Trade Under Edward III*, ed. G. Unwin, Manchester, Eng., 1918, cited by Joseph and Frances Gies, *Merchants and Moneymen*, New York, 1972, pp. 170–171.

12. Contamine, *La Guerre au Moyen Age*, pp. 416–417.

13. *Chroniques de J[ean] Froissart*, ed. by Simeon Luce, 10 vols., Paris, 1849, cited by Luce, *Du Guesclin*, Vol. III, p. 31.

14. Cuvelier, *Chronique*, Vol. I, p. 28, lines 657–663.

15. Ibid., pp. 29–31, lines 291–771; Jamison, citing the *Chronique (anonyme)*, gives a slightly different version.

16. Cuvelier, *Chronique*, Vol. I, pp. 31–32, lines 789–809.

17. Ibid., pp. 34–40, lines 865–1040.

18. Jamison, *Du Guesclin*, pp. 80–81, citing P. H. Morice, *Histoire écclésiastique et civile de Bretagne*, 2 vols., Paris, 1750, Vol. I, pp. 283–284.

19. For data on pay scales, see Contamine, *Guerre, état, et société*, pp. 95–121, 250. On the indenture system: A. E. Prince, "The Indenture System Under Edward III," in *Historical Essays in Honor of James Tait*, ed. by J. G. Edwards, V. H. Galbraith, and E. F. Jacob, Manchester, Eng., 1933, pp. 283–298; P. S. Lewis, "Decayed and Non-feudalism in Later Medieval France," *Bulletin of the Institute of Historical Research* 37 (1964), pp. 156–184; J. W. Sherborne, "Indentured Retinues and English Expeditions to France, 1369–1380," *English History Review* 79 (1964), pp. 727–730; N. B. Lewis, "The Organization of Indentured Retinues in Fourteenth-Century England," *Transactions of the Royal Historical Society*, 4th Ser., 27 (1945).

20. Cuvelier, *Chronique*, Vol. I, pp. 45–47, lines 1180–1238.

21. Ibid., pp. 82–96, lines 2235–2606.

22. R. Delachenal, *Histoire de Charles V*, 5 vols., Paris, 1916, Vol. II, pp. 113, 294, Vol. I, p. 383; Luce, *Du Guesclin*, pp. 120, 247–248.

23. Cuvelier, *Chronique*, Vol. I, pp. 130–132, lines 3617–3660; Delachenal, *Charles V*, Vol. II, pp. 117–118.

24. Vercel, *Bertrand of Brittany*, p. 89.

25. Ibid., p. 90.

26. Cuvelier, *Chronique*, Vol. I, pp. 121–122, lines 3431–3459. Tiphaine Raguenel's eminence as an astrologer was preserved in the writings of Simon de Phares, court astrologer of Charles VIII a century later, according to E. Charrière (Cuvelier, *Chronique*, Introduction, p. 1v).

27. Delachenal, *Charles V*, Vol. II, p. 353, note 1.

28. *Chronique des quatre premiers Valois, 1327–1343,* ed. by Simeon Luce, Paris, 1862, p. 140.

29. Delachenal, *Charles V,* Vol. III, pp. 359–361; *Chronique des quatre premiers Valois,* p. 138. Jamison, *Du Guesclin,* pp. 163–166, citing Froissart's somewhat different account (Froissart, *Chronique,* Vol. VI, pp. 102–105.)

30. Cuvelier, *Chronique,* Vol. I, pp. 158–182, lines 4292–4905; Delachenal, *Charles V,* Vol. III, pp. 36–44, citing variant Froissart versions and Christine de Pisan, *Livre des faits et bonnes moeurs du sage roy Charles;* Jamison, *Du Guesclin,* pp. 168–180, citing several sources.

31. Froissart, *Chronique,* ed. by Luce, Vol. VI, pp. 157–171.

32. Jamison, *Du Guesclin,* pp. 239–247.

33. Ibid., pp. 246–247.

34. Cuvelier, *Chronique,* Vol. I, p. 265, lines 7303–7321.

35. Vercel, *Bertrand of Brittany,* p. 142.

36. On the changing composition of the companies: Contamine, *Guerre, état, et société,* pp. 12–25. On horse and foot soldiers of this period: Sherborne, "Indentured Retinues."

37. Froissart, Cuvelier, and other sources give varying figures and kinds of coin for Du Guesclin's huge ransom, but 100,000 doubloons of fine gold is specified in Du Guesclin's letter to Charles V: Cuvelier, *Chronique,* Vol. II, p. 402, "Obligation de Du Guesclin envers Charles V."

38. Cuvelier, *Chronique,* Vol. II, p. 12, lines 13645–13648.

39. Ibid., Vol. II, pp. 28–35, lines 14095–14300; Vercel, *Bertrand of Brittany,* p. 183.

40. Delachenal, *Charles V,* Vol. III. 469–492.

41. Cuvelier, *Chronique,* Vol. II, p. 132, lines 17165–17228.

42. Vercel's rendition (p. 196) of a cryptic passage in Cuvelier, *Chronique,* Vol. II, p. 135, lines 17227–17228.

43. Perroy, *The Hundred Years' War,* p. 159.

44. Ibid., pp. 162–163.

45. Christine de Pisan, *Livre des faits,* p. 256, cited in Jamison, *Du Guesclin,* p. 403.

46. Froissart, *Chroniques,* ed. by Luce, Vol. VII, p. 255.

47. Cuvelier, *Chronique,* Vol. II, p. 157, lines 17900–17910.

48. Ibid., Vol. II, p. 136, lines 17257–17267.

49. Jamison, *Du Guesclin*, pp. 409–412; Cuvelier, *Chronique*, Vol. II, pp. 168–178, lines 18130–18505; Froissart, *Chroniques*, ed. by Luce, Vol. VIII, pp. 1–5.

50. Delachenal, *Charles V*, Vol. IV, pp. 416–417.

51. J. C. d'Orronville, *Vie de Louis de Bourbon*, p. 181, cited in Jamison, *Du Guesclin*, p. 429; Cuvelier, *Chronique*, Vol. II, pp. 216–217, lines 19666–19690.

52. Froissart, *Chroniques*, ed. by Luce, Vol. VIII, pp. 33–115.

53. Ibid., Vol. VIII, pp. 161–162.

54. Morice, *Histoire de Bretagne*, Vol. I, p. 374, cited by Jamison, *Du Guesclin*, p. 572, credits Du Guesclin with a son named Michel who served in the war; Du Chastelet, *Preuves de Du Guesclin*, p. 466, also cited by Jamison, gives him, by a Spanish servant woman, two sons who became members of the Castilian nobility.

55. Vercel, *Bertrand of Brittany*, p. 236.

56. Ibid., p. 240.

57. Ibid., pp. 240–241; Cuvelier, Froissart, and Jamison, citing several sources, give variant forms of Du Guesclin's alleged last words.

58. Froissart, *Chroniques*, ed. by Luce, Vol. IX, pp. 232–233; Vercel, *Bertrand of Brittany*, p. 243.

59. Contamine, *Guerre, état, et société*, gives extensive information on pay scales from 1200 to 1500 in Annexe VI, pp. 619–636, and Annexe VII, pp. 637–638.

8 / ENGLISH KNIGHTS OF THE FIFTEENTH CENTURY: SIR JOHN FASTOLF AND THE PASTONS

1. K. B. McFarlane, *The Nobility of Later Medieval England*, Oxford, 1973, p. 45; McFarlane, "The Investment of Sir John Fastolf's Profits of War," *Transactions of the Royal Historical Society*, 5th Ser., 7 (1957), pp. 104, 114. Fastolf's father's will is printed in *Norfolk Archaeology* 4 (1855), pp. 319–320.

2. McFarlane, *Nobility*, p. 83.

3. William Worcester, *Itineraries*, ed. by John H. Harvey, Oxford, 1969, p. 183.

4. Fastolf's will, in *The Paston Letters*, ed. by James Gairdner, 6 vols., New York, 1965, Vol. III, p. 155.

5. McFarlane, *Nobility,* p. 237; McFarlane, "Investment," p. 116; McFarlane, "William Worcester: A Preliminary Survey," in *Studies Presented to Sir Hilary Jenkinson,* ed. by J. Davies, London, 1957, pp. 205, 215; H. S. Bennett, *The Pastons and Their England,* Cambridge, Eng., 1970, p. 111.

6. McFarlane, *Nobility,* pp. 83, 183.

7. Worcester, *Itineraries,* pp. 353–354; McFarlane, *Nobility,* pp. 34–35. On the second phase of the Hundred Years' War: see references in Chapter 7, note 2; also, A. H. Burne, *The Agincourt War,* London, 1956; C. T. Allmand, ed., *Society at War, the Experience of England and France during the Hundred Years War,* New York, 1973; Allmand, ed., *War, Literature, and Politics in the Late Middle Ages,* Liverpool, 1973.

8. See references in Chapter 7, note 19; also, K. B. McFarlane, " 'Bastard Feudalism,' " *Bulletin of the Institute of Historical Research* 20 (1943–1945), pp. 161–180.

9. N. B. Lewis, "An Early Indenture of Military Service, 27 July 1287," *Bulletin of the Institute of Historical Research* 13 (1935–1936), p. 89.

10. M. R. Powicke, "Lancastrian Captains," in *Essays in Medieval History Presented to Bertie Wilkinson,* Toronto, 1969, pp. 373–375.

11. Contamine, *Guerre, état, et société,* pp. 228–230; M. G. A. Vale, "New Techniques and Old Ideals," in Allmand, ed., *War, Literature, and Politics,* pp. 64, 69–70.

12. Denys Hays, "The Division of the Spoils of War in Fourteenth-Century England," *Transactions of the Royal Historical Society* 4 (1954), pp. 91–109.

13. M. M. Postan, "The Costs of the Hundred Years' War," *Past and Present* 27 (1964), p. 44.

14. *Paston Letters,* Vol. III, pp. 185–186.

15. Blair, *European Armour,* pp. 79–86, 182.

16. *Dictionary of National Biography,* Oxford, 1967–1968, Vol. VI, p. 1099.

17. C. A. J. Armstrong, "Sir John Fastolf and the Law of Arms," in Allmand, ed., *War, Literature, and Politics,* pp. 46–56; Benedicta J. H. Rowe, "A Contemporary Account of the Hundred Years' War from 1415 to 1429," *English History Review* 11 (1926), pp. 504–513; *Paston Letters,* Vol. III, pp. 58, 64; Edward Hall, *Chronicle Containing the History of England during the Reign of Henry the Fourth and the Succeeding Monarchs to the End of the Reign of Henry the Eighth,* New York, 1965, pp. 120, 141. Armstrong identifies Fastolf's prize as Passy-en-Valois, but it may have been Pacy-sur-Eure, south of Rouen.

18. McFarlane, "Investment," p. 95.

19. *Paston Letters,* Vol. III, pp. 58–59, 64, 73–74.

20. Joseph Stevenson, ed., *Letters and Papers Illustrative of the Wars of the English in France during the Reign of Henry VI, King of England,* 2 vols., London, 1861, 1864, Vol. II, i, pp. 44–50. An earlier Fastolf indenture, for his appointment as governor of the Bastille, appears in: John Gough Nichols, "An Original Appointment of Sir John Fastolfe to be Keeper of the Bastille of St. Anthony at Paris in 1421," *Archaeologia* 44 (1873), pp. 113–122.

21. Lewis, "Decayed Feudalism," pp. 175–176; McFarlane, *Nobility,* pp. 162–163; Elias Ashmole, *The Institution, Laws and Ceremonies of the Most Noble Order of the Garter,* London, 1971 (facsimile of 1672 edition).

22. McFarlane, "Investment," pp. 95–100.

23. Jules Quicherat, *Procès de condamnation et de réhabilitation de Jeanne d'Arc, dite la Pucelle,* 5 vols., Paris, 1841–1849, Vol. III, p. 212.

24. Ibid., Vol. III, p. 95.

25. Jean Wavrin du Forestal, *Anciennes chroniques d'Angleterre,* ed. by M. Dupont, Paris, 1858, pp. 280–295.

26. Enguerrand de Monstrelet, *Chronique,* 6 vols., ed. by L. Douet d'Arcq, Paris, 1857–1862, Vol. IV, pp. 331–332.

27. *The Dictionary of National Biography* (Vol. VI, 1967–1968, p. 1100) cites John Anstis, the eighteenth-century historian of the Garter and expert on heraldry.

28. McFarlane, "William Worcester," p. 200.

29. L. W. Vernon Harcourt, "The Two Sir John Fastolfs," *Transactions of the Royal Historical Society* 4 (1910), pp. 47–62.

30. Stevenson, *Letters and Papers,* Vol. II, ii, pp. 579–581.

31. Reginald Brill, "The English Preparations Before the Treaty of Arras: A New Interpretation of Sir John Fastolf's Report, September, 1435, *Studies in Medieval and Renaissance History* 7 (1970), pp. 213–247.

32. Desmond Seward, *The Hundred Years War, the English in France, 1337–1453,* New York, 1978, p. 242.

33. *Journal du siège d'Orléans,* in Quicherat, *Procès,* Vol. IV, p. 105.

34. Quicherat, *Procès,* Vol. III, pp. 214–215.

35. *The Tree of Battles of Honoré Bonet,* trans. by G. W. Coopland, Cambridge, Mass., 1949.

36. Ibid., pp. 21–25; N. A. R. Wright, "The *Tree of Battles* of Honoré Bouvet and the Laws of War," in Allmand, ed., *War, Literature, and Politics*, pp. 12–13.

37. McFarlane, "William Worcester," pp. 210–211; McFarlane, "Investment," p. 116; M. H. Keen, "Chivalry, Nobility, and the Man-at-Arms," in Allmand, ed., *War, Literature, and Politics*, pp. 35–36; Keen, *The Laws of War in the Late Middle Ages*, London and Toronto, 1965.

38. Keen, "Chivalry, Nobility, and the Man-at-Arms," pp. 34–36; Wright, "*Tree of Battles*," pp. 12–31.

39. *Tree of Battles*, p. 125.

40. Ibid., p. 153.

41. Ibid., p. 189.

42. Ibid., pp. 120–121.

43. Ibid., pp. 121–122.

44. Ibid., p. 131.

45. Ibid., p. 132.

46. Ibid., p. 131.

47. Ibid., p. 135.

48. McFarlane, *Nobility*, pp. 36, 83–84; McFarlane, "Investment," pp. 101–106.

49. McFarlane, *Nobility*, p. 92; McFarlane, "Investment," pp. 115–116.

50. H. D. Barnes and W. Douglas Simpson, "The Building Accounts of Caister Castle, A.D. 1432–1435," *Norfolk Archaeology* 30 (1952), pp. 178–188.

51. *Paston Letters*, Vol. III, pp. 166–174.

52. Ibid., Vol. II, p. 280.

53. Ibid., Vol. IV, p. 233.

54. McFarlane, "William Worcester," p. 124.

55. Worcester, *Itineraries*, p. 223; *Paston Letters*, Vol. III, p. 157.

56. *Paston Letters*, Vol. II, p. 154.

57. Ibid., Vol. III, p. 15.

58. Ibid., Vol. II, p. 152.

59. Ibid., Vol. II, p. 160.

60. Ibid., Vol. III, p. 89.

61. McFarlane, " 'Bastard Feudalism,' " pp. 167–180; McFarlane, *Nobility*, pp. 102–121.

62. *Paston Letters*, Vol. I, pp. 28–29.

63. Ibid., Vol. II, p. 239.

64. Ibid., Vol. I, pp. 153–154; Vol. II, pp. 113–116.

65. Ibid., Vol. III, pp. 152–157.

66. Ibid., Vol. III, pp. 144–145.

67. Ibid., Vol. IV, pp. 236–245.

68. Ibid., Vol. III, pp. 163–164.

69. Ibid., Vol. III, pp. 134–135, 276–277, 280.

70. Sylvia L. Thrupp, *The Merchant Class of Medieval London, 1300–1500*, Ann Arbor, Mich., 1948, pp. 275–278.

71. *Paston Letters*, Vol. I, pp. 200, 206.

72. Arthur B. Ferguson, *The Indian Summer of English Chivalry: Studies in the Decline and Transformation of Chivalric Idealism*, Durham, N.C., 1960, pp. 11–12, 113–114.

73. *Paston Letters*, Vol. I, pp. 238–239, 268, 307–308.

74. Norman Davis, ed., *The Paston Letters*, 2 vols., Oxford, 1971, Vol. I, pp. lix–lxi.

75. Francis Worship, "An Account of a MS Genealogy of the Paston Family," *Norfolk Archaeology* 4 (1855), pp. 1–55.

76. R. W. Ketton-Cremer, *The Story of the Pastons*, Norwich, Eng., 1953 (guide to a Paston exhibition in Norwich in the coronation year of Elizabeth II).

9 / THE LONG TWILIGHT OF CHIVALRY

1. Sir George Sitwell, "The English Gentleman," *Ancestor* 1 (1902), quoted in A. W. Redd, "Chivalry and the Idea of a Gentleman," in *Chivalry*, ed. by E. Prestage, London, 1928, p. 209.

2. Lyon, *From Fief to Indenture*, pp. 253–269; Contamine, *Guerre, état, et société*, pp. 277–551.

3. Jean de Bueil, *Le Jouvençel*, ed. by C. Favre and L. Lecestre, 2 vols., Paris, 1887, Vol. I, pp. 21–22.

4. Ibid., Vol. I, p. 26.

5. Ibid., Vol. I, p. 14.

6. Ibid., Vol. II, pp. 45–54.

7. Ibid., Vol. II, pp. 95–96.

8. Ibid., Vol. I, pp. 210–211.

9. Ibid., Vol. II, p. 100.

10. Ibid., Vol. II, pp. 20–21.

11. *Les Mémoires de Messire Martin du Bellay*, in *Collection complète des mémoires relatifs à l'histoire de France*, ed. by M. Petitot, Vols. 17–19, Paris, 1821, p. 451. Bayard's sixteenth-century biographer does not repeat the story: Jacques de Mailles, *La Très joyeuse, plaisante, et récréative histoire du gentil seigneur de Bayart, composée par le loyal serviteur*, ed. by M. J. Roman, Paris, 1878.

12. Ferguson, *The Indian Summer of English Chivalry*. See also: Raymond L. Kilgour, *The Decline of Chivalry as Shown in the French Literature of the Late Middle Ages*, Cambridge, Mass., 1937; J. Huizinga, *The Waning of the Middle Ages*, Garden City, N.Y., 1956 (originally published in 1924); Huizinga, "The Political and Military Significance of Chivalric Ideas in the Late Middle Ages," in *Men and Ideas, History, the Middle Ages, the Renaissance*, trans. by James S. Holmes and Hans van Marle, London, 1960, pp. 196–206.

13. Blair, *European Armour*, p. 192.

14. Clephan, *The Tournament*, pp. 78–80.

15. William Caxton, trans., *The Book of the Ordre of Chyvalry*, in Herlihy, *The History of Feudalism*, pp. 343–344.

16. *The Chronicles of Jean Froissart in Lord Berners' Translation*, ed. by Gillian and William Anderson, London, 1963, p. xvii.

17. Cripps-Day, *The History of the Tournament*, pp. 111–113.

18. Clephan, *The Tournament*, pp. 122–123; Cripps-Day, *History of the Tournament*, pp. 121–122.

19. *Queene Elizabethes Achademy*, ed. by F. J. Furnivall, London, 1869.

20. *The Poetical Works of Edmund Spenser*, London, 1932, p. 142 (Book III, Canto 1, Stanza 13).

21. Ludovico Ariosto, *Orlando Furioso*, trans. by William Stewart Rose, Indianapolis, 1968, p. 95 (Canto XI, Stanzas LXIV–LXXVII).

22. George Fenwick Jones, "The Tournaments of Tottenham and Lappenhausen," *Proceedings of the Modern Language Association* 46 (1951), pp. 1123–1140.

23. Roger Ascham, *The Scholemaster,* in *English Works of Roger Ascham,* ed. by W. A. Wright, Cambridge, 1904, pp. 230–231.

24. Miguel de Cervantes, *Don Quixote de la Mancha,* trans. by Walter Starkie, London, 1957, pp. 1045, 1048, 1050.

25. Lionel Gossman, *Medievalism and the Ideologies of the Enlightenment, the World and Work of La Curne de Sainte-Palaye,* Baltimore, 1968.

26. Mark Girouard, *The Return to Camelot, Chivalry and the English Gentleman,* New Haven, Conn., 1981.

27. Sir Walter Scott, "Chivalry," *Encyclopaedia Britannica,* 1823 Supplement, Vol. III.

28. "Guinevere," in *The Idylls of the King, The Works of Tennyson,* New York, 1918, p. 454.

29. "Gareth and Lynette," *The Idylls of the King, The Works of Tennyson,* p. 313.

30. Ian Anstruther, *The Knight and the Umbrella, An Account of the Eglinton Tournament,* 1839, London, 1959.

31. Edward FitzGerald, "Euphranor, a Dialogue on Youth," (1851), in *The Variorum and Definitive Edition of the Poetical and Prose Writings of Edward FitzGerald,* ed. by George Bentham, 7 vols., New York, 1967, Vol. I, p. 147.

32. William Cory, *Extracts from the Letters and Journal,* ed. by Francis Warre Cornish, London, 1897, pp. 459–460.

BIBLIOGRAPHY

Ackerman, Robert W., "The Knighting Ceremonies in the Middle English Romances," *Speculum* 19 (1944).

Allmand, C. T., ed., *Society at War, the Experience of England and France During the Hundred Years War*, New York, 1973.

———, *War, Literature, and Politics in the Late Middle Ages*, Liverpool, 1976.

Andraud, Paul, *La Vie et l'oeuvre du troubadour Raimon de Miraval*, Paris, 1902.

Anonymi gesta Francorum et aliorum Hierosolymitanorum, trans. and ed. by Rosalind Hill, London, 1962.

Anstruther, Ian, *The Knight and the Umbrella, an Account of the Eglinton Tournament, 1839*, London, 1959.

Ariosto, Ludovico, *Orlando Furioso*, trans. by William Stewart Rose, ed. by Stewart A. Baker and A. Bartlett Giamatti, Indianapolis, 1968.

Armstrong, C. A. J., "Sir John Fastolf and the Law of Arms," in Allmand, ed., *War, Literature, and Politics.*

Ascham, Roger, *The Scholemaster*, in *English Works of Roger Ascham*, ed. by W. A. Wright, Cambridge, Eng., 1904.

Ashmole, Elias, *The Institution, Laws, and Ceremonies of the Most Noble Order of the Garter*, London, 1971 (facsimile of 1672 edition).

Bachrach, Bernard S., "Charles Martel, Mounted Shock Combat, the Stirrup and Feudal Origins," *Studies in Medieval and Renaissance History* 7 (1970).

———, *Merovingian Military Organization, 481–751*, Minneapolis, 1972.

———, "Military Organization in Aquitaine under the Early Carolingians," *Speculum* 49 (January 1974).

Barber, Malcolm, *The Trial of the Templars*, Cambridge, Eng., 1978.

Barber, Richard, *The Knight and Chivalry*, London, 1970.

Baret, Eugene, *Les Troubadours et leur influence sur la littérature du Midi de l'Europe*, Geneva, 1969.

Barnes, A. S., "The Teutonic Knights and the Kingdom of Prussia," *Dublin Review*, October 1915.

Barnes, H. D., and Simpson, W. Douglas, "The Building Accounts of Caister Castle, A.D. 1432–1435," *Norfolk Archaeology* 30 (1952).

Battaglia, Otto Forst de, "The Nobility in the European Middle Ages," *Comparative Studies in Society and History* 5 (1962–1963).

Beeler, John, *Warfare in Feudal Europe 730–1200*, Ithaca, N.Y., 1971.

Bennett, H. S., *The Pastons and Their England*, Cambridge, 1922.

Benninghoven, Friedrich, *Der Orden der Schwertbrüder: Fratres Milicie Christi de Livonia*, Graz and Köln, 1965.

Benton, John F., "The Court of Champagne as a Literary Center," *Speculum* 36 (1961).

Bezzola, Reto R., *Les Origines et la formation de la littérature courtoise en Occident (500–1200)*, 3 vols., Paris, 1944–1963.

Billet, Leon, *Bernard de Ventadour, troubadour du XIIe siècle, promoteur de l'amour courtois, sa vie, ses chansons d'amour*, Tulle, 1974.

Bivar, A. D. H., "Cavalry Equipment and Tactics on the Euphrates Frontier," *Dumbarton Oaks Papers* 26 (1972).

———, "The Stirrup and Its Origins," *Oriental Art* N.S. 1 (1955).

Blair, Claude, *European Armour circa 1066 to circa 1700*, Batsford, Eng., 1958.

Bloch, Marc, *Feudal Society*, trans. by L. A. Manyon, 2 vols., Chicago, 1961.

Bogin, Meg, *The Women Troubadours*, New York, 1976.

Bonenfant, P., and Despy, G., "La Noblesse en Brabant aux XIIe et XIIIe siècles," *Le Moyen Age* 64 (1958).

Bonet, Honoré, *The Tree of Battles*, trans. by G. W. Coopland, Cambridge, Mass., 1949.

Bonnaud-Delamare, R., "Fondement des institutions de paix au XIe siècle," in *Mélanges d'histoire du moyen âge dédiés à la mémoire de Louis Halphen*, Paris, 1951.

———, "Les institutions de paix en Aquitaine au XIe siècle," *Recueils de la société Jean Bodin*, 14 (1961).

Bonner, Anthony, ed. and trans., *Songs of the Troubadours*, New York, 1972.

Bordonove, Georges, *La Vie quotidienne des Templiers au XIIIe siècle*, Paris, 1975.

Borst, Arno, "Rittertum im Hochmittelalter: Idee und Wirklichkeit," *Saeculum* 10 (1959).

Bosl, Karl, " 'Noble Unfreedom.' The Rise of the *Ministeriales* in Germany," in *The Medieval Nobility*, ed. and trans. by Timothy Reuter, Amsterdam, 1978.

Bouchard, Constance B., "The Origins of the French Nobility: A Reassessment," *American Historical Review* 86, No. 3 (June 1981).

———, "The Structure of a Twelfth-Century French Family: The Lords of Seignelay," *Viator* 10 (1979).

Boussard, J., "Les mercenaires au XIIe siècle. Henry II Plantagenet et les origines de l'armée de métier," *Bibliothèque de l'École des Chartes*, 1945–1946.

Boutière, Jean, and Schutz, A.-H., *Biographies des troubadours, textes provençaux des XIIIe et XIVe siècles*, Toulouse and Paris, 1950.

Brill, Reginald, "The English Preparation before the Treaty of Arras: A New Interpretation of Sir John Fastolf's 'Report,' September, 1435," *Studies in Medieval and Renaissance History* 7 (1970).

Bruel, Alexandre, *Recueil des chartes de l'abbaye de Cluny*, 6 vols., Paris, 1876–1903.

Brundage, J. A., "The Army of the First Crusade and the Crusade Vow," *Medieval Studies* 33 (1971).

——, "The Votive Obligation of the Crusader: The Development of a Canonistic Doctrine," *Traditio* 24 (1968).

Bueil, Jean de, *Le Jouvençel*, ed. by C. Favre and L. Lecestre, 2 vols., Paris, 1887.

Bullough, D. A., "Early Medieval Social Groupings: The Terminology of Kinship," *Past and Present* 45 (1969).

Bumke, Joachim, *The Concept of Knighthood in the Middle Ages*, trans. by W. T. H. Jackson and Erika Jackson, New York, 1982.

Cam, H. M., *The Hundred and the Hundred Rolls*, London, 1930.

Canello, Ugo A., *La vita e le opere del trovatore Arnaldo Daniello*, Halle, 1883.

Carcopino, Jérôme, *Daily Life in Ancient Rome*, New York, 1971.

Cervantes, Miguel de, *Don Quixote of La Mancha*, trans. by Walter Starkie, New York, 1979.

Chrétien de Troyes, *Lancelot or the Knight of the Cart*, ed. and trans. by William W. Kibler, New York, 1981.

——, *Le Roman de Perceval ou le conte du Graal*, ed. by William Roach, Geneva, 1956.

The Chronicle of Jean Froissart in Lord Berners' Translation, ed. by Gillian and William Anderson, London, 1963.

The Chronicle of Matthew of Edessa, trans. by A. Dostourian, University Microfilms, 1972.

Chronicon Monasterii de Bello, ed. by J. S. Brewer, London, 1846.

Chronique de Bertrand du Guesclin par J[ean] Cuvelier, trouvère du XIVe siècle, ed. by E. Charrière, 2 vols., Paris, 1839.

Clephan, R. Coltman, *The Tournament: Its Periods and Phases*, London, 1919.

Cline, Ruth Huff, "The Influence of Romances on Tournaments of the Middle Ages," *Speculum* 20 (1945).

Contamine, Philippe, "The French Nobility and the War," in *The Hundred Years War*, ed. by K. Fowler, London, 1971.

——, *La Guerre au moyen age*, Paris, 1980.

——, *La Guerre de Cent Ans*, Paris, 1968.

——, *Guerre, état, et société à la fin du moyen âge*, Paris, 1972.

Cory, William, *Extracts from the Letters and Journal*, ed. by Francis Warre Cornish, Oxford, 1897.

Cowdrey, H. E. J., "The Genesis of the Crusades," in Thomas Patrick Murphy, ed., *The Holy War*, Columbus, Ohio, 1974.

————, "The Peace and the Truce of God in the Eleventh Century," *Past and Present* 46 (1970).

Cripps-Day, Francis Henry, *The History of the Tournament in England and in France*, London, 1982 (reprint of 1918 edition).

Curzon, Henri de, *La Maison du Temple de Paris*, 1888.

————, *La Règle du Temple*, Paris, 1886.

Dante, *De vulgari eloquentia*, ed. by Pier Vincenzo Mengaldo, Padua, 1968.

David, C. W., *Robert Curthose*, Cambridge, Mass., 1920.

Dawson, Christopher, *Medieval Essays*, New York, 1959.

Delachenal, R., *Histoire de Charles V*, 5 vols., Paris, 1916.

Denholm-Young, N., "Feudal Society in the Thirteenth Century: The Knights," *History* 29 (1944).

————, "The Tournament in the Thirteenth Century," in *Studies in Mediaeval History Presented to F. M. Powicke*, Oxford, 1948.

————, *Seignorial Administration in England*, London, 1937.

Denomy, A. J., "Concerning the Accessibility of Arabic Influences to the Earliest Provençal Troubadours," *Medieval Studies* 15 (1953).

————, "Courtly Love and Courtliness," *Speculum* 28 (1953).

Dillon, Viscount, "On a MS Collection of Ordinances of Chivalry of the Fifteenth Century," *Archaeologia* 57 (1900).

Douglas, David C., *William the Conqueror*, Berkeley, Calif., 1967.

Dronke, Peter, *Medieval Latin and the Rise of the European Love Lyric*, Oxford, 1965.

————, *The Medieval Lyric*, London, 1968.

Du Bellay, Martin, *Les Mémoires de Messire Martin du Bellay*, in *Collection complète des mémoires relatifs à l'histoire de France*, ed. by M. Petitot, Vols. 17–19, Paris, 1821.

Duby, Georges, *The Chivalrous Society*, trans. by Cynthia Poston, Berkeley, Calif., 1977.

————, *The Knight, the Lady, and the Priest*, trans. by Barbara Bray, New York, 1983.

————, *Medieval Marriage*, trans. by Elborg Forster, Baltimore, 1978.

————, *La Société aux XIe et XIIe siècles dans la région mâconnaise*, Paris, 1955.

Edelman, Nathan, *Attitudes of Seventeenth-Century France Toward the Middle Ages*, New York, 1946.

Erdmann, Carl, *The Origin of the Idea of Crusade*, trans. by Marshall W. Baldwin and Walter Goffart, Princeton, 1982.

The Exempla of Jacques de Vitry, ed. by Thomas Frederick Crane, London, 1890.

Fedden, Robin R., and Thomson, John, *Crusader Castles*, London, 1957.

Ferguson, Arthur B., *The Indian Summer of English Chivalry: Studies in the Decline and Transformation of Chivalric Idealism*, Durham, N.C., 1960.

Ferrante, Joan M., *Woman as Image in Medieval Literature from the Twelfth Century to Dante*, New York, 1975.

Fletcher, Robert Huntington, *The Arthurian Material in the Chronicles, Especially Those of Great Britain and France*, New York, 1965 (reprint of 1905 edition).

Forquet, J., "La chanson chevaleresque allemande avant les influences provençales," in *Mélanges de linguistique romane et de philologie médiévale offerts à M. Maurice Delbouille*, Gembloux, Belgium, 1964.

Fowler, K. A., ed., *The Hundred Years War*, New York, 1971.

Frank, I., "Du role des troubadours dans la formation de la poésie lyrique moderne," in *Mélanges de linguistique et de littérature romanes offerts à Mario Roques*, 3 vols., Paris, 1950–1953.

Frappier, Jean, *Chrétien de Troyes: The Man and His Work*, trans. by Raymond J. Cormier, Athens, Ohio, 1982.

Freed, John B., "The Origins of the European Nobility: The Problem of the Ministerials," *Viator* 7 (1976).

Froissart, Jean, *Chroniques de J[ean] Froissart*, ed. by Simeon Luce, 10 vols., Paris, 1849.

Gabrielli, Francesco, *Arab Historians of the Crusades*, trans. from the Italian by E. J. Costello, Berkeley, Calif., 1969.

Ganshof, F. L., *Feudalism*, trans. by Philip Grierson, New York, 1961.

Génicot, Leopold, "La Noblesse au moyen âge, dans l'ancienne 'Francie,' " *Annales, Economies, Sociétés, Civilisations* 17 (1961).

———, "La Noblesse au moyen age dans l'ancienne 'Francie': Continuité, rupture ou évolution?" *Comparative Studies in Society and History* 5 (1962–1963).

———, "La noblesse dans la société médiévale," *Le Moyen Age* 71 (1965).

———, "Noblesse, ministérialité et chevalerie en Gueldre et Zutphen," *Le Moyen Age* 71 (1965).

———, "Recent Research on the Medieval Nobility," in *The Medieval Nobility*, trans. and ed. by Timothy Reuter, Amsterdam, 1978.

Geoffrey of Monmouth, *The History of the Kings of Britain*, trans. by Lewis Thorpe, Harmondsworth, Eng., 1966.

Gibb, H. A. R., *Damascus Chronicle of the Crusades*, London, 1932.

Girouard, Mark, *The Return to Camelot, Chivalry and the English Gentleman*, New Haven, Conn., 1981.

Gossman, Lionel, *Medievalism and the Ideologies of the Enlightenment, the World and Work of La Curne de Sainte-Palaye*, Baltimore, 1968.

Gotein, S. D., "Contemporary Letters on the Capture of Jerusalem by the Crusaders," *Journal of Jewish Studies* 3 (1952).

Grant, Michael, *The Army of the Caesars*, London, 1974.

———, *The World of Rome*, New York, 1960.

Gutton, Francis, *L'Ordre d'Alcantara*, Paris, 1975.

———, *L'Ordre de Santiago*, Paris, 1972.

Hall, Edward, *Chronicle Containing the History of England during the Reign of Henry the Fourth and the Succeeding Monarchs to the End of the Reign of Henry the Eighth*, New York, 1965.

Harcourt, L. W. Vernon, "The Two Sir John Fastolfs," *Transactions of the Royal Historical Society*, 3rd Ser., Vol. IV (1910).

Harvey, Sally, "The Knight and the Knight's Fee in England," *Past and Present* 49 (1970).

Hatto, A. T., "Archery and Chivalry: A Noble Prejudice," *Modern Language Review* 35 (1940).

Hay, Denys, "The Division of the Spoils of War in Fourteenth-Century England," *Transactions of the Royal Historical Society* 4 (1954).

Herlihy, David, "The Agrarian Revolution in Southern France and Italy," *Speculum* 33 (1958).

———, ed., *The History of Feudalism*, New York, 1970.

Hill, Raymond T., and Bergin, T. G., *Anthology of the Provençal Troubadours*, 2 vols., New Haven, Conn., 1973.

L'Histoire de Guillaume Maréchal, ed. by Paul Meyer, 3 vols., Paris, 1901.

Holmes, Urban Tigner, and Klenke, Sister M. Amelia, *Chrétien, Troyes and the Grail*, Chapel Hill, N.C., 1959.

Holt, J. C., "Feudalism Revisited," *Economic History Review*, 2nd Ser., 14 (1961–1962).

Huizinga, Johan, *Men and Ideas, History, the Middle Ages, the Renaissance*, trans. by James S. Holmes and Hans van Marle, London, 1960.

———, *The Waning of the Middle Ages*, Garden City, 1956 (first published in 1924).

Irsigler, Franz, "On the Aristocratic Character of Early Frankish Society," in *The Medieval Nobility*, ed. and trans. by Timothy Reuter, Amsterdam, 1978.

Jamison, D. F., *Bertrand du Guesclin et son époque*, trans. from the English by J. Baissac, Paris, 1866.

Jeanroy, A., *La Poésie lyrique des troubadours*, 2 vols., Toulouse, 1934.

Joinville, Jean de, *Vie de St. Louis*, in *Joinville and Villehardouin, Chronicles of the Crusades*, trans. by M. R. B. Shaw, Baltimore, 1963.

Jones, George Fenwick, "The Tournaments of Tottenham and Lappenhausen," *Publications of the Modern Language Association* 66 (1951).

Jordan, William Chester, *Louis IX and the Challenge of the Crusade*, Princeton, N.J., 1982.

Keen, Maurice H., "Brotherhood in Arms," *History* 47 (1962).

———, *Chivalry*, New Haven, Conn., 1984.

———, "Chivalry, Nobility, and the Man at Arms," in C. T. Allmand, ed., *War, Literature, and Politics in the Late Middle Ages*, Liverpool, 1976.

———, *The Laws of War in the Late Middle Ages*, London and Toronto, 1965.

Kilgour, Raymond L., *The Decline of Chivalry as Shown in the French Literature of the Late Middle Ages*, Cambridge, Mass., 1937.

Krey, A. C., *The First Crusade: The Accounts of Eye-Witnesses and Participants*, Princeton, 1921.

Lavaud, René, *Les Poésies d'Arnaut Daniel*, Toulouse, 1910.

Lazar, Moshe, *Bernard de Ventadour, troubadour du XIIe siècle: chansons d'amour*, Paris, 1966.

Lefebvre des Nouettes, Richard, *L'Attelage, le cheval de selle à travers les âges*, Paris, 1931.

Lewis, N. B., "The Organization of Indentured Retinues in Fourteenth-Century England," *Transactions of the Royal Historical Society*, 4th Ser., 27 (1945).

Lewis, P. S., "Decayed and Non-Feudalism in Later Medieval France," *Bulletin of the Institute of Historical Research* 37 (1964).

——, *Later Medieval France: The Polity*, London, 1968.

Loomis, Roger Sherman, ed., *Arthurian Literature in the Middle Ages*, Oxford, 1959.

——, *Arthurian Tradition and Chrétien de Troyes*, New York, 1949.

——, "Chivalric and Dramatic Imitations of Arthurian Romance," in *Medieval Studies in Memory of A. K. Porter*, Cambridge, Mass., 1939.

——, "Edward I, Arthurian Enthusiast," *Speculum* 28 (1953).

Lucas, Robert H., "Ennoblement in Late Medieval France," *Medieval Studies* 39 (1977).

Luce, Simeon, *Histoire de Bertrand du Guesclin et de son époque, La Jeunesse de Bertrand (1320–1364)*, Paris, 1876.

Lull, Raymond, *The Book of the Ordre of Chyvalry*, ed. by Alfred T. P. Byles, London, 1926.

Lyon, Bruce D., *From Fief to Indenture, the Transition from Feudal to Non-Feudal Contract in Western Europe*, Cambridge, Mass., 1957.

McFarlane, K. B., "Bastard Feudalism," *Bulletin of the Institute of Historical Research* 20 (1943–1945).

——, "A Business Partnership in War and Administration, 1421–1445," *English History Review* 78 (1963).

——, "The Investment of Sir John Fastolf's Profits of War," *Transactions of the Royal Historical Society*, 5th Ser., 7 (1957).

——, *The Nobility of Later Medieval England*, Oxford, 1973.

——, "William Worcester: A Preliminary Survey," in *Studies Presented to Sir Hilary Jenkinson*, ed. by J. Davies, London, 1957.

McKisack, May, *The Fourteenth Century*, Oxford, 1959.

Mailles, Jacques de, *La Très joyeuse, plaisante, et récréative histoire du gentil seigneur de Bayart composée par le loyal serviteur*, ed. by M. J. Roman, Paris, 1878.

Mansi, G. D., *Sacrorum conciliorum nova et amplissima collectio*, Florence, 1759–1798.

Maran, René, *Bertrand du Guesclin, l'épée du roi*, Paris, 1960.

Martindale, Jane, "The French Aristocracy in the Early Middle Ages: A Reappraisal," *Past and Present* 75 (1977).

Mathew, Gervase, "Ideals of Knighthood in Late Fourteenth-Century England," in *Studies in Medieval History Presented to Frederick Maurice Powicke*, ed. by R. W. Hunt, W. A. Pantin, and R. W. Southern, Oxford, 1948.

Mayer, Hans Eberhard, *The Crusades*, translated by John Gillingham, Oxford, 1972.

Melville, Marion, *La Vie des Templiers*, Paris, 1951.

Miko, Stephen J., "Malory and the Chivalric Order," *Medium Aevum* 25 (1966).

Miller, Timothy S., "The Knights of Saint John and the Hospital of the Latin West," *Speculum* 53 (1978).

Monstrelet, Enguerrand de, *Chronique*, 6 vols., ed. by L. Douet d'Arcq, Paris, 1857–1862.

Moore, John C., *Love in Twelfth-Century France*, Philadelphia, 1972.

Moore, Olin H., "The Young King, Henry Plantagenet, 1155–1183, in History, Literature, and Tradition," *Ohio State University Studies*, Vol. II, No. 12 (1925).

Moorman, Charles, "The First Knights," *Southern Quarterly* 1 (1962).

Morris, W. A., *The Medieval English Sheriff to 1300*, Manchester, Eng., 1927.

Munro, Dana C., *Letters of the Crusaders, University of Pennsylvania Translations and Reprints from the Original Sources of European History*, Vol. I, No. 4, Philadelphia, 1896.

———, *Urban and the Crusaders, University of Pennsylvania Translations and Reprints from the Original Sources of European History*, Vol. I, No. 2, Philadelphia, 1895.

Newman, F. X., ed., *The Meaning of Courtly Love*, papers of the first annual conference of the Center for Medieval and Early Renaissance Studies, State University of New York at Binghamton, Albany, N.Y., 1968.

Nichols, John Gough, "An Original Appointment of Sir John Fastolfe to be Keeper of the Bastille of St. Anthony at Paris in 1421," *Archaeologia* 44 (1873).

Nykl, A. R., *Hispano-Arabic Poetry and Its Relations with the Old Provençal Troubadours*, Baltimore, 1946.

O'Callaghan, Joseph, *The Spanish Military Order of Calatrava and Its Affiliates*, London, 1975.

Ogg, F. A., *A Source Book for Medieval History*, New York, 1907.

Oman, C. W., *The Art of War in the Middle Ages* (revised edition), Ithaca, N.Y., 1953.

O'Neil, Bryan Hugh St.-John, *Castles and Cannon*, Oxford, 1960.

L'Ordene de chevalerie, ed. by Roy Temple House, Chicago, 1918.

Ordericus Vitalis, *The Ecclesiastical History of England and Normandy,* trans. by Marjorie Chibnall, 6 vols., Oxford, 1975.

Painter, Sidney, "Castle Guard," *American Historical Review* 40 (1935).

———, *French Chivalry, Chivalric Ideas and Practices in Mediaeval France,* Ithaca, N.Y., 1940.

———, "The Ideas of Chivalry," *Johns Hopkins Alumni Magazine* 23 (1935).

———, *William Marshal, Knight-Errant, Baron, and Regent of England,* Baltimore, 1933.

Paris, Gaston, "Lancelot du Lac: 2, Le conte de la charette," *Romania* 12 (1883).

Paris, Matthew, *English History from the Year 1235 to 1273 (Chronica Majora),* trans. by J. A. Giles, 3 vols., London, 1854.

Parker, Thomas W., *The Knights Templars in England,* Tucson, Ariz., 1963.

Pasquet, D., *An Essay on the Origin of the House of Commons,* trans. by R. G. D. Laffan, Cambridge, Eng., 1925 (reprinted 1964, Exeter, Eng.).

The Paston Letters, ed. by James Gairdner, 6 vols., New York, 1965.

The Paston Letters, ed. by Norman Davis, 2 vols., Oxford, 1971.

Paterson, Linda M., *Troubadours and Eloquence,* Oxford, 1975.

Payen, Jean-Charles, "La crise du mariage à la fin du XIIIe siècle d'après la littérature française du temps," in *Famille et parenté dans l'Occident médiéval,* Rome, 1977.

Perroy, Edouard, *La Féodalité en France du X. au XII. siècle,* Paris, 1956.

———, "Gras profits et rançons pendant la Guerre de Cent Ans: L'Affaire du Comte de Denia," in *Mélanges d'histoire du moyen âge dédiés à la mémoire de Louis Halphen,* Paris, 1951.

———, *The Hundred Years' War,* trans. by W. B. Wells, London, 1951.

———, "Social Mobility among the French *Noblesse* in the Later Middle Ages," *Past and Present* 21 (1962).

Peters, Edward, ed., *The First Crusade: The Chronicle of Fulcher of Chartres and Other Source Materials,* Philadelphia, 1971.

Petrarch, *Rime, canzoniere, trionfi, estravaganti,* ed. by Attilio Nulli, Milan, 1956.

Piquet, Jules, *Des Banquiers au moyen âge: les Templiers,* Paris, 1939.

The Poetry of Arnaut Daniel, ed. and trans. by James J. Wilhelm, New York, 1981.

The Poetry of William VII, Count of Poitiers, IX Duke of Aquitaine, ed. and trans. by Gerald A. Bond, New York, 1982.

Postan, M. M., "The Costs of the Hundred Years' War," *Past and Present* 27 (1964).

Pound, Ezra, *Personae,* New York, 1926.

———, *Translations,* London, 1953.

Poupardin, René, "Les Grandes familles comtales à l'époque Carolingienne," *Revue Historique* 72 (1900).

Powicke, F. M., "Distraint of Knighthood and Military Obligation under Henry III," *Speculum* 25 (1950).

Powicke, Michael R., "The English Aristocracy and the War," in Fowler, ed., *The Hundred Years War*, New York, 1971.

———, "Lancastrian Captains," in *Essays in Medieval History Presented to Bertie Wilkinson*, Toronto, 1969.

———, *Military Obligation in Medieval England: A Study in Liberty and Duty*, Oxford, 1962.

Prestage, E., ed., *Chivalry*, London, 1928.

Prestwich, J. O., "War and Finance in the Anglo-Norman State," *Transactions of the Royal Historical Society* V, 4 (1954).

Prince, A. E., "The Indenture System under Edward III," in *Historical Essays in Honour of James Tait*, ed. by J. G. Edwards, V. H. Galbraith, and E. F. Jacob, Manchester, Eng., 1933.

Queene Elizabethes Achademy, ed. by T. J. Furnivall, London, 1869.

Quicherat, Jules, *Procès de condamnation et de réhabilitation de Jeanne d'Arc, dite la Pucelle*, 5 vols., Paris, 1841–1849.

Raymond d'Aguilers, *Historia Francorum qui ceperunt Iberusalem*, trans. by John Hugh Hill and Laurita L. Hill, Philadelphia, 1968.

Recueil des historiens des croisades, Historiens occidentaux, 5 vols., Paris, 1844–1895.

Reed, A. W., "Chivalry and the Idea of a Gentleman," in Prestage, ed., *Chivalry*, London, 1928.

Reuter, Timothy, ed. and trans., *The Medieval Nobility: Studies on the Ruling Classes of France and Germany from the Sixth to the Twelfth Century*, Amsterdam, 1978.

Ribera y Tarrago, Julian, *Music in Ancient Arabia and Spain*, trans. by Eleanor Hague and Marion Leffingwell, New York, 1970.

Richey, Margaret F., *Essays on the Medieval German Love Lyric*, Oxford, 1943.

———, *Selected Poems of Walther von der Vogelweide*, Oxford, 1948.

———, *Studies of Wolfram von Eschenbach, with Translations*, Edinburgh, 1957.

Riley-Smith, Jonathan, *The Knights of St. John in Jerusalem and Cyprus, c. 1050–1310*, New York, 1967.

———, *What Were the Crusades?* Totowa, N.J., 1977.

Robinson, I. S., "Gregory VII and the Soldiers of Christ," *History* 58 (1973).

Rosenthal, Joel T., *Nobles and the Noble Life, 1295–1500*, New York, 1976.

Rowe, Benedicta J. H., "A Contemporary Account of the Hundred Years War from 1415 to 1429," *English History Review* 41 (1926).

Runciman, Steven, *A History of the Crusades*, 3 vols., Cambridge, 1951–1954.

Salmon, P. B., *Literature in Medieval Germany*, London, 1967.

Sancti Bernardi opera, ed. by J. Leclercq and H. M. Rochais, Rome, 1963.

Sawyer, P., and Hilton, R., "Technical Determinism: The Stirrup and the Plough," review of Lynn White, Jr., *Medieval Technology and Social Change, Past and Present* 24 (1963).

Schmid, Karl, "The Structure of the Nobility in the Earlier Middle Ages," in Reuter, ed., *The Medieval Nobility*, Amsterdam, 1978.

Schofield, William Henry, *Chivalry in English Literature: Chaucer, Malory, Spenser and Shakespeare*, Cambridge, Mass., and London, 1912.

Scott, Walter, "Chivalry," *Encyclopaedia Britannica*, 1823 Supplement, Vol. III.

Setton, Kenneth M., ed., *A History of the Crusades*, 4 vols., Madison, Wis., 1955–1977.

Shellabarger, Samuel, *The Chevalier Bayard, a Study in Fading Chivalry*, New York, 1971.

Sherborne, J. W., "Indentured Retinues and English Expeditions to France," *English History Review* 79 (1964).

Sitwell, Sir George, "The English Gentleman," *Ancestor* 1 (1902).

Smail, Richard C., *Crusading Warfare 1097–1192*, Cambridge Studies in Medieval Life and Thought, Vol. III N.S., Cambridge, 1956.

Sommer, H. Oskar, ed., *The Vulgate Version of the Arthurian Romances, Edited from Manuscripts in the British Museum*, 6 vols., New York, 1969.

Spufford, Peter, ed., *Origins of the English Parliament*, New York, 1967.

Stenton, F. M., "The Changing Feudalism of the Middle Ages," *History* N.S., 19 (1935).

Stephenson, Carl, "The Origins and Significance of Feudalism," *American Historical Review* 46 (1941).

Stevenson, Joseph, ed., *Letters and Papers Illustrative of the Wars of the English in France during the Reign of Henry VI, King of England*, 2 vols., London, 1861, 1864.

Strayer, Joseph R., *Feudalism*, Princeton, N.J., 1965.

Strubbe, E. I., "La Paix de Dieu dans le nord de la France," *Recueils de la société Jean Bodin* 14 (1961).

Suger, *Vie de Louis VI le Gros*, in *Oeuvres complètes*, ed. by A. Lecoy de La Marche, Paris, 1867.

Taylor, Ronald J., *The Art of the Minnesinger*, 2 vols., Cardiff, Wales, 1968.

Thrupp, Sylvia L., *The Merchant Class of Medieval London, 1300–1500*, Ann Arbor, Mich., 1948.

Toja, G., ed., *Arnaut Daniel, Canzoni*, Florence, 1960.

Tomkinson, A., "Retinues at the Tournament of Dunstable," *English History Review* 74 (1959).

Topsfield, L. T., *Chrétien de Troyes, a Study of the Arthurian Romances*, Cambridge, Eng., 1981.

———, *Troubadours and Love*, Cambridge, 1975.

Treharne, R. F., "The Knights in the Period of Reform and Rebellion, 1258–67: A Critical Phase in the Rise of a New Class," *Bulletin of the Institute for Historical Research* 21 (1946).

Tumler, P. Marian, *Der deutsche Orden im Werden, Wachsen und Wirken bis 1400*, Vienna, 1955.

Upton, Nicholas, *De Studio Militari*, ed. by F. P. Bernard, Oxford, 1931.

Vale, M. G. A., "New Techniques and Old Ideals," in Allmand, ed., *War, Literature, and Politics*, Liverpool, 1976.

Van der Werf, Hendrik, *The Chansons of the Troubadours and Trouvères, a Study of the Melodies and Their Relation to the Poems*, Utrecht, 1972.

Van Luyn, P., "Les *milites* dans la France du XIe siècle," *Le Moyen Age* 77 (1971).

The Variorum and Definitive Edition of the Poetical and Prose Writings of Edward FitzGerald, ed. by George Bentham, 7 vols., New York, 1967.

Vercauteren, Fernand, "A Kindred in Northern France in the Eleventh and Twelfth Centuries," in Reuter, ed., *The Medieval Nobility*, Amsterdam, 1978.

Vercel, Roger, *Bertrand of Brittany*, London, 1934.

Wace and Layamon, *Arthurian Chronicles*, trans. by Eugene Mason, London, 1978 (reprint of 1912 edition).

Wagner, Anthony Richard, *Heralds and Heraldry in the Middle Ages: An Inquiry into the Growth of the Armorial Functions of Heralds*, London, 1956.

Warlop, E., *The Flemish Nobility before 1300*, trans. by J. B. Ross, 4 vols., Kortrijk, Belgium, 1975–1976.

Warren, W. L., *Henry II*, Berkeley, Calif., 1973.

Wavrin du Forestal, Jean, *Anciennes chroniques d'Angleterre*, ed. by M. Dupont, Paris, 1858.

White, Lynn, Jr., *Medieval Technology and Social Change*, Oxford, 1962.

Wilhelm, James J., *Medieval Song: An Anthology of Hymns and Lyrics*, New York, 1971.

———, *Seven Troubadours, the Creators of Modern Verse*, University Park, Pa., 1970.

William of Malmesbury, *Chronicle of the Kings of England*, trans. by J. A. Giles, New York, 1968 (reprint of 1847 edition).

William of Tyre, *A History of Deeds Done Beyond the Sea*, trans. by Emily Atwater Babcock and A. C. Krey, 2 vols., New York, 1943.

Worcester, William, *Itineraries*, ed. by John H. Harvey, Oxford, 1969.

The Works of Tennyson, New York, 1913.

Yates, Frances A., "Elizabethan Chivalry: The Romance of the Accession Day Tilts," *Journal of the Warburg and Courtauld Institutes* 20 (1957).

index

Grateful acknowledgment is made for permission to reprint:

Excerpts from Geoffrey of Monmouth, *The History of the Kings of Britain*, translated by Lewis Thorpe (Penguin Classics, 1966). Copyright © Lewis Thorpe, 1966; and Joinville & Villehardouin: *Chronicles of the Crusades*, translated by Margaret R. B. Shaw (Penguin Classics, 1963). Copyright © M. R. B. Shaw, 1963. Reprinted by permission of Penguin Books Ltd.

Excerpt from *Personae* by Ezra Pound. Copyright 1926 by Ezra Pound; and from *Translations* by Ezra Pound. Copyright © 1963 by Ezra Pound. Reprinted by permission of New Directions Publishing Corporation and Faber and Faber Ltd.

Excerpt from *The Trial of the Templars* by Malcolm Barber. Reprinted by permission of Cambridge University Press.

Excerpt from *Arab Historians of the Crusades* by Francesco Gabrielli. Reprinted by permission of The University of California Press.

Excerpts from Wace and Layamon, *Arthurian Chronicles*, translated by Eugene Mason. Reprinted by permission of J. M. Dent & Sons Ltd.

Excerpts from *The Poetry of Arnaut Daniel*, edited and translated by James Wilhelm and *The Poetry of William VII, Count of Poitiers, IX Duke of Aquitaine*, edited and translated by Gerald Bond. Reprinted by permission of Garland Publishing, Inc.

Excerpts from *The Tree of Battles of Honoré Bonet*, edited and translated by G. W. Coopland. Reprinted by permission of Liverpool University Press.

Excerpts from Raymond d'Aguilers' *Historia Francorum qui Ceperunt Iherusalem*, translated by John Hugh Hill and Laurita L. Hill. Reprinted by permission of the American Philosophical Society.

Excerpts from Cervantes, *Don Quixote*, translated by Walter Starkie. Reprinted by permission of Macmillan Ltd.

Excerpts from *Songs of the Troubadours* by Arnaut Daniel, translated by Anthony Bonner. Copyright © 1972 by Schocken Books, Inc. Reprinted by permission of Schocken Books Inc.

Excerpts from *Anonymi gesta Francorum et aliorum Hierosolymitanorum*, translated by Rosalind Hill. Copyright © 1962 by Clarendon Press. Reprinted by permission of the Clarendon Press.

Excerpts from Fulcher of Chartres, *Historia Hierosolymitana*, translated by Martha E. McGinty, and Dana C. Monro, *Urban and the Crusaders*, both printed in *The First Crusade: The Chronicle of Fulcher of Chartres and other Source Materials*, edited by Edward Peters. Copyright © 1971 by the University of Pennsylvania Press. Reprinted by permission of the University of Pennsylvania Press.